St. Teresa of Avila

"In these letters, beautifully rendered, the voice is very much alive, conveying the spiritual force (and rich humor) that changed so many hearts—and so changed the course of history."

Mike Aquilina
Author of *A History of the Church in 100 Objects*

"Through her writings, St. Teresa often had heart-to-heart conversations with those she loved. *Her Life in Letters* is not to be read as an academic treatise; rather, St. Teresa's letters invite us to sit with her and learn from her experience, her grace, and her heart. Those who do just might find a new, lifelong friend."

From the preface by **Regina Marie Gorman, O.C.D.**
Vicar general of the Carmelite Sisters
of the Most Sacred Heart of Los Angeles

"A saint who is one of the peaks of Christian spirituality of all time."

Pope Benedict XVI

St. Teresa of Avila

Her Life in Letters

Preface by Regina Marie Gorman, O.C.D.
Translated and introduced by Kieran Kavanaugh, O.C.D.

Christian Classics ✠ *Notre Dame, Indiana*

Founded in 1865, Ave Maria Press is a ministry of the United States Province of Holy Cross.

www.christian-classics.com

Paperback: ISBN-13 978-0-87061-313-5

E-book: ISBN-13 978-0-87061-314-2

Cover image © North Wind Picture Archives, Gettyimages.com.

Cover and text design by Katherine Robinson.

Printed and bound in the United States of America.

Contents

The Letters

Preface

What does a sixteenth-century cloistered nun have to say to us today?

St. Teresa of Jesus was the catalyst, the reformer, the unstoppable spiritual entrepreneur whose writings teach us to draw near to the humanity of Jesus and not fear the light and darkness within our own humanity. From her we learn that personal friendship with Christ is the cornerstone of true prayer. Her wisdom still resonates within our souls today.

Progress in the spiritual life is often explained in the classical terms of the purgative, illuminative, and unitive ways. In the purgative way we make a decision to break with sin; in the illuminative way we more fully embrace God's light and grace in our daily lives; finally, we reach the unitive way of infused contemplation, which leads to mystical union with God. In St. Teresa's writings, she explains these three ways through down-to-earth, understandable analogies, symbols, and images such as the interior castle, the four waters, and the transformation of a chrysalis into a butterfly.

Many people benefit from reading these straightforward comparisons; St. Teresa concretizes abstract spiritual concepts—much like our Lord did with the gospel parables.

It is one grace to have a spiritual experience; it is another gift to understand that experience and a third to know how to explain it. After all, how can one define the supernatural with mere words? This is exactly what St. Teresa did, and, thanks be to God, we still have her writings available to us so that we, too, can learn from her wisdom.

Although most people have heard of St. Teresa's books, many people are not acquainted with her letters. There is something about personal correspondence that provides a precious window into the soul of the writer.

St. Teresa's hand written letters reveal her prodigious acumen, her intimate relationship with God, her knowledge and understanding of human nature, and her own spiritual experiences. She asks and answers questions, offers counsel, and clarifies Catholic teaching. She writes to members of the Church hierarchy, to family and friends, and to persons involved in her business dealings, so necessary in the opening of new monasteries.

So, here we are, five hundred years after her death, still publishing her letters. Through her writings, St. Teresa often had heart-to-heart conversations with those she loved. *Her Life in Letters* is not to be read as an academic treatise; rather, St. Teresa's letters invite us to sit with her and learn from her experience, her grace, and her heart.

Those who do just might find a new, lifelong friend.

Regina Marie Gorman, O.C.D.

Editor's Note

References to St. Teresa's other writings are from *The Collected Works of St. Teresa of Avila*, translation by Kieran Kavanaugh, O.C.D., and Otilio Rodriguez, O.C.D., 3 volumes (Washington, DC: ICS Publications, 1976–85).

The Book of Her Foundations (vol. 3)
The Interior Castle (vol. 2)
The Book of Her Life (vol. 1)
Meditations on the Song of Songs (vol. 2)
A Satirical Critique (vol. 3)
Spiritual Testimonies (vol. 1)
The Way of Perfection (vol. 2)

The brief biographies at the end of this volume provide additional information about Teresa's correspondents and people mentioned in the correspondence. The present work is an abridged version of *The Collected Letters of St. Teresa of Avila, Volumes 1 and 2*, also published by ICS Publications, 2001, 2007. For more information, please refer to those volumes.

Introduction

St. Teresa's correspondence makes up nearly one half of her known writings. Her letters have left us with a treasure trove of vivid narratives about her times, along with illuminating insights into her personality. Only those letters written by Teresa in the last few decades of her life have reached us, however, those decades representing the same period in which she wrote her major works. It is not difficult to admit that her career as a spiritual author flowed from her mystical experience of God. But while spiritual needs prompted Teresa's classic works, it was the many other needs of her daily life that drove her to letter writing. Her letters, as a rule, do not give us the kind of teaching and testimony we have grown accustomed to in her other works. Rather, they show us a different facet of Teresa, a Teresa immersed in the relationships and grim business matters thrust upon her by her vocation as a foundress and reformer.

Certainly she had written honestly and openly the story of her life and work in her two books, *The Book of Her Life* and *The Book of Her Foundations*. Despite the openness of these works, however, she wrote in the knowledge they would be read by her confessors and eventual censors. Her letters exhibit an even greater candor, and we benefit from many more details that were not meant for the public, nor even for her confessors or censors. Even at that, many personal details in her *Life* were not meant for broadcast. A keen observer of the reality around her as well as within, Teresa focuses light on many of the struggles in both the Carmelite order and the Church of sixteenth-century Spain. She introduces us to major personalities who have left their marks on history.

In addition, historians benefit from the letters because many of the gaps in the outline of events that is presented in her *Foundations* are filled in through her letters. Through them we also gain better knowledge of the chronology of events in her life and of how she related to the diverse people she dealt with. A number of everyday particulars that compilers and editors of those times considered unimportant are today prized. Her worries, her troubles and triumphs, her expressions of sadness and joy, can all be discerned there. With a compelling spontaneity, the letters disclose a Teresa in a complex variety of circumstances. We walk with her year by year, day by day—even hour by hour sometimes. Without question, we have before us a rich collection of documents, unbroken in their sequence, revealing in confidential tones a personal history that touches the furthest reaches of her soul.

Despite the fact that the letter writing was a necessity, any reader can easily see that, though a lover of solitude and prayer, Teresa possessed a heart magnanimously open to others. Ever willing to communicate with them on many levels different from the decidedly spiritual level mainly found in her other writings, she pours herself out to her family members, her religious sisters and brothers, to friends, theologians, advisors, patrons of the nobility, and businesspeople. She had to travel and buy and sell. The ever-present burden of fund-raising wearied her. Problems sprang up over jurisdiction, stirring her to write to Rome and even to King Philip II. She had to choose prioresses, advise and comfort them, and discuss the nettlesome pros and cons ever present in the selection of new postulants, as well as doubts about dowries and other material needs. People's health was always a disquieting concern for her.

A Daily Torment

The extraordinary gifts of grace bestowed by God on this Spanish Madre fortified her for a demanding ministry of service, which entailed heavy responsibilities that drew her contemplative soul into a maelstrom of activities. Because of the limited means for travel and communication in the sixteenth century, the organization of a reform like hers, with its unavoidable business matters, had to be dealt with chiefly through correspondence, a chafing duty that became one of Teresa's greatest trials. She wrote, "With so many duties and troubles . . . I wonder how I'm able to bear them all. The biggest burden is letter-writing" (February 4, 1572). This is the often-repeated confession of a woman overwhelmed with worries. Difficult as writing a book was for her, she preferred it to the letter writing, a drudgery that cost her more than all the pitiful roads and sorry weather experienced on her journeys through Spain.

What proved painful for Teresa has proved a treasure for us, a collection claimed by scholars to be unparalleled in Spanish literature even to this day. With their humor and delicacy, the letters on the surface do not betray the inner self-coercion they hide. Held bondage by her correspondence, Teresa worked at it day after day, often far into the night by the light of a poor little oil lamp. The pile of letters to be answered was enough to drive her mad. Yet, even though she could be busy answering them until two in the morning, she was up with the rest of the community at five in summer, and six in winter.

Eventually the burden and the lack of sleep took their toll, and she fell into the alarming exhaustion of 1577, precisely in the most intense period of her correspondence. "But I wrote you yesterday, and the labor of letter-writing this winter has so weakened my head that I have been truly sick" (March 1–2, 1577). The doctor issued orders that she not continue writing after midnight and that she get a secretary. Subsequently following this advice, whenever she felt especially exhausted she turned for help to a secretary. When a letter from Teresa is written in another's hand, we can usually attribute it to poor health at the time. "I beg your forgiveness that this is written in someone else's hand, for the bloodletting has left me weak, and my head can't do anything more" (middle of August, 1570).

The use of a secretary became more common after the exhaustion of 1577. "You should know, *mi padre*, that my heavy correspondence and many other duties that I tried to handle all alone have caused a noise and weakness in my head. And I have been given orders that unless it's very necessary I should not be writing letters in my own hand" (February 28, 1577). Sometimes Teresa began a letter herself, gave it to the secretary to continue, and then added some final words in her own hand. If she needed a special guarantee because of the uncertainty that surrounded the mail, she again turned for help to a secretary to make copies. She would order duplicates, triplicates, and even quadruplicates to be made and sent by different means. In that way she could sustain some hope that at least one would reach its destination.

Even in her tortuous travels she seized every moment she could find to work on her correspondence. With her longing for the day when she could be free for more prayer and solitude, her forced confinement in the Carmel in Toledo would have been like a paradise—except for the heavy load of correspondence. It is hardly a surprise that sometimes she didn't know what day it was, that she nearly sent to Gracián's mother a letter she wrote to the Bishop of Cartagena, or that she did actually get some addresses mixed up.

The Quantity of Letters

How many letters did Teresa write? The answer to that question is not an easy one, unless you respond that no one knows. Most of her letters have not survived. Some of them she directed to be destroyed, those that if intercepted could have given her trouble. Fortunately Gracián paid little heed to her warnings and saved a good part of Teresa's correspondence. But Anne of Jesus, submissive to Teresa's orders, burned what must have been a captivating collection. One of the letters to her, however, a severe letter, did escape the fire, although by Anne's mistake. On another occasion, in an act of renunciation, it is told, John of the Cross burned a cherished packet of letters from Teresa. Whether or not this is so, none of her letters to John have been conserved.

But how could many of Teresa's correspondents have known the value that a letter from Teresa of Jesus would one day have? Teresa herself generally destroyed letters written to her. Today we regret the loss of all that must have scintillated in her letters to St. John of Avila, Doña Guiomar de Ulloa, St. Peter of Alcántara, St. Francis Borgia, St. Luis Beltrán, St. Pius V, and many other collaborators, friends, and benefactors.

Undoubtedly, because of the defects of the postal system, numerous letters were clearly lost. Judging by Teresa's own complaints, a quantity of her letters simply vanished along the road. At times they vanished because someone suspected that money was enclosed. Simple carelessness, the way in which autographs have been treated by their owners down through the centuries, further contributed to the loss of letters. In sum, Teresa wrote hundreds of letters more than those that have reached us.

Kieran Kavanaugh, O.C.D.
Carmelite Monastery
Washington, DC

The Letters

Her Forties

To Don Lorenzo de Cepeda,[1] Quito (Ecuador)
Avila, December 23, 1561

Teresa is living outside her monastery in the home of Doña Guiomar de Ulloa in Avila. From there she is supervising the renovation of the house bought for her first foundation. She is in dire financial need. Unexpectedly, several Indians who are Lorenzo's friends bring letters and money. A mysterious promise made by St. Joseph is fulfilled. Deeply moved, Teresa writes in haste before Lorenzo's messenger leaves.

1. Jesus. Señor. May the Holy Spirit be always with your honor, amen, and repay you for the care with which you have so diligently come to the help of all. I hope in the majesty of God that you will gain much in his eyes. Certainly all those to whom you sent money received it at such an opportune moment that I was greatly consoled. I believe that it was God who stirred you to send me so much. The amount of money brought by Juan Pedro de Espinosa and Varrona (which I think is the name of the other merchant) would have been enough to keep a poor worthless nun like myself who goes about in patches—which I now consider an honor, glory to God—out of need for some years.

2. I have already written you a long letter about a matter that for many reasons I could not escape doing, since God's inspirations are the source. Because these things are hard to speak of in a letter, I mention only the fact that saintly and learned persons think I am obliged not to be cowardly but do all I can for this project—a monastery of nuns. There will be no more than fifteen nuns in it, who will practice very strict enclosure, never going out or allowing themselves to be seen without veils covering their faces. Their life will be one of prayer and mortification as I have written more at length in a letter to you. I will write another for Antonio Morán to bring when he leaves.

3. That lady, Doña Guiomar,[2] who is also writing to you, is a help to me. She is the wife of Francisco Dávila, of Salobralejo, if you recall. Her husband died nine years ago. He had an annual income of 1 million maravedis. She, for her part, has an entailed estate in addition to what she has from her husband. Although she was left a widow at the age of twenty-five, she has not

married again but has devoted herself very much to the Lord. She is deeply spiritual. For more than four years we have been devoted friends, closer than if we were sisters. She still helps me very much, for she contributes a good portion of her income. At present she is without funds, so it is up to me to buy and prepare the house. With God's favor I have received two dowries beforehand and have bought the house, although secretly. But I did not have the means to pay for the work that still needed to be done. So by trusting in God alone (for God wants it to be done and will provide), I entered into an agreement with the workers. It seemed a foolish thing to do. But then His Majesty comes along and moves you to provide for it. And what amazes me is that the forty pesos you added was just what I needed. I believe that St. Joseph—after whom the house will be named—wanted us to have the money, and I know that he will repay you. In sum, although the house is small and poor, the property has a field and some beautiful views. And that's sufficient.

4. They have gone to Rome for the papal bulls, for although the house belongs to my own religious order, we are rendering our obedience to the bishop.[3] I hope the foundation will give the Lord much glory, if he allows it to come about. I believe without a doubt that it will, for the souls that are planning to enter will give an excellent example of humility, as well as penance and prayer. They are choice souls. Will you all pray to God for this project, for by the time Antonio Morán departs, everything will be completed, with God's favor.[4]

5. Antonio Morán came here and was a great consolation to me. He seemed to be a loyal and highly gifted man. I was especially consoled to learn about all of you, for one of the great favors the Lord has granted me is that he has given you understanding of what the world is, and so you have chosen to live quiet lives. Now I know, too, that you have taken the path of heaven. This is what I wanted most to know, for up until now I was always in dread. Glory to the One who does all. May it please him that you always advance in his service. Since there is no measure to his remunerations, we should never stop trying to serve the Lord. Each day we will advance at least a little further, and with fervor. It seems, and so it is, that we are always at war, and until we are victorious, we must not grow careless.

6. All those with whom you have sent money have been reliable men. But Antonio Morán has surpassed them all. He has sold the gold at a higher price without charge, as you will see, and has brought the money here from Madrid despite his poor health— although today he is better, for it was caused by an accident. I notice that he thinks highly of you. He also brought the money from Varrona and did so with great care. Rodríguez came here too, and has done everything well. I will write to you through him, for perhaps he will be the first to leave. Antonio Morán showed me the letter you had written him. Believe me, I think that all this care is not only the fruit of his virtue, but also the result of God's inspiration.

7. Yesterday my sister María[5] sent me the enclosed letter. When they bring her the other money, she will write again. The help came just in time for her. She is a very good Christian and undergoes many trials. If Juan de Ovalle[6] initiates a lawsuit, it would destroy her children. Certainly he doesn't have as much a claim as he thinks he does, even though the sale of everything went badly and proved a disaster. But Martín de Guzmán also had good intentions—God rest his soul—and the judge ruled in his favor, even though not well enough. I cannot bear that anyone should now claim what my father—may he enjoy eternal glory— sold. And the rest, as I say, would only kill María, my sister. God deliver me from the self-interest that brings so much harm to one's relatives. It has reached the point here that it's a wonder if there's a father who cares about his son or a brother who cares about his brother. Thus I'm not surprised by Juan de Ovalle; rather, he has done well by setting this litigation aside for now out of love for me. He is by nature good, but in this case it would be unwise to trust in that. When you send him the 1,000 pesos, you should ask him for a written promise to be given to me; and the day that he reintroduces the lawsuit, 500 ducats will go to Doña María.[7]

8. The houses at Gotarrendura are still not sold, but Martín de Guzmán received 300,000 maravedis from them, and it was only right that this amount went to Juan de Ovalle. Along with the 1,000 pesos you sent, he is taken care of and will be able to live here. For this is what he has done, he has come here and now needs to remain. He would be unable to live here other than

badly and for only short periods of time without help from over there.[8]

9. His marriage is a good one. But I must tell you that Doña Juana is so honorable and trustworthy that she makes you want to praise God, and she has the soul of an angel. I've turned out to be the worst sister; the way I am, you ought not even acknowledge me as your sister. I don't know why you're all so fond of me. I say this in all truthfulness. Juana has undergone many trials and borne them well. If you can send the money without placing yourself in need, do so quickly, even if little by little.

10. The money you sent was allocated as you will see from the letters. Toribia[9] is dead as is also her husband. It was a great help for her children, who are poor. The Masses have been said according to your intentions—some of them before the money arrived—and by the best persons I could find, all of them excellent. I was edified by the intentions for which you had them said.

11. I am staying in the house of Señora Doña Guiomar during these business affairs.[10] It makes me happy to be with persons who speak to me about you; indeed, it is my pleasure. One of this lady's daughters, who is a nun in our monastery, had to come out and stay with her mother, and our provincial ordered me to be her companion. Here, more than at my sister's house, I am at liberty to do the many things I need to do. All the conversation here is about God, and we live in great recollection. I will remain here until given other orders, even though it would be better for me to stay here so as to handle the above business matters.

12. Now to speak of my dear sister, Señora Doña Juana,[11] for although I mention her last, she is not so in my heart. That is certain, for I pray to God for her as intensely as I do for you. I kiss both your hands a thousand times for all the kindnesses you have shown me. I don't know how to repay you other than by praying fervently for our little boy.[12] And this is being done, for the saintly friar Peter of Alcántara has promised to do so (he is the discalced friar about whom I wrote you), and the Theatines[13] and other persons whom God will hear are doing so. May it please His Majesty to make the child better than his parents, for good as you are, I want more for God. Continue writing to me

about your joy and resignation to God's will, for that makes me very happy.

13. I mentioned that when Antonio Morán leaves I will send along for you a copy of the patent letters of nobility,[14] which they say couldn't be better. I'll take great care in doing this. And if this time it gets lost on the way, I'll keep sending others until one arrives. For some foolish reasons it was not sent (it was the responsibility of a third party who did not want to—I'll say no more). I'll also send you some relics, for the reliquary isn't worth much. I kiss my brother's hands a thousand times for what he has sent me. If it had come at a time when I wore gold jewelry, I would have been very envious of the medal, for it is extremely beautiful. May God keep you and your wife for many years. And may he give you a happy new year, for tomorrow is New Year's Eve for 1562.[15]

14. Since I spent a long time with Antonio Morán, I began this letter late; otherwise I would say more, but he wants to leave tomorrow. I will write again through Jerónimo de Cepeda,[16] and since I'll be doing so soon, it doesn't matter that I don't say more here. Always read my letters yourself. I went to great lengths to use good ink. This letter was written so quickly; and, as I say, it is so late that I cannot take time to read it over. My health is better than usual. May God give you health in body and soul, as I desire, amen.

15. I'm not writing to Hernando de Ahumada or Pedro de Ahumada[17] for lack of time; I will do so soon. Your honor should know that some very good persons who are aware of our secret—our new undertaking—have considered it a miracle that you sent so much money at such a time. I hope that when there is need for more, God will put it into your heart to help me, even though you may not want to.

> Your devoted servant,
> Doña Teresa de Ahumada

To the Lords of the Town Council, Avila
Avila, December 5, 1563

This letter speaks of the consolation the sisters find in their hermitages, places of solitude in their garden where they can praise God and pray for the city. A lawsuit was initiated against the nuns because one of the hermitages was constructed at a site harmful to the city's water supply.

Most Honorable Lords:

1. Since we received information that the little hermitages constructed on our property would cause no damage to the city's waterways, and the need was very great, we never thought your honors would be disturbed. What we did only serves for God's praise and provides us with a place apart for prayer, for it's in these hermitages that we beg God in a special way to preserve this city in his service.

2. Aware that your honors are displeased—which distresses us all—we beg you to come and see. We are prepared to comply with all the documents, promises, and pledges your lawyers might require so as to be sure that no damage will be done at any time; and we have always resolved to act in this way.

3. If despite this your honors are not satisfied and want the hermitages removed, may you first consider the benefit and not the harm that may come from them. What we want most to avoid is that you be displeased. We would be distressed if we had to go without the consolation we find in them, for it is spiritual.

4. May our Lord keep and preserve you, most honorable gentlemen, in his service, amen.

> *Your unworthy servants who respectfully kiss your hands,*
> *The poor sisters of San José*

To Juan de San Cristóbal, Avila
Avila, April 9, 1564

This served as a letter of agreement for the sale of some dovecotes. Since the request in the last letter was rejected, Teresa decided to make this purchase and convert the dovecotes into other hermitages that would not be a threat to the city's water supply.

---

1. This day, Quasimodo Sunday,[1] 1564, Juan de San Cristóbal and Teresa of Jesus entered into agreement on the sale of a group of dovecotes for 100 ducats free of tithes or duties.

2. The amount will be paid in this manner: 10,000 maravedis now and 10,000 by Pentecost Sunday; the remainder will be paid by St. John's feast of this year.

In confirmation of the above, I place my signature.
Teresa of Jesus

To Padre García de Toledo, Avila(?)
Avila, 1565

This letter accompanied the second draft of Teresa's The Book of Her Life *and appears in that work as the epilogue. García de Toledo, one of her directors, had urged Teresa to expand on the first draft and now was in a hurry to read what she had written in her second draft.*

1. May the Holy Spirit be always with your honor, amen.

It wouldn't be wrong for me to exaggerate this service[1] I have rendered you in order that you feel obliged to take great care to pray to our Lord for me. For I certainly must have the right to ask this of you from what I have undergone in writing about myself and calling to mind so many of my miseries; although I can truthfully say it was more difficult for me to write about the favors His Majesty granted me than about my offenses against him.

2. I did what you commanded me and enlarged upon the material.[2] I did this on the condition that you do what you promised by tearing up what appears to you to be bad. I hadn't finished reading it after the writing was done when you sent for it. It could be that some of the things are poorly explained and others put down twice, for I had so little time I couldn't read over what I wrote. I ask you to correct it and have it transcribed if it is to be brought to Padre Maestro Avila, for it could happen that someone might recognize my handwriting.[3] I urgently desire that he be asked for his opinion about it, since this was my intention in beginning to write. If it seems to him I am walking on a good path, I shall be very consoled; then nothing else would remain for me than to do what lies within my power. Nevertheless, do what you think best, and remember you are obliged to one who has so entrusted her soul to you.

3. I shall recommend your soul to our Lord for the rest of my life. So do me the favor of hurrying to serve His Majesty; for you will see, from what is written here, how well one is occupied when one gives oneself entirely—as you have begun to do—to him who so immeasurably gives himself to us.

4. May he be blessed forever! I hope in his mercy that you and I will see each other there where we shall behold more clearly the great things he has done for us, and praise him forever and ever, amen.

This book was finished in June 1562.[4]

The Letters

Her Fifties

To Don Gaspar Daza, Avila
Toledo, March 24, 1568

Gaspar Daza was a priest in Avila of whom Teresa speaks in her
Life. *Now he is an admirer and defender of the little monastery of St.*
Joseph's. Writing from the palace of Doña Luisa de la Cerda in Toledo,
Teresa had just come from Alcalá where she had assisted María de Jesús
in a foundation for Carmelite nuns there.

---

1. The relics of the young shepherd saints[1] that were brought to
Alcalá move us to praise our Lord. May he be blessed for everything. Indeed, sir, it is so easy for His Majesty to make saints that
I don't know why you are so amazed up there that he should
grant some favors to those who live in solitude. May it please
the Lord that we know how to serve him, for he knows so well
how to repay.

2. I was most happy that you were pleased . . . which will not
be enjoyed save by one who truly understands how sweet the
Lord is. May it please God to preserve you for me many years
as a help to those sisters.[2]

3. Do not allow them to speak with one another about the kind
of prayer they experience, nor should they get involved in such
matters, or speak about Concepción,[3] for each one will want to
add some foolishness of her own. They should let her be, for
when she cannot do all the work, they can find another and the
two can share the work, for God will provide food . . .

4. Your mother and sister must remember little of me. I will write
to the abbess,[4] if I can. May God give her health. I already wrote
to Madrid for the coarse wool. I don't know whether I am forgetting something. At least, I won't forget to pray for you. Please
do the same for me and ask the Lord that this new house[5] for his
service may be founded. Next Tuesday, I think, we will be going
for certain. Today is the vigil of Our Lady of the Incarnation. My
regards to Padre Lárez, Brother Cristóbal, and to Maridíaz.

Your unworthy servant and daughter,
Teresa of Jesus, Carmelite

To Doña Luisa de la Cerda, Antequera
Toledo, May 27, 1568

Teresa is writing late at night from the Toledan palace of Doña Luisa de la Cerda. She had received a letter sent from Andalusia by Doña Luisa, but nothing was said in it about her book (the Life*). She presents a positive report on life at the palace and gives information about Malagón and the plans for a school of Christian doctrine. Having arrived very sick and been confined to bed, Teresa improved after being bled twice.*

---

1. May Jesus be with your ladyship. Today, the feast of the Ascension, the licentiate[1] gave me your letter. When I learned that he had come, I was very anxious, until I read it, for I wondered about its contents. Glory to our Lord that you are doing well, as is also Don Juan, and my lords.[2]

2. As for the rest, don't worry in the least about it. But even though I say this, I myself was disturbed and told him that he had done the wrong thing. He is very confused, in my opinion; indeed, one cannot understand him. On the one hand he desires to serve and says that he loves you very much, which is true, and on the other hand he doesn't know how to behave consistently. He also suffers from a little melancholy, just as Alonso de Cabria.[3] But what contradiction in the things of this world! He could be serving you and doesn't want to; and I, who would enjoy doing so, cannot. Things like these, and other worse things, we as mortals have to endure. We never manage to understand the world, but we don't want to leave it.

3. I'm not surprised that you are distressed. I've already understood that you would have to suffer much, seeing that you have not the kind of temperament that gets along with everyone. But since this is for the service of the Lord, try to bear it and talk it over with this Lord, for he will not leave you alone. That the licentiate has left you will not seem bad to anyone here, but they will feel sorry for you. Try to cast aside your worries. See how much we care about your health. Mine has been very bad these past days. Were it not for all the comfort you have provided for me in this house, it would have been worse. I needed this, for with the sun along the road, the pain I was suffering when you

were in Malagón increased to such a point that when I arrived in Toledo they had to bleed me twice. I wasn't able to move in bed because of the pain moving up from my shoulders to the back of my head. The next day I had to undergo a purge. And so I was delayed here eight days as of tomorrow, for I came Friday.[4] I'm leaving in a very weakened condition—for they drew much blood—but feeling better. I felt very lonely when I found myself here without you, my friend. May the Lord be served by everything. Everyone has treated me very well, including Reolín.[5] Indeed, I was delighted over how you took such care of me up here, even though you are down there. I pray fervently to the Lord for you. I am well now, although weak.

4. The priest from Malagón accompanied me;[6] it is remarkable how indebted I am to him. Alonso de Cabria does so well under his administrator[7] that he didn't feel like coming with me. He said that the administrator would miss him very much. Since I had such good company and he was tired from the previous trip, I did not press him. You should know that the administrator does a superb job. They say he's beyond all expectations. Alonso de Cabria never finishes praising him, and so, too, the others. Lord Don Hernando[8] is also very happy with him.

5. Carleval has left, and I don't think he'll return . . .[9] They say that the Lord has wanted Alonso de Cabria to work for the monastery and that the hospital would pay the expenses. And that is true because Carleval's brother[10] came. I tell you that I am most happy to leave him there. Other than my Padre Pablo,[11] I don't know who I could have left that would match him. We are lucky to have him. He is a man of prayer, with deep experiences of it. He is very happy, but it's necessary to make some further provisions for him. Because I've written to you in Malagón about all this, I'll say no more. Here they tell me great things about this *padre* I'm speaking of.

6. The sisters are elated. We agreed to bring in a woman who is very much a *teatina*.[12] The house will provide her meals—since we must give alms we might as well do it this way—and she will teach needlework gratis to young girls with the intent of teaching them Christian doctrine and how to serve the Lord, something highly beneficial. Padre Carleval also sent for a young man, and Huerna, as they call him, to assist them. And he and the parish

priest will teach the doctrine. I hope in the Lord that this will be of great benefit. Truly, I have come away highly pleased, and may you be so also. Be assured that my absence will take nothing away from the religious observance of the house, for with the spirit of the sisters and with such a confessor,[13] and the priest, who will not neglect them, I hope in God they will advance each day, and I don't doubt that.

7. As for the other chaplain, no one wants to tell him not to say Mass.[14] You might write to him about it, although Padre Pablo is looking for someone to tell him, but I would not want you to forget to do so yourself. The administrator says that he will arrange things so well for him that he will be much better off than previously; but since it is he who must console him, he does not want to be the one to tell him. I beg you not to forget this. They have already given a third of the money to the licentiate; Miranda gave it to him. Send your instructions in writing about who should reimburse Miranda for these payments. May the devil not concoct a scheme that would make us lose a man like this. And he certainly will try, for Miranda will do him as much harm as he possibly can. May you understand the importance of this, and not allow it.

8. I was so busy today that I didn't have time to write; now it's late into the night, and I feel very weak. I brought the lady's saddle that you kept in the fortress—I hope you won't mind—and I bought another good one here. I already know that you will be happy that it is a help to me on these journeys since it was there without being used. At least, I'll be traveling with something that is yours. I hope in the Lord that I shall be returning on it; and if not, I will send it to you as soon as you return.

9. I've already written to you in Malagón that I think the devil is trying to prevent Maestro Avila from seeing what I entrusted to you.[15] I wouldn't want him to die before seeing it; that would be too much to bear. Since you are so near him, I beg you that through one of your messengers you send it to him sealed. Write to him and highly recommend it to him, for he wants to read it and will do so as soon as he can. Fray Domingo[16] now wrote to me here that when I arrive in Avila I should send it to him by a private messenger. I'm distressed—I don't know what to do, for, as I told you, I would be greatly harmed, if they found out.[17] For

love of our Lord, please attend to this quickly; realize that if you do, you will be rendering our Lord a service. And as a favor to me, be brave in those strange lands. Recall how our Lady and our Father St. Joseph went about in Egypt.

10. I'm going to go by way of Escalona, for the marchioness is there and she has sent for me.[18] I told her that you had bestowed so many kindnesses on me that I didn't need anything further from her, but that I would stop to see her on the way. It will be for only half a day, if possible, no more. I'm doing this because Fray García,[19] who promised her, urged me to do so, and I won't be going out of my way. Señor Don Hernando and Señora Doña Ana[20] graciously came to see me, and Don Pedro Niño[21] and Señora Doña Margarita[22] as well; and other friends and various people came, some of whom tired me out. Those from your house are very recollected and solitary. Would you write to the señora directress;[23] you now see what you owe her. I did not see her, although she sent me gifts, for I was confined to bed most of the time. I must go to see the señora prioress[24] tomorrow before leaving, for she is insisting that I come to see her.

11. I was not going to speak about the death of my lady the Duchess of Medinaceli[25] in case you had not heard about it. Afterward, I thought that by the time this reaches you, you will know about it. I would not want you to grieve over it, for the Lord has granted a favor to all those who truly loved her—and granted one to her—in that he brought her so quickly to himself; with the sickness she had, they would have seen her die a thousand deaths. Such was her ladyship's life that she will live forever, and the hope of seeing her again, you and I together, helps me to live deprived of her presence. I kiss the hands of all my lords; Antonia[26] kisses yours. Give my best regards to Señor Don Juan; I pray for him very much. May His Majesty keep watch over you for me and guide you always. I'm very tired, and so I'll say no more.

Your unworthy subject and servant,
Teresa of Jesus, Carmelite

12. They've already given authorization to our "eternal *padre*."[27] That's the way it is: on the one hand I'm annoyed, and on the other I see that the Lord wants it so and that you suffer trials

alone. The *padre* will surely write to you when he finds a messenger. I will leave this letter with Doña Francisca[28] giving her urgent instructions. If I find someone going that way, I will write from Avila. I forgot to mention that our *padre* told me of a nun who is very devoted to reading and gifted in ways pleasing to him. She has no more than 200 ducats, but the nuns are so much alone and the needs of a monastery in its beginning so great that I said they should take her. I prefer having her to taking in foolish nuns, and if I could find another like her, I wouldn't take any more. May your ladyship remain with God; I'd rather not bring this to an end, nor do I know how I'm going to bear being so far from someone to whom I'm so indebted and love so much.

Doña Luisa de la Cerda, Antequera
Avila, June 9, 1568

Teresa, in an exhausted condition, had arrived in Avila eight days prior to the date of this letter. She had traveled from Malagón to Toledo and through Escalona to Avila. She writes about her arrival, but also mentions again the matter of her manuscript, The Book of Her Life.

1. Jesus be with your ladyship. I arrived here in Avila very tired on the Wednesday before Pentecost, for, as I wrote to you,[1] I was in such a dreadful state of health that I wasn't ready for traveling. And so we journeyed at a slow pace. The priest[2] accompanying us was a great comfort to me; he's so gracious about everything. A relative of mine is passing through; as a child, he suffered from stone and was cured by the waters of the spring down there[3] and has never suffered a relapse. This good news made me so happy, because I hope in our Lord the same thing will happen to Señor Don Juan. May His Majesty heal him, which is what we here are begging him to do. I kiss his honor's hands and those of all my lords.

2. I've found out that Doña Teresa, the daughter of the Marchioness of Velada, has become a nun[4] and is very happy. I visited the Marchioness of Vellena last Sunday. She was most gracious, but since my Señora Doña Luisa is all I need, the courtesy mattered little to me. May the Lord bring you here to me safely and in good health. In regard to what I entrusted with you,[5] I beg you once more, for reasons about which I've already written you, not to neglect it, for it is a very important matter for me. Since I left a long letter in Malagón for you and another in Toledo, this one is for no other purpose than to let you know that I arrived safely, and so I've nothing further to say.

Today is Wednesday.

Your ladyship's unworthy subject and servant,
Teresa of Jesus, Carmelite

To Doña Luisa de la Cerda, Antequera
Avila, June 23, 1568

Teresa is preparing for her journey to Valladolid to make her fourth foundation. She is still concerned about her book, which has now been delivered to St. John of Avila. She is happy with her Carmels in Avila and Malagón.

---

1. May Jesus be with your ladyship. The messenger is in such a hurry that I don't know how I'm going to manage sending you even these few lines, although my love for you is helping me find the time. Oh, my lady, how often I think of you and of your trials, and so I take care in praying to our Lord for you. May it please His Majesty to give health quickly to those lords so that I will not feel so far away from you, for if I knew you were in Toledo, I think I'd be content. I am well, glory be to God. I will go from here to Valladolid after the feast of St. Peter.

2. Remember, since I entrusted my soul[1] to you, that you send it to me by messenger as quickly as you can, but not without a letter from that holy man,[2] so that we may know his opinion, as we agreed in our conversation together. I'm afraid that when the *presentado* Fray Domingo[3] comes, for they say he is coming this summer, I'll be caught red-handed.[4] For love of our Lord, after that saint has seen it, send it to me, for there will be time for us to see it together when I return to Toledo. Don't worry about having Salazar[5] see it, unless an exceptional opportunity arises, for it's more important that you send it back to me.

3. From your monastery[6] they write me that everything is going very well and that they are making progress, and I believe it. Everyone here thinks that those sisters are so very fortunate in having such a confessor—for they know him.[7] They marvel and so do I at the manner in which the Lord brought him there. I think the Lord did so for the benefit of souls in that place, for they say he does much good. And this he has done wherever he has been. Surely, he is a man of God. Everyone here esteems the house in Malagón highly, and the friars[8] are very happy. May the Lord bring me back there with you.

4. I find that the sisters here have made exceptional progress. All of them kiss your hands, and I, those of both Señor Don Juan[9] and my ladies, for I have no time to write more. Tomorrow is the feast of St. John; we will pray fervently to him for our foundress and patroness, and for our patron.[10]

Your ladyship's unworthy servant,
Teresa of Jesus

Unless you want them to pass through the superior, address your letters, and what I entrusted to you, here.

To Don Francisco de Salcedo, Avila
Valladolid, September 1568

Francisco de Salcedo collaborated with Gaspar Daza in the spiritual direction of Teresa at the beginning of her mystical life. Teresa is now sending John of the Cross to Avila with letters of recommendation from her to her friends to prepare for the foundation in Duruelo.

To The Most Honorable Señor Francisco de Salcedo.
My lord,

1. Jesus be with you. Glory to God that after six or eight letters dealing with business matters that couldn't be avoided, I have a little time to rest from them by writing these lines to let you know I receive much consolation from your letters. Do not think that writing to me is time lost, for now and then I need this, provided that you don't keep telling me that you are old, which leaves me in total dismay. As though there were some security in being young! May God let you remain here until I die; afterward, so as not to be there without you, I will beg the Lord to bring you there quickly.

2. Would you speak to this *padre*,[1] I beg you, and help him in this matter, for although he is small, I know that he is great in the eyes of God. Certainly we will miss him very much here, for he is wise, and just right for our way of life. I believe our Lord has called him for this task. There's not a friar who does not speak well of him, for he had been living a life of great penance, even though he is young. It seems the Lord is watching over him carefully, for although in trying to get everything settled we met with a number of troubles—and I myself must have caused trouble at times by becoming annoyed with him—we never saw an imperfection in him. He's courageous, but since he is alone, he needs all that our Lord gives him for taking this work so much to heart. He will tell you how we are getting along here.

3. The generous sum of six ducats seemed to be no small thing, but I would give much more to see you. Surely you are worth a higher price than I; who is going to value a poor lowly nun? In addition, you are to be prized more in that you can give *aloja*,[2] wafer cookies, radishes, and lettuce, that you have an orchard

and take the place of your servant—I know about it—to bring us apples. The *aloja* here, they say, is very good, but since I don't have Francisco de Salcedo here, we don't know what it tastes like nor do we have the means of knowing. I'm telling Antonia[3] to write you, for I'm not able to go on at length. Remain with God. I kiss the hands of Señora Doña Mencía[4] and Señora Ospedal.[5]

4. May it please the Lord that the improved health of that married gentleman continue. You shouldn't be so incredulous, for prayer can do all things, and the kinship he has with you will do a lot. Here, we will help with our widow's mite. May the Lord bring it about as he can. Indeed, I think the illness of his wife is more incurable. The Lord can cure it all. I beg you, tell Maridíaz, and the Flemish woman, and Doña María de Avila[6]—for I would very much want to write her, and surely I don't forget her—when you see them, to recommend me and this monastery to God. May His Majesty keep your honor many years for me, amen. For, in passing, it might be said that this year could go by without my seeing you again, the Princess of Eboli[7] being in such a hurry.

Your lordship's true and unworthy servant,
Teresa of Jesus, Carmelite

5. I beg again as an alms of you that you speak to this *padre* and counsel him on what you think about his mode of life. The spirit the Lord has given him has greatly encouraged me, and his virtue, among so many troubles, makes me think we have a good beginning. His prayer is deep and he has good intelligence. May the Lord lead him on.

To Doña Juana de Ahumada, Alba
Avila, Middle of December 1569

Juan de Ovalle has arrived in Toledo on his way back from Seville. He has collected a good sum of money sent by Lorenzo to be deposited in Spain. He has also collected a hundred pesos each for Juana and Teresa. As a result, Teresa speaks to her sister about money matters and her own thinking regarding the demands of poverty.

---

1. Jesus be with your honor. I would be foolish to deprive you of the joy of reading a letter from me by not spending some time to write you when so good a messenger[1] is available. Blessed be the Lord who has arranged things so well. May it please His Majesty to do the same in everything else.

2. Don't you see how, even though you didn't want it, circumstances made it necessary for my brother[2] to come here? And it may be that he will have to come again to get the money,[3] although there may be someone through whom he can send it. He will bring you news about your son.[4] Everything that could bring one joy is going well now; may the same be true regarding the soul's progress. Go to confession in preparation for Christmas and pray for me.

3. Don't you see that however much I try, His Majesty doesn't want me to be poor?[5] I tell you, indeed, that in a certain sense this gives me great displeasure, but it removes the scruples I undergo when I have to spend something. I am thinking now of some little things I got for you, of what I paid and what was left and the greater amount I spent on the needs of the order, and, so as not to go around with these scruples, to keep account of what I have to spend otherwise. For if I do have money, I cannot keep anything when I see the great need at the Incarnation.[6] And no matter how much I try, I cannot get fifty ducats for what I claim is necessary, not for getting what I want but for what pertains to the greater service of God. That is the truth. May His Majesty guide us and make you holy and give you a happy Christmas.

4. I don't like these plans of which my brother[7] speaks. It would involve going outside your own house and spending more than

he would make. And you would be alone, and we would all be anxious. Let us wait now to see what the Lord does. Try to please the Lord, for he will take care of your affairs. And don't forget that all things come to an end. Don't fear that your children will be left in want if you seek to please His Majesty. My regards to Beatriz.[8] May he watch over you all. Amen.

5. One thing I ask you out of charity is that you do not love me for the sake of what you can gain in the world but because I pray for you. When it comes to anything else, there's nothing I can do—regardless of what Señor Godínez[9] says—and it distresses me. I follow the one who governs my soul, and not whatever happens to enter the head of this one or another. I say this so that you may respond when something is said to you. You should understand that if we consider how the world is now and the state the Lord has placed me in, the less you think I do for you the better it is for me; and this is fitting for the service of the Lord. Certainly, even if I should do nothing, it would be enough for someone to imagine the least little thing so as to say about me what I hear said about others. So you have to be careful in regard to the little thing you mentioned to me.

6. Believe me that I truly love you and that sometimes I put together some trifle for a moment in which it will bring you pleasure. But explain when someone mentions it to you that I must spend what I have at my disposal for the order, for it belongs to the order. And how do others have a say in this matter? Realize that someone as exposed to the world as I am has to be careful even in the way she practices virtue. You'd be unable to believe the trouble I have. But, then, I do things so as to serve God. His Majesty will watch over you and your affairs for me.

7. May God keep you; I've gone on at length and the bell for Matins has rung. I assure you that when I see a postulant bringing with her something of value, I think of you and Beatriz, but I would never take anything, not even by paying for it with my money.

Yours,
Teresa of Jesus

To Diego Ortiz, Toledo
Toledo, Middle of August 1570

Diego Ortiz did not want to speak to Teresa about the meaning of some stipulations made in the contract for the foundation in Toledo. On the eve of her departure for Avila, she writes to him to clarify her understanding of what was stipulated. She has been ill and uses a secretary for this letter, with the exception of the last paragraph.

To the very magnificent Señor Diego Ortiz, my lord.

1. Jesus. May our Lord bestow his divine grace on your honor. I had very much wanted to meet with you during these days, and so I sent word beseeching you in this regard. Since you are not going to grant me this favor and the time has arrived for my departure (which I believe will be tomorrow), I want to tell you about what we began discussing the other day in regard to the sung Masses on Sundays and feast days. I have been thinking about the matter these days, for I had not given it much thought before you spoke to me; nor did I think it necessary to speak about it, for my intention seemed clear in the written agreement. But they tell me I must clarify some things.

2. What I intended was that the chaplains be obliged to sing a Mass on feast days, for then our constitutions prescribed this, but not that the nuns be obliged to sing, for in their rule this is optional. Even if the constitutions do prescribe singing, they do not on this matter bind under any sin. How could I make this an obligation for the nuns! I wouldn't do it for anything, nor did you or anyone ask me for such a thing. I spoke in this way for the sake of our convenience.[1] If in writing this down I made an error, it wouldn't be right to demand of them what should be voluntary. And since they are willing to serve you and ordinarily sing the Masses, I beg you that when some need arises for them you consider it a good thing to allow them their freedom. I beg your forgiveness that this is written in someone else's hand,[2] for the bloodletting has left me weak, and my head can't do anything more. May our Lord keep you.

3. Señor Martín Ramírez[3] pleased me very much. May the Lord be pleased to make him his servant and keep you for the good of all. You will be doing me a great favor if you clarify the matter concerning the Masses. And since the Mass is sung almost every day without the nuns being obliged, it would be right for you to remove this scruple of ours and make the nuns and me happy in a matter that has so little importance, for we all want to serve you.[4]

Your unworthy servant,
Teresa of Jesus

To Doña Catalina Hurtado, Toledo
Avila, October 31, 1570

Doña Catalina Hurtado was the mother of two young women who had entered the Carmel in Toledo the previous July. Having befriended Teresa, she began sending her gifts. Teresa is ill and cannot express her gratitude in her own handwriting.

1. Jesus. The grace of the Holy Spirit be with your honor and watch over you for me, amen, and repay you for the care you take in giving me gifts. The butter was exquisite, like everything your hands have made for me. Whenever you have some more that is good, I will accept it with pleasure if you remember me, for it is very beneficial to me. The quince were also exquisite; it seems you have no other care than to give me gifts. On my part it is a gift to see a letter from you and know that you are well. As for me, I am not so well right now. I have a pain in my jaw and my face is a little swollen, and that is why this letter is not in my handwriting. But I don't think this will matter at all to you.

2. Pray for me, and don't think it provides me little joy to have a daughter[1] like the one I have had up until now and will have always. I will not forget to pray for you, and the sisters will do the same. All those in this house kiss your hands, especially the subprioress,[2] who owes you so much. Pray for her, for her health is not good. May the Lord keep you for me and give you his Holy Spirit.

October, the end of the month.

I beg for the prayers of those ladies, your sisters. May God give health to the one who is ill, for I am beseeching him to do this, and I ask the same for you, my daughter.

Your honor's unworthy servant,
Teresa of Jesus

To Doña Isabel de Jimena, Segovia
Salamanca, End of 1570

Teresa replies to an aspirant who sought to enter one of her monasteries. Teresa writes warmly to Doña Isabel, who was giving up her wealth in order to serve God.

To the very magnificent Señora Doña Isabel de Jimena, my lady.

1. Jesus. May the Holy Spirit be with your honor always and give you the grace to understand how much you owe the Lord. Despite dangers so dangerous as youth, wealth, and freedom, the Holy Spirit gives you light to want to leave them aside. And the things that usually frighten souls, such as penance, enclosure, and poverty, enabled you to understand their value and also the delusion and loss that would have been yours had you followed after the former dangers. May the Lord be blessed and praised forever.

2. This is the reason you have so easily persuaded me that you are very good and capable of being one of our Lady's daughters by entering her holy order. May it please God that you will advance so far in your holy desires and works that I won't have to complain of Padre Juan de León.[1] He sent me information that left me so satisfied that I didn't need to know anything more. I am so consoled with the thought that you will become a great saint that I would be very satisfied in just having you without anything more.

3. May the Lord repay you for the alms you have resolved to give wherever you enter, for the amount is large.[2] Doing this must be very consoling to you since you are doing what the Lord counsels—to give yourself to him—and what you have to the poor for love of him.[3] Considering what you have received, I don't think you could have fulfilled your obligation with a smaller amount. Since you are doing all you can, your offering is no small matter nor will what you receive in return be small.

4. Since you have seen our constitutions and rule, I have nothing to say but that if you carry on with this decision you may enter at whatever time you settle on, and you may choose from among

our houses the one you prefer. In all of this I want to please my Padre Juan de León, leaving the choice to you. Truly, I would have liked you to take the habit in the house where I am living, for I certainly desire to make your acquaintance. May our Lord direct everything for his greater service and glory, amen.

Your honor's unworthy servant,

Teresa of Jesus, Carmelite

To Diego Ortiz, Toledo
Avila, May 27, 1571

Diego Ortiz was insisting on his right to have certain Masses sung in the church of the Carmelite nuns in Toledo at which the nuns would participate. His letters, filled with justifications for his requests, are severe in tone. Teresa's answer is tactful but firm.

1. Jesus. The grace of the Holy Spirit be with your honor, amen. You show me so much kindness and charity through your letters that even were your last letter more severe, I would have felt well repaid and obliged once more to serve you. You say that you sent me a letter through Padre Mariano[1] that I might know the reasons for your request. Because you have given me such good ones and you know so well how to put forth the value of what you want, I'm afraid my reasons are of little weight. And so I'm not thinking of defending myself, but as with those who have a hopeless case I will shout and cry out and remind you that you are always more obliged to favor orphan daughters and minors over chaplains. For, in the end, everything is yours—how much so—even the monastery and those living in it, but not those who, as you say, are in a hurry to finish quickly, and sometimes with little devotion.

2. You have done me a great favor in agreeing to that matter concerning Vespers, for it's a subject about which I can do nothing. As for the rest, I am writing to Mother Prioress[2] to do as you ask, and I am sending her your letter. Perhaps by leaving everything in her hands and those of Señor Alonso Alvarez,[3] we will gain more. The two of them can work out an agreement among themselves. I kiss your honor's hands many times. I was very sorry to learn of the pain in your side from which you suffered. Here we offered it to the Lord, and so I pray for all of you and for those angels.[4] May God make them his own and preserve them.

3. There is one thing that would seriously inconvenience the nuns and be burdensome to them: a Mass to be said before the High Mass when a saint's feast is being celebrated, especially if there is a sermon. I don't know how that can be arranged. It should matter little to all of you that on such a day the feast be

celebrated at the High Mass; and a little before it, the low Mass by the chaplain could be celebrated. The need for this will not arise often. Try to put up with this opposition to your desire and do me this favor, even though the day may be a festive one; of course, I'm not referring to ceremonies requested by one of you. Know that this matter is not important, and you will be doing the nuns a good deed and me a great favor.

4. After the letter to our Father General[5] went out, I realized that there was no reason for it; anything Father Visitor[6] does is as valid as something done by the pope, for no general or general chapter can undo it. The visitor is very learned and well informed, and your honor will enjoy dealing with him. I think that without doubt he will make a visitation of the monastery there this summer, and he will be able to set up firmly what you ask for. I will speak to him about this when he passes through here. Well, I will not depart in the slightest from what you see as serving best for greater stability nor from anything by which I might serve you. I am sorry I am not in a place where I could show you my good will from close at hand. I earnestly recommend myself to the prayers of Señora Doña Francisca Ramírez.[7] I no longer have a fever, glory to God.

5. You can indeed write to me all that you want, for I know the spirit in which you write. My only pain would be to cause you pain. For surely I would not want to cause you any or that anyone in that house do so. As for the rest, nothing that you have ever said has caused me any harm, nor will it. May our Lord bestow on you all the spiritual blessings that I ask His Majesty for, and may he always guide you.

Today is the Sunday after the Ascension.

Your honor's unworthy servant,
Teresa of Jesus

To Doña Luisa de la Cerda, Paracuellos
Avila, November 7, 1571

Doña Luisa de la Cerda's son (who was thought to be suffering from kidney stones) had died sixteen days previous to this letter, and Teresa writes to console her friend. She has been prioress at the Incarnation in Avila for about a month, sent there under obedience. Her responsibilities for the 130 nuns are many and troublesome, but an inner calm remains with her.

To the very illustrious Señora Doña Luisa de la Cerda.

My lady in Paracuellos,

1. Jesus. May the grace of the Holy Spirit be with your ladyship. Since I have been in this house of the Incarnation—a little over three weeks now—I have written you three times.[1] I don't think any of my letters has reached you. I share so much in your trials that when this suffering is added to the many I have here, I'm no longer worrying about asking our Lord for any more. May he be blessed for everything, for it truly seems that you are among those who will enjoy his kingdom since he gives you to drink from the chalice through so many illnesses, both your own and of those you love.

2. I once read in a book that the reward for trials is the love of God. For so precious a return, who will not love them? So I beg you to do so and to note how all things pass away quickly; journey by detaching yourself from everything that does not last forever.

3. I had already learned that you were ill, and so today I have tried in every way to learn about your health. May the Lord be blessed that you have improved. Come away from that region, for the love of God, for it is clearly bad for the health of all.[2] My health is good—may he be blessed—compared to what it usually is. But with all the work I have, I wouldn't be able to hold up without better health than I usually have. My responsibilities are so many and so pressing, inside and outside the house, that I have little time even to write this.

4. May our Lord repay you for your kindness and the consolation your letter brought me, for I tell you that I need some of this. Oh, my lady, as one who has known the calm of our houses and now finds herself in the midst of this pandemonium, I don't know how one can go on living, for everywhere there is suffering. Nonetheless, glory to God, there is peace, which is no small thing. Gradually I am taking away the nuns' diversions and freedom, for even though these nuns are so good—certainly there is much virtue in this house—changing a habit is death, as they say. They bear it well and show me much respect. But where there are 130 nuns, you will understand the care that is necessary to keep things in order. I am somewhat concerned about our own monasteries; but since I was obliged to come here under obedience,[3] I hope that our Lord will not allow me to fail in my duty, but that he will care for them. It doesn't seem that my soul is disturbed in the midst of this whole Babylon, which I take to be a favor from the Lord. Human nature grows tired, but it is all little next to my offenses against the Lord.

5. I was sorry to learn of the death of the good Doña Juana.[4] May God take her to himself, and indeed he will, for she was most worthy. I really don't know why we should feel sorry about those who depart for a safe haven, whom God draws out of this world with its dangers and instability. We are loving ourselves rather than those who go to enjoy a greater good. I commend myself to the prayers of my ladies.

6. I tell you that I keep you ever present and that it was not necessary for you to awaken me with your letter; I would rather be half asleep than see myself so imperfect as to fail to be afflicted over your sufferings. May our Lord give you eternal happiness and rest because for some time now you have given up happiness and rest in this life, though you do not yet appreciate the value of suffering. The day will come when you will understand what you have gained and that for nothing in the world should you ever want to lose it.

7. I'm very much consoled in knowing that my Padre Duarte[5] is there. Now that I am not able to serve you, it brings me joy to know that you have so much good support to help you undergo your trials. The messenger is waiting, so I cannot go on any longer, save to kiss the hands of my ladies many times.

8. May our Lord lead you by his hand and take those fevers away quickly. May you be given the strength to please His Majesty in everything, as I beg of him, amen.

Written at the Incarnation in Avila, 7 November.

Your ladyship's unworthy servant and subject,
Teresa of Jesus

To Doña Juana de Ahumada, Galinduste
Avila, February 4, 1572

Teresa writes from the monastery of the Incarnation, which was in financial straits. She has had bad health since she arrived.

1. Jesus be with your honor. It seems as though you are in another world, living far off in that place. God deliver me from it and from this place as well, for almost from the time of my arrival I've had poor health. So as not to be telling you about this, I've preferred not to write. Before Christmas I suffered from fevers and a sore throat, and was bled and purged twice. Since before Epiphany I've been down with the quartan fevers, but I've not experienced any nausea; and on days when I've been free of them, I've been able to go to choir with the others and sometimes to the refectory. I don't think the fevers will last. Since I see the improvement the Lord has brought about in this house,[1] I try not to stay in bed except when I have the fever, which lasts all night. The chills begin about two, but they are not excessive. Everything else is going well, with so many duties and troubles that I wonder how I'm able to bear them all. The biggest burden is letter-writing. I have written four times to the Indies, for the fleet is leaving.

2. I'm amazed by your indifference in seeing me with so many trials. I've been waiting each day for Señor Juan de Ovalle, who, I'm told, will be passing through here on his way to Madrid, for it is important to send my brother what he has requested.[2] Now it's too late, nor do I know what to say. Everything should be easy for you; certainly it will not look well.

3. I've been told that Señor Juan de Ovalle and Señor Gonzalo de Ovalle are those who oppose giving a narrow passageway to the monastery.[3] I can't believe it. I wouldn't want us to become involved in haggling. This doesn't look right for women, even though there may be a reason, and those lords would be greatly discredited, especially since the matter pertains to me. Furthermore, I don't think the nuns were aware of the reason; at least one should not turn their simplicity into a fault. Would you inform me about what is going on, for, as I say, this is the news

that reached me, and it could be incorrect. Do not be sorry about my illness, for I don't think it will amount to anything; at least it is not interfering much with my duties, even though it does cost me somewhat.

4. I miss you here very much, and I find myself alone. I need some *reales*, for I don't take any food from the monastery provisions except bread;[4] try to send me some. I kiss the hands of those lords and of Beatriz. I would be very happy to have her here. I already know that Gonzalo is well. May God watch over him. Agustín de Ahumada is with the viceroy; Fray García has written me about it. My brother has arranged marriages for two of his nieces—and very good ones at that. They will be secure on his departure. The clock will soon strike twelve and I'm very tired so—no more.

Yesterday was the feast of St. Blase; the day before, of our Lady.

Your honor's devoted servant,
Teresa of Jesus

To Doña Juana de Ahumada, Galinduste
Avila, February–March 1572

Teresa encourages her sister to bear her trials and assures her of prayers. Her sister's husband Juan de Ovalle has just passed through Avila on his return from Madrid.

1. Jesus . . . the Lord. The muleteer is coming . . . thus there is no time to say more. You should reflect that in one way or another those who are going to be saved will have trials, and God does not give us a choice in the matter; and perhaps he gives you who are weak the smallest. I couldn't know better what you are going through, even if you were to try to explain or write it in a letter; and so I pray to God for you with great care. It seems I love you more now than ever, although my love for you is always great.

2. You will be receiving another letter from me. I don't think you have become worse, even though it seems so to you. I beg you for the love of God and me to go to confession frequently. May he be with you, amen. Señor Juan de Ovalle will tell you the rest; he left in a hurry.

Send the turkeys since you have so many.

Your unworthy servant,
Teresa of Jesus

To Padre Antonio Lárez, Avila
Avila, 1572

This is a fragment from a note of condolence written to the Jesuit rector of San Gil in Avila after the sudden death of a brother Jesuit.

Your lordship ought not grieve the sudden death of Padre Hernandálvarez del Aguila, for there is someone who has seen him in heaven among the holy confessors there.

To Doña Juana de Ahumada, Alba de Tormes
Avila, September 27, 1572

The situation at the Incarnation continues to improve, and Teresa's health is fairly good. The nuns are benefiting a great deal from Fray John of the Cross's spiritual direction. But the financial problems are still a cause for worry. Teresa and her sister Juana are awaiting the arrival of Lorenzo from America, which they think might be any day now.

---

1. Jesus be with your honor. Blessed be God that Señor Juan de Ovalle is well, for the weakness will pass. The tertian fever has been everywhere. Around here,[1] that's all one finds, although it has left me alone. Everything is daily getting better, glory to God. I have been well this summer. I don't know what the winter will bring, for it is already starting to cause me some disturbance; but when there's no fever, one can put up with it all.

2. Regarding the purchase of the house, I would like to know what was done.[2] From Oropesa they wrote me of the news that the fleet had arrived in Sanlúcar, although this is not certain. I know nothing more. As soon as I know anything about my brother, I will inform you. I have the Perálvarez house ready for him.[3]

3. I am displeased by those fasts of the prioress.[4] Tell her so, and that this is why I do not want to write to her or have anything to do with her. God deliver me from anyone who wants to do her own will rather than obey. If I can be of help to Señora Doña Ana, out of consideration for Señor Don Cristóbal, I'll do so gladly.[5] We have discussed her staying in the house where Doña Sancha used to live, but it is in such a state that no one could live in it. Here in the Incarnation, no one may enter except as far as the portress's office,[6] nor can the service women go out. Her sisters, I believe, though they would like to help her, could do little for her. Because for five years they have eaten nothing but the bread supplied by the monastery, they are drained of energy—and Doña Inés is almost always sick.[7] They deeply regret their lack of energy. As for myself, you already know they are so bound by precepts that there is little I can do.[8]

4. Give my best regards to the subprioress. I don't have time to write any more. Isabel Juárez is the one who came from Malagón, and most unwillingly, according to what they say. But having once expressed the desire, she was sent by the prioress; and I think that at some other time the prioress herself will come. I have many cares—may God provide for them. My regards to Señor Juan de Ovalle and to my dear children. You don't tell me what Beatriz's illness was. May God be with them.

Today is 27 September.

Yours,
Teresa of Jesus

The discalced friar who is confessor here is doing great good; he is Fray John of the Cross.[9]

To Madre Inés de Jesús, Medina del Campo
Avila, Beginning of May 1573

The prioress in Medina consulted Teresa with respect to a nun whom they believed was possessed. Teresa responded by sending St. John of the Cross, who had gained a reputation in Avila as an exorcist. His most noted exorcism took place in May 1574.

My daughter: I am very sorry about Sister Isabel's[1] sickness. I am sending you the saintly Fray John of the Cross, for God has given him the grace to cast out devils from persons having them. Just recently here in Avila he has driven out three legions of devils from a person, demanding that they identify themselves, and they obeyed at once. What they fear in him is so much grace accompanied by so much humility.

To King Don Philip II, Madrid
Avila, June 11, 1573

Teresa writes from the Incarnation, where she has been prioress for almost two years. She wants a favor from the king, but we do not know the details of what it was. The letter presents to the king her intermediary, Juan de Padilla, an influential but somewhat over-zealous reformer.

To His Sacred, Catholic, Imperial Royal Majesty, the Lord King.

1. Jesus. The grace of the Holy Spirit be always with your majesty, amen. I truly believe that your majesty is aware of the everyday care I take to recommend you to our Lord in my poor prayers. Since I am so miserable a person, this may be of small service, but by stirring the sisters of these discalced monasteries of our order to do so, I may be of some help to you; for I know that they serve our Lord. And in this house where I now reside, the same is done,[1] together with praying for our lady the queen and for the prince[2] —may God give him long life. And the day in which his highness was pronounced heir, special prayers were offered. This we will do always. Thus, the more this order increases, the more your majesty will gain.

2. As a result, I dare to beg your majesty for your favor in certain matters about which the licentiate Juan de Padilla,[3] in whom I'm confiding, will speak to you. Would you give credence to him. Seeing his true zeal, I felt confident in entrusting this affair to him. If it were made public, great harm would be done to what we are aiming after, which is all for the glory and honor of our Lord. May His Divine Majesty preserve you for many years, as many as are needed by Christendom. It is a great relief that in its trials and persecutions, our Lord God has as great a defender and help for his Church as is your majesty.

From this house of the Incarnation in Avila, 11 June 1573.

> *Your majesty's unworthy servant and subject,*
> *Teresa of Jesus, Carmelite*

To Pedro de la Banda, Tozos (Salamanca)
Salamanca, August 2, 1573

Pedro de la Banda had offered his house to the Carmelite nuns for the foundation in Salamanca. Since it belonged to an entailed estate, a license from the king was required. Teresa had arrived two days before writing this letter. She has the license from the king, but the owner is absent.

1. Jesus. May the grace of the Holy Spirit be always with your honor, amen. I have come here to proceed at once toward getting these sisters settled. I don't have much time and because of this and also because the desirable season for constructing walls is nearly over, I was sorry not to find you here. The license from the king has arrived, and it's necessary to have it verified at once.

2. I beg you please to come quickly; since the matter is so important, I hope in God that you will not become irritated with me. May the Lord guide everything for his greater service and may he always lead you by the hand.

3. The house seems good to me, although more than 500 ducats will be necessary before entering it. Nonetheless, I am pleased and I hope in our Lord that you will be pleased in seeing it put to such good use. May the Lord grant you many years. Remember, the work has to begin during the good season and so it's a pity to see these days wasted.

4. For the love of God do us the favor of coming at once. And if you delay, I beg you to agree to our beginning to make the partition walls, for more than two hundred are needed; this will do no harm to the house. If afterward the agreement is not finalized (which is why I hope in God you will come quickly), the loss will be ours.

5. When you arrive, everything can be worked out. May His Majesty give you a long life so that you may ever gain more merit for eternal life.[1]

Today is 2 August.

> *Your honor's unworthy servant, who kisses your hands,*
> *Unworthy,*
> *Teresa of Jesus*

To Pedro de la Banda, Salamanca
Salamanca, October 8, 1573

The nuns moved into the house owned by Pedro de la Banda on September 28. Eight days later Teresa signed the purchase and sales agreement. But the demands of the former owner continue, and Teresa responds with this note. Three years later the purchase of the house was still not finalized.

To the Illustrious Señor Pedro de la Banda, my lord.

1. Everything your honor said is being carried out according to your wishes. From what everyone says, I am not obligated to all of this until the license arrives. But our having entered the house obliges me to comply with your orders, and please God you will be satisfied with everything.

2. May our Lord give you calm[1] that you may serve him better, and may he always lead you by his hand.

Today is 8 October.

Your honor's unworthy servant,
Teresa of Jesus

To Padre Domingo Báñez, Valladolid
Salamanca, Beginning of January 1574

Although Teresa is sick with the quartan fevers, her manner is sprightly. The letter deals with four separate dramas going on at this time in Teresa's life: the question of a school for girls in Medina; the capricious Princess of Eboli; the bizarre story of Casilda de Padilla; and the purchase of a house in Salamanca. She jests with Báñez over his letter-writing habits.

To my Padre and Señor, Maestro Fray Domingo Báñez.

1. Jesus. May the grace of the Holy Spirit be with your honor and in my soul. When I was sick I wrote you a long letter telling you about the ups and downs of my health, and sent it by way of Medina—I don't know why they didn't deliver it. Now I would also like to write at length, but I have many letters to write and I am feeling cold, for it is the day of the quartan fever.[1] I've been without it, or half without it, for two days. But since the pain I used to have along with it hasn't returned, it all amounts to nothing.

2. I praise our Lord for the news I hear about your sermons, and I am very envious. And now, since you are the superior of that house, I feel a longing to be there. But when have you ceased being my superior? If I were there, though, it seems to me I would experience a new joy. But since I don't deserve anything but the cross, I praise him who gives it to me always.

3. I was delighted with those letters of Father Visitator to you, *mi padre.*[2] Not only is that friend of yours a saint, but he knows how to show it, and if his words do not contradict his deeds, he proceeds very wisely. And although what he says is true, he will not fail to admit her,[3] because between lords and lords the difference is great.

4. The Princess of Eboli as a nun was something to cry over.[4] That angel there,[5] as a nun, can be of benefit to other souls, and the greater the outcry, all the more! I find no drawbacks. The worst that can happen is that she leave, but the Lord in the meantime will have drawn out, as I say, other benefits and perhaps have

stirred some soul who otherwise without this means might have been condemned. Great are God's judgments, and there is no reason for us to deny admission to one who loves him so authentically when she is in the danger that all these illustrious people are in. Nor should we refuse to bear the trial of some disturbance in exchange for so great a good. To make her wait, it seems to me, would be like going along with the world and copying its ways, and it would be a torment to her. It is clear that even if she did change her mind[6] during the thirty days, she would not say so. But if such a delay would placate her parents, justify her cause, and provide for the waiting period your honor desires—it would be no more, I repeat, than a delay—may God be with her. For it is impossible for whoever gives up much not to receive much from God since he gives so much to us who have given up nothing.

5. I am greatly consoled that you are there to lend support to the prioress and that she may do what is right in all matters. May he be blessed who has thus arranged everything. I hope in His Majesty that all things will go well. This business with Pedro de la Banda[7] is never-ending. I believe I'll have to go first to Alba so as not to lose time, for there is a danger in this matter that the conflict is between him and his wife.[8]

6. I greatly pity the nuns in Pastrana. Even though the princess has returned home, they are like captives, for the prior of Atocha[9] went there and did not dare visit them. Now she is also mad at the friars.[10] I don't know why they should have to put up with such slavery. I am doing well with Padre Medina.[11] I think that if I were to speak with him often, everything would soon be smoothed over. He is so busy that I hardly see him . . .

Doña María Cosneza[12] told me that I shouldn't prize him as highly as I do you . . .

7. Doña Beatriz[13] is well. Last Friday she repeatedly offered to do something for me; but now I don't need anything, thanks be to God. She told me about the goodness you have shown her. The love of God permits many things; if it is in the least bit lacking, everything would be finished. Your difficulty, it seems, is to write at length; mine is to be brief. Nonetheless, you do me a great favor because I do not grow sad when I see a bundle of letters

and yours is not among them. May God keep you. . . . May it please God that my excess will not be tempered by your silence.

Your honor's servant and daughter,
Teresa of Jesus

To Madre Ana de la Encarnación, Salamanca
Alba de Tormes, Middle of January 1574

Ana de la Encarnación (Tapia), Teresa's cousin, was a nun from the Incarnation. Teresa at this time was prioress in Salamanca and was again sick. She sends kind regards and messages of concern, adding that she is sending a trout to Padre Medina.

For Mother Prioress in Salamanca.

1. Jesus be with your reverence. Let me know how you are and how all the nuns are as well, and give them my regards. Tell them I would like to be enjoying their company along with that of the nuns here. I believe I will have less difficulty here than I thought. And from my hermitage,[1] and also from where I sleep, there's a view of the river—I can enjoy it while in bed, a most refreshing experience for me. I have felt better today than usual. Doña Quiteria[2] has her customary fever; she says she misses all of you. They have brought a doctor here for Señora Doña Jerónima, for she is still sick. Pray for her there, as we are doing so here; I am worried about her. May God guide you.

2. The duchess sent me this trout today. It looked so good that I got this messenger to deliver it to my Padre Maestro Fray Bartolomé de Medina.[3] If it arrives at dinner time, send it to him at once through Miguel, and this letter as well. And if it arrives later, send it to him anyway to see if he's willing to write a few lines.

3. Don't neglect to write me about how you are, and don't neglect to eat meat these days. Tell the doctor about your infirmity and give him my best regards. Anyway, may God be always with you, amen.

4. Give my regards to my Padre Osma and tell him I greatly miss him here. Let me know how Juana de Jesús[4] is, for she had a very pale face the day I left.

Today is Wednesday after the twelfth, and I am yours,

Teresa of Jesus

5. How is the countess? And the magistrate's wife? Send someone to find out and let me know about it. I will write about how your sister is, for I did not want to send Navarro[5] until I knew; through him I will also send you something. He will bring these sixteen *reales*, if I remember tomorrow, for today I also forgot. If Lescano should ask for something, give it to him, for I will repay you. I told him that if he needs something you would give it to him. I'm quite sure he will not ask.

To Don Alvaro de Mendoza, Valladolid
Alba de Tormes, January–February 1574

This letter reflects two family dramas: the Padilla family's opposition to young Doña Casilda's becoming a discalced Carmelite nun (a matter in which Don Alvaro and his sister don't dare interfere); and the marriage of Don Fadrique with Doña Magdalena de Guzmán, which Don Alvaro opposes. Teresa learns of the first through the prioress in Valladolid and of the second from the Duchess of Alba.

1. Jesus. The grace of the Holy Spirit be always with your lordship. Blessed be God that you are in good health. May it please His Majesty that you continue to improve, as I beg him.

2. It would be a consolation for me if I had the time to write you at length, but I have so little that I didn't want to begin. María Bautista[1] will give you news of me, since I cannot do so here in this letter. When she writes, she gives me the news that I desire and informs me about you, glory to God, and with this I can get along without seeing any letter from you. I have written some letters. With one of them, I already know that, for a certain reason, they did not give it to you; with the others I don't know what happened. I have received only one from you since I have been here. (I mean I received it in Salamanca.)[2]

3. I have already told the duchess what you directed me to tell her. She gave me an account of the matter and said that she had never thought you knew about the recent events. She certainly deserves that one not lose her friendship.[3] Nor can I write to Señora Doña María.[4] I kiss her ladyship's hands many times, but it seems to me that our Lady defends her daughters better than her ladyship does her subjects, judging from what they tell me about her silence in these matters. May the Lord help that little angel,[5] for what he is doing for her is now something truly new in the world. I think this is the reason he has ordained that she find herself alone and with these struggles: that his favor toward her be better known. This makes me praise His Majesty greatly.

4. Now, since you have many saints there, you are beginning to recognize those who are not, and so you are forgetting me.

Nonetheless, I believe that in heaven you will see that you owe the sinner[6] more than you do them. I would be more willing to send best wishes to Señora Doña María and my lady the countess if it were for something else than this wedding; although I am consoled that it is taking place so quickly.

5. May it please our Lord that it be for his service, and may your lordship and Señora Doña María rejoice in it for many years. I kiss the hands of Señora Doña Beatriz and my lady the duchess many times.[7] May our Lord always guide you.

Your lordship's unworthy servant and subject,
Teresa of Jesus

6. I beg you to inform me whether Father Visitator has given the permission for me to spend some days at St. Joseph's; the prioress will write to me.[8]

To Some Aspirants, Avila
Segovia, Middle of March 1574

Two young women in Avila wanted to enter St. Joseph's even though their parents would not give them permission. Teresa counsels them to wait and pray for their parents' change of heart.

---

1. Jesus. The grace of the Holy Spirit be in your souls, and may he grant that your good desires be lasting ones. It seems to me, my ladies, that Doña Mariana, the daughter of Francisco Juárez, has had more courage, since for six years she has had to bear the displeasure of her mother and father and has been relegated to a small town.¹ How much she would give to have the freedom you have in being able to confess at San Gil.²

2. It is not as easy as you think to receive the habit in this way. Even though you are determined in your desire, I do not think you are so holy that you will not afterward grow tired of suffering the loss of your father's favor. Thus, it is preferable that you pray to our Lord for your father and leave the matter to His Majesty, who can change hearts and provide other means. And when we are most detached, he will so arrange things that everyone will be pleased. Right now, what must be fitting is to wait. His judgments are different from ours.

3. Be content with knowing that a place is being reserved for you, and abandon yourselves into God's hands so that his will may be done in you. This is what perfection consists of, and the rest could be a temptation.

4. May His Divine Majesty bring about what he sees as best. Certainly, if it were a matter of my will alone, I would at once comply with your desires. But, as I said, there are many things that have to be considered.

Your honors' servant,
Teresa of Jesus

To Antonio Gaytán, Alba de Tormes
Segovia, May 30(?), 1574

Antonio Gaytán met Teresa in Alba de Tormes. Undergoing a conversion of life, he became her collaborator. Teresa here reports on the situation of the foundation in Segovia, of which he was a part. She also responds to his questions about prayer and in this respect calls him "my son."

---

1. Jesus. May the Holy Spirit be with your honor, my son. I'm not fortunate enough to have the time to write you at length, but I assure you I have the desire to do so. Your letters bring me happiness in knowing about the favors the Lord grants you, which each day become greater. He is repaying you now for all the work you have done here.

2. You should not tire yourself with a great deal of thinking, nor should you be concerned about meditation. If you haven't forgotten, I have often told you what you should do and how this is a greater favor from the Lord. And to be always praising him and desiring that everyone do so is the greatest effect of the soul's being occupied with His Majesty. May it please the Lord that you, and I as well, may know how to repay something of what we owe him and may he give us much to suffer, even if it comes from fleas, goblins, and traveling.

3. Antoño Sánchez[1] was ready to give us the house without further word, but I don't know what you and Padre Julián de Avila[2] had done with your eyes that you wanted to buy it in the condition that it was in. It's a good thing he had not wanted to sell it. Now we are negotiating to buy one near San Francisco, on the Calle Real in the best part of the suburb, near the marketplace. It is very nice. Let us pray for this.[3]

4. All the nuns send their best regards. I am better; I was going to say "well," because when I am without the usual ailments, this means good health for me. May the Lord give you health and preserve you for us.

Your honor's servant,
Teresa of Jesus

To Madre María Bautista, Valladolid
Segovia, End of June 1574

In this confidential letter Teresa shares with María Bautista intimate thoughts that would be understood only by the recipient. She comments on other matters concerning her Carmels and sends some medicine for the prioress of the Dominican nuns.

---

1. Jesus. May the Holy Spirit be with your reverence, my daughter. If the prioress of Medina[1] had not informed me that you are well, I would have been feeling sorry for you, thinking that you must be ill since you haven't written for so long. May God be blessed, for I greatly desire your good health. Let those who are are ill bear it cheerfully so that, God willing, it will be beneficial to their souls.

2. You perhaps know that the Lord took to himself Isabel de los Angeles,[2] the one about whom there was all that trouble in Medina, and by such a death that if any nun were to undergo a similar one she would be considered a saint. Certainly she went to be with God, and here I remain, someone who has become useless. Three weeks ago I had a terrible cold along with many other ailments. Now I am better, although not entirely well, and very happy about the news I am writing to Padre Fray Domingo.[3] May they give thanks to the Lord, for we have done this here. May he be praised for everything.

3. Would you send this letter to the prioress of the convent of the Mother of God,[4] for I am enclosing here some medicine that I think helped me. I am distressed about her illness, since I have suffered so much from it in these recent years; that pain is without mercy. But what an idea you had to send me the scorzonera![5] I hardly ate any, for I had been left with a loathing for anything sweet. Nonetheless, I have greatly prized your care in sending things to the sisters and to Isabel,[6] who already through her courtesy and love seems fully mature.

4. How foolish you are in the excuses you make regarding the hands and all the rest! Until we meet once again, I don't dare tell you about the intention I have in everything. You should know

that every day I feel greater freedom, and if I were sure that that person commits no offense against God, I would have no other fears. I have seen many great falls and many dangers in this matter, and I greatly love that soul—it seems God has given me this concern. And the simpler she is, the more fear I have for her. So, I am happy that she is pleased to be in a safe place, although in this life there is no such thing; nor is it good that we feel safe, for we are at war and surrounded by many enemies.

5. Look, my daughter, when I am without such a serious illness as I have had here, I become very frightened if I feel the least stirring of attraction toward something. This is for you alone, because those who do not understand me will have to be guided according to their own spirit. And indeed, if there is anyone with whom I can allow this stirring, it is with the one to whom I am writing, but however small this may be, a free soul feels it very strongly, and perhaps God wants it to feel this to safeguard the part that is necessary for his service. Oh, my daughter! We are in a world that you will never completely understand, even when you are as old as I. I don't know why I am writing these things without having a trustworthy person to send this letter with; I'll give a good tip.

6. Everything you do for Doña Guiomar[7] is well done, for she is holier than you realize, and has her fill of trials. It's good the other one left in such peace. May it please God that things go better with the other one we received, despite my fear. Those who give up their own home to come to us don't find it easy to adapt to ours, although for now it seems she will do all right. Isabel[8] will write to you about it.

7. I had written as far as this and not found a messenger. Now they tell me there is one and that I should send my letters at once . . .[9]

To Don Teutonio de Braganza, Salamanca
Segovia, July 3, 1574

Don Teutonio has been ill and is undergoing a cure. Teresa pleads with him not to use pompous titles in addressing her. She assures him of her prayers and urges him not to worry. In answer to his questions, she gives him some advice about prayer.

To the Very Illustrious Señor Don Teutonio de Braganza, my lord.

1. Jesus. The grace of the Holy Spirit be with your lordship. I tell you definitely that if you address your letter to me again with those titles, I won't reply.[1] I don't know why you want to displease me, although I was not so aware of this displeasure until today. Find out from Father Rector[2] how he addresses letters to me, and don't add anything more, because the titles you use are against the spirit of our order. I am glad that he is well, for I was concerned about him. I beg you to give him my best regards.

2. This seems a difficult time of the year for you to be seeking a cure. May it please the Lord that the cure be successful, as I am begging him. May His Majesty bring back your servants in good condition. I am already beseeching him for this. But I would rather you weren't so troubled—what will this distress do to your health? Oh, if we understood well these truths, few things would trouble us on this earth.

3. I sent the letter at once and wrote to Father Rector[3] telling him how important it was to me that he act quickly. I owe him a great deal. He arranged everything for a house we have already bought,[4] glory to God—tell Father Rector[5]—which is a very good one, close to the one where we are living now, which is in a good location. It belongs to a gentleman named Diego de Porres. Padre Acosta[6] will describe it for you; give him my regards and tell him that his novices grow happier each day, and we with them. They ask for your prayers and for those of the nuns. But what bad manners I have to be asking you to deliver these messages. Truly, it's your humility that bears with all this.

4. With regard to the desire you experience to cut short your prayer, pay no attention to it. Instead praise the Lord for the

desire you have for prayer and believe that this is what your will wants—and love to be with God. Melancholy dislikes being treated with severity. It is best to use less severe means and at times relax outdoors where you can walk and see the sky; your prayer will suffer no loss because of this; it's necessary that we bear our weakness and not try to constrain our nature. Everything amounts to seeking God, since it is for him that we search out every kind of means, and the soul must be led gently. In this regard and in everything else, my Father Rector[7] will better discern what is appropriate for you.

5. They are awaiting Father Visitator,[8] for he is on his way. May God reward you for your care in wanting to favor us.[9] I will write to you when I find out where he is. What is important is that you speak with him, for he will pass through there. I am better now; may it please the Lord that you will be so also and that the cure will be of great benefit to you.

Today is 3 July.

Your lordship's unworthy servant and subject,
Teresa of Jesus, Carmelite

To Madre María Bautista, Valladolid
Segovia, July 16, 1574

In the morning Teresa received letters from María Bautista and Báñez; she now hurries to send off her reply in the afternoon of the same day. María Bautista longs to see her but Teresa cannot go to Valladolid.

For my daughter, Madre María Bautista, prioress of the Conception monastery.

1. Jesus be with you, my daughter. Your annoyance made me smile. I assure you it is no pleasure for me to have to give up seeing you. In fact, it would be such a pleasure for me that it seems to me a lack of perfection to try to go there without any compelling reason. Moreover, if Padre Maestro[1] is there, what need is there for me? So, if I am given orders to go there, I will go; if not, I'll have nothing to say. I really think I can be of service wherever I go, even when it seems there is no need. But since you are so prudent, perhaps I'd have nothing more to do than rest. I'm no longer good for much else.

2. With regard to the lay sister, there is nothing to say; the deed is done. But I tell you it is a hard thing to have to see so many lay sisters for every three nuns, as they say. It makes no sense. I believe we will have to get Father Visitator to set a limit as we have for the choir nuns.[2] I don't know what excuse you have for not telling me how sick you are; this grieves me. It's very foolish for you to be worried about perfection when you should be pampering yourself, for your health is important to us. I don't know what *mi padre* is doing; take note that I will be very annoyed if you do not obey María de la Cruz in this case.

3. I am very discreet in similar things. The truth of the matter is that I have never been very perfect, and now I think I have a greater motive, since I am old and tired; it would frighten you to see me. These days my stomach has been weak, so the nuts you sent arrived at a good time. Although there were still some left from others that had been sent to me, these are very good. You eat the ones that remain for love of me, and give my best regards to the Countess of Osorno.[3] It seems to me that I received

only one letter from her, and I wrote one; but I will write again as soon as I can. Today they brought me three packets of letters and yesterday a good number of them. Since my confessor is at the grille and says I should send this messenger boy off quickly, I won't be able to write at length.

4. Oh, how the letter from *mi padre* saddens me! You should find out at once whether the power the visitator has is in writing. How these canons weary me; and now they want authorization from the prelate so as to oblige us to pay rent on the land. If *mi padre* is able to give it, it must be in writing and notarized. He should consider how far his powers extend; and if he can give it, let him send it to me at once, for goodness' sake, if he doesn't want the canons to be annoyed with me. We would now be in the house if it were not for a miserable 3,000 maravedis, and perhaps there would be time left over for me to be sent to your monastery. I would like that, even if it were just to see what this nun of yours is like. Tell María de la Cruz that her letter made me happy and that the gift I now ask of her is that she surround your reverence with care.

5. Don't fail to communicate with the rector, for I assure you he may be a greater friend of yours than anyone else may be; indeed, these fathers are helpful. The rector here made the purchase, and he went to the chapter about it, and took care of everything very well. May God likewise take care of you, my daughter, and do not be angry with me, for I have told you why I am not coming to Valladolid. It would be a lie for me to say I don't want to. If I were to come, all the dealings with the nobility and all the commotion would greatly tire me; but I would put up with it all in order to see you.

6. Last night I wrote you a few lines, and now I've written a lot considering the hurry I am in to finish. All the nuns send their regards. May God make you holy. The replies that you make in the letter from *mi padre* are very amusing; I don't know whom to believe. Don't tire yourself trying to get him to write to me; if you tell me how his health is, I will be very satisfied with that.

7. Tell me where he is from because if it is Medina, he will be doing wrong not to pass by this way. This messenger boy came

today, 16 July, at ten o'clock. I am sending him back at four. Why don't you tell me about the business affairs of Señora Doña María. Give her my best. May God keep you.

Your servant and still . . .
Teresa of Jesus

To Madre María Bautista, Valladolid
Segovia, September 11, 1574

The visitator ordered Teresa to return to Avila to prepare for a foundation in Beas de Segura, ruining the chances of a trip to see María Bautista in Valladolid. Teresa is hoping that the nuns in Segovia will be in their house before she has to leave. Her health is better. She is in immediate need of money.

---

1. Jesus. May the Holy Spirit be with your reverence, my daughter. From the letter of Padre Maestro Fray Domingo, you will see what is happening and how the Lord has arranged matters in such a way that I will be unable to see you. I assure you I deeply regret this, for it is one of the things that would now give me consolation and pleasure. But this disappointment will pass away also, as do all the things of this life; when I think of this, I can bear well anything that displeases me.

2. My best regards to my dear Casilda (for I also regret not being able to see her) and to María de la Cruz. On some other occasion the Lord will so arrange things that more time will be available than there would have been at present. Take care of your health (now you see how important that is and how it saddens me that you are ill); and try to be very holy, for I tell you, holiness will be necessary if you are going to bear the trial you have there. I no longer have the quartan fevers. When the Lord wants me to do something, he then gives me better health.

3. I will be going at the end of this month; and I am still afraid that the nuns here won't be established in their house when I leave. We have agreed to give the chapter[1] six hundred ducats at once; from one of the sisters we have a very good title to an income worth six hundred and thirty. Well, we haven't been able to find anything about this title; no one will accept it or take it as collateral. Pray for this; it would make me very happy not to have to leave the nuns before they are settled in their house. If Señora Doña María had given the money, they would have readily accepted the title, for it is very good and safe. Let me know if this might be possible, or if there is anyone who might accept it or who would give us a loan on good collateral worth

St. Teresa of Avila: Her Life in Letters

more than a thousand. And pray for me, since I have to make such a long trip and in winter.

4. The end of this month, at the latest, I will go to the Incarnation. If you want to send something, write to me, and don't be sad about not seeing me. Perhaps it would make you sadder to see me, I'm so old and worn-out. Give my regards to all. Isabel de San Pablo would very much like to see you. These canons have mortified us all. May God forgive them.

5. Do you know anyone there who could lend me some *reales*? I don't want them as a donation but only until I am paid what my brother[2] gave me, for they say it has now been collected. To go to the Incarnation without a cent would be a mistake.[3] And here there is nothing available since they have renovations to complete on the house. Whether little or much, try to get something for me.

6. Now they have spoken to me of two nuns with very good dowries who would like to enter here. They would bring more than two thousand ducats each; this could go to pay for the house, which cost four thousand, and to pay the six hundred to the canons, and still more. I am telling you this that you might praise the Lord, for he has granted me a favor; and the two women being received are so good. I have not heard anything about Doña María's business affairs; write to me about them, and send her greetings from me, and let us see if she sends something.

7. Glory to God that my Padre Fray Domingo is well. If by chance Padre Maestro Medina[4] passes through, give him this letter from me for he thinks I am angry with him, according to what Father Provincial says,[5] because of a letter he wrote me. It was a letter deserving thanks rather than anger. He must be wondering also if I know what he said to the other person, although I said nothing to him about it. Our Father Visitator told me she was already a nun and had no more than a thousand ducats for a dowry. Write to me about how she is doing and what Father Visitator says. Well, since she is from his order, he will be patient.

8. I wrote to you a short while ago. I don't know whether you received it. It is not right for you to go so long without writing to me, for you know how delighted I am with your letters. May

God be with you. It's strange how difficult I am finding it not to be able to see you—I had still been hopeful.[6]

Today is 11 September.

Yours,
Teresa of Jesus

To Don Antonio Gaytán
Segovia, Final Months(?) 1574

Antonio Gaytán had written for counsel about prayer and his desire for solitude.

To the Magnificent Señor Antonio Gaytán, my lord.

1. Jesus be with your honor and repay you for the book you sent, which is just right for me. I would need more time to answer your question—I mean about what touches on prayer—although the substance of the answer is that this is a very common way of proceeding by those who have reached contemplation. I have often told you this, but you forget it. You have to realize that just as there are different seasons on this earth, so there are in the interior life, and it cannot be otherwise. So don't be troubled— you are not at fault.

2. As for the rest, I cannot be a judge, since I am an interested party; and also my natural inclination has always been toward the state of solitude, although I have not merited to have it, and since this is the state proper to our order, I could be giving counsel appropriate for myself but not for what is fitting for you. Speak about this clearly with Father Rector, and he will see what is best; and try observing to which one your spirit has the greater leaning. May God keep you, for I am writing so many letters that I don't know how I have been able to say this much, and the messenger is waiting.

3. As to my departure, there is nothing new; I don't know how it could be possible this year. God can do all. Pray much to His Majesty for me, as I do for you, and keep me always informed about yourself.

Your honor's unworthy servant,
Teresa of Jesus

To Padre Domingo Báñez, Valladolid
Avila, December 3, 1574

For two months Teresa had been back in Avila after having made the foundation in Segovia. Báñez is preparing the community in Valladolid for their coming elections. Teresa's health is better despite the cold weather of Avila.

---

1. I tell you, *mi padre*, I think my joys are no longer of this kingdom, for what I want I do not have, and what I have I do not want. What is missing is that the happiness I used to experience in dealing with my confessors is no longer present; one would have to be more than a confessor. Anything less than what the soul desires does not fulfill it. Certainly, it has been a relief for me to write this. May God grant that your honor always find your relief in loving him.

2. Tell your "poca cosa,"[1] who is concerned about whether the sisters will vote for her or not, that she is thereby meddling and lacking in humility. For what you and those of us who look after the welfare of that house believe is best will be done rather than what one nun thinks, for we have more interest in a good choice. It is necessary that the nuns be made to understand these things. When you see Señora Doña María, give her my regards for I have not written for some time. It is a good thing that I am better in the midst of this cold weather.

I think it is 3 December, and I am your honor's daughter and servant.

Teresa of Jesus

To Doña Ana Enríquez, Toro
Valladolid, December 23, 1574

Ana Enríquez was the daughter of the marquises of Alcañices and a good friend of Teresa's. The difficulties with the family of Casilda de Padilla occasioned the visit by Teresa to Valladolid. Her health is good; she is happy with the community and, especially, with the sermons of Domingo Báñez.

1. Jesus. The grace of the Holy Spirit be with your honor always. It would have been a great consolation for me to find you here, and I would have considered the journey well spent had it given me the opportunity to enjoy your company for a longer time than in Salamanca. I do not deserve this favor from our Lord. May he be blessed forever. This prioress[1] has enjoyed your company fully. After all, she is better than I and most dedicated to serving you.

2. I was most happy that you had my Padre Baltasar Alvarez[2] there for several days to provide you with some relief from so many trials. May the Lord be blessed that you are enjoying better health than usual. Mine is now much better than it has been in recent years, and that is saying a lot for this time of year. I have found souls of such quality in this house that I had to praise the Lord. And although Estefanía[3] certainly is a saint in my opinion, the talent of Casilda[4] and the favors the Lord has granted her after she took the habit have pleased me greatly. May His Majesty lead her forward. For we should have high regard for souls that he takes to himself in so short a time.

3. Estefanía's simplicity in everything except what pertains to God amazes me, for I perceive through her words the wisdom she has in regard to the Truth.[5]

4. Father Provincial[6] has visited this house, and the election has taken place. They have reelected the prioress,[7] and from St. Joseph's in Avila we are going to bring the subprioress elected by them, whose name is Antonia del Espíritu Santo. Señora Doña Guiomar knows her; she is a very good soul.

5. The foundation in Zamora has been set aside for now, and I am going to make the long trip for which I had left before.[8] I

have already thought of giving myself the joy of passing through your region so as to pay my respects to you. I haven't received a letter from my Padre Baltasar Alvarez in a long time. Nor have I written to him; certainly not so as to mortify myself, for I never make any progress in this or, it seems, in anything else. But I haven't written because of the torment of having to write so many letters, and when I think of writing one just for my own satisfaction, there is never time. Blessed be God, for we will have security in our eternal enjoyment of him. Here below, certainly, with this flux of separation and change of every kind, we cannot rely much on anything. With this hope for the end, I go through life; they say we do so with many trials, but it doesn't seem so to me.

6. Mother Prioress here is telling me about my "custodian." His affability is as pleasing to me as it is to her. May our Lord make him very holy. I beg you to give him my regards. I often pray to the Lord for him and for Señor Don Juan Antonio as well. Don't forget me in your prayers, for love of the Lord, for I am always in need. We can now be at ease about Doña Guiomar, as you say and she herself confirms. I would love to know something about the successful event so as to make a better judgment and share in your joy. May our Lord in this Christmas season grant your soul all the great joys that I beg of him for you.

7. On this feast of St. Thomas, Padre Fray Domingo preached a sermon here in which he spoke of trials in such terms that I found myself wanting to have many and that the Lord would give them to me in the future. His sermons are for me a sheer joy. They have elected him prior. It is not known whether he will be confirmed.[9] He is so busy that only briefly have I been able to benefit from his presence. But if I were able to see you for as much time, I would be happy. May the Lord bring this about, and may he give you as much health and rest as is necessary to gain that which has no end.

Tomorrow is Christmas Eve.

Your honor's unworthy servant and subject,
Teresa of Jesus

To Doña Inés Nieto, Madrid
Valladolid, December 28, 1574

Doña Inés Nieto was the wife of Don Juan de Albornoz, secretary to the Duke of Alba. She had just sent some good news to Teresa, perhaps of the return of her husband and the duke from Flanders. Teresa speaks of the monastery's need for a dowry from aspirants and thanks Inés for a statue.

---

1. Jesus. The grace of the Holy Spirit be with your honor. Although I have not written until now, you can be sure that I do not forget you in my poor prayers before our Lord, and learning of your happiness made me happy. May it please our Lord that you will enjoy many years in his service, for I hope in His Majesty that nothing will impede you from this service, even though there may be obstacles. All those things considered good in this miserable life are obstacles. That you spent these past years for God will be of great benefit to you in judging each thing according to its true worth and counting it as something that will soon pass away.

2. Some time ago Señora Isabel de Córdoba[1] spoke to the prioress of this house,[2] who considers her to be very dedicated to God's service. And so I arranged to speak to her. She told me she is a rather close relative of Señor Albornoz's,[3] which is the reason why I would like her to enter here. However since this house is in the process of being adapted and Doña María Mendoza[4] is the foundress, we will need the help of some alms in order to receive her. Since she told me that Señor Albornoz had promised to help her become a nun, I told her that I thought he would be even more willing to do so if she were to enter this house. Indeed, even were I to want a different arrangement, I wouldn't be able to do anything, because of Doña María and also the nuns. Since the number of nuns is small and there are many aspirants, and they are in need, it would be harmful for the nuns not to take in those who can help them. She told me that she has property but that it is of a kind, she is informed, that cannot be sold. When some means are found, even if less than what could be received from others, I will do what I can, for I certainly want to serve

you and Señor Albornoz as I ought, for whose prayers I beg. In my prayers, although miserable, I will do what you have asked.

3. May our Lord reward you for the statue. You indeed owe it to me. I beg you to keep it well protected until I ask you for it. That will be when I am more settled in one monastery than I am now; there I will be able to enjoy it. May you do me the favor not to forget me in your prayers. May our Lord grant you all the spiritual blessings that I beg of him, amen.

Today is the feast of the Holy Innocents.

Your honor's unworthy servant,
Teresa of Jesus, Carmelite

To Don Teutonio de Braganza, Salamanca
Valladolid, January 2, 1575

Teresa answers a letter from Don Teutonio, who has just returned from a business trip that was not entirely successful. He is interested in the Teresian foundations and has a number of possible sites in mind. He had defended Teresa's travels outside the cloister, for which she was being criticized. He had warned her to be careful in dealing with a certain person. And finally, he had sought advice about some difficulties in his spiritual life.

---

1. Jesus. The grace of the Holy Spirit be with your lordship always and give you many more good years, as many as I desire, and with the holiness I beg for you. I have been waiting a long time to see your handwriting and find out whether you are in Salamanca, for I didn't know where to write to you. And now I don't know if I'll have the time to write at length, as I desire, since I have a very reliable messenger for this letter. I praise our Lord that you are better. My health has been good, which is a lot for this time of year.

2. May His Majesty repay you for the care with which you undertook all that I had asked of you. Well, it seems to me that our Lady, the Blessed Virgin, has chosen you to be the protector of her order. It is consoling for me to know that she will repay you in more ways than I could think of mentioning in my prayers, although I continue to pray for you.

3. The monastery in Zamora has been set aside for now: first, because this is not a suitable time of year (it's the time for going to a much warmer region); second, because it doesn't seem that the one who was to give us the house responded to all that we expected of him, and he is absent. However, we have not given up. Furthermore, I have also been considering how troublesome it is for a house founded in poverty to have a founder who is not much inclined to helping, especially if he has the right to build the monastery.[1] It seems to me that it would be better to begin in a different way, by buying a house, but this would require more time. The Lord will provide when it pleases him to do so. You have done me a great favor in obtaining the authorization for me

at the right time. When a messenger is available you can send it to me, but it is not necessary to hire one immediately.

4. With regard to Torrijos, don't go to any bother about it. In no way does the place appeal to me. I would accept it to comply with your wishes. But for persons of this kind to be received just because we need the dowry would be something unacceptable in these houses, because then we would not be able to send them away at once if they were not suited to our order.

5. I am sorry that the reason for your having undertaken the trip was not realized. Nevertheless, I hope in the Lord that your words will bear much fruit, even though their effect is not seen immediately. May it please the Lord that the business in Rome will go well. I have prayed hard for this, if it be for his service; what I hope is that if it is, he will bring it about, because so many prayers are being offered for that intention.

6. With respect to the countess's monastery, I don't know what to say, for I have been hearing about it for a long time. I tell you I would rather found four monasteries of our nuns than try to convert these blessed souls, however holy, to our manner of living, for within fifteen days from the start our manner of life can be set up so that those who enter do not have to do anything more than what they see is done by the other nuns. I spoke with two of them in Toledo and know that they are doing well in the way of life they have chosen. On the other hand, I certainly don't know how I could receive them under my charge, for I believe they conduct themselves with more rigor and penance than mortification and prayer; I mean in general. Nonetheless, if the Lord so desires, I will find out more, since that is what you seem to want.

7. It was most fortunate that you had the marquis so much on your side, for that is important. May it please the Lord that you receive good news. Regarding the business here, now that you are in the midst of it, I hope in him that all will go well. I will not have to worry any more about letters that displease Padre Olea since it is to you that one ought to write.[2] I have been sorry about it, for much is owed to him and in my opinion my letters got into the hands of others. The prioress of Segovia must not have been on guard, thinking that the matter was not important.

It made me happy to know how I can write to you when it is necessary and that when the occasion arises you will speak in favor of my travels.³ Certainly traveling is one of the things that wearies me in life and one of life's greater trials, and above all when I am judged by others to be doing something bad. I have often thought how much better off I would be remaining at rest and not having the general's command.⁴ At other times, when I see how the Lord is served in these houses, everything seems small to me. May His Majesty direct me in doing his will.

8. I tell you there are souls in this house⁵ that almost continually, or very frequently, stir me to the praises of God. Although Estefanía is great and, in my opinion, a saint, Sister Casilda de la Concepción amazes me. Certainly I don't find anything in her, exteriorly or interiorly, that would keep her from becoming (with God's assistance) a great saint. What he is doing in her is clearly seen. She is very talented (beyond all possibility for her age) and deeply prayerful, for since she took the habit the Lord has favored her. Her happiness and humility are remarkable; it's a strange thing. Both of them say they will pray for your lordship in a special way.

9. I have not wanted her to write to you: first, because we are being very careful not to let her think we are showing her any special attention (although, indeed, in her simplicity she has little need for this; in many ways she's like another Fray Junípero);⁶ second, because I wouldn't want you to pay attention to what we poor women tell you, for you have a good *padre* who awakens and teaches you and a good God who loves you.

10. With regard to Madrid, I don't know the reason, but even though I see that it would be appropriate to have one of these houses there, a strange resistance wells up in me; it must be a temptation. I still haven't seen a letter from Prior Covarrubias. It would be difficult to make a foundation without permission from the ordinary, because the patent letter I have requires this, and also the Council. But I believe we would have the permission, if this were the only thing in need of our attention. May the Lord advance the project.

11. I will be leaving here after the feast of Epiphany. I am going to Avila along the road passing through Medina, where I don't

think I'll stay for more than a day or two; the same goes for Avila, in that I am going on at once to Toledo. I want to finish up this business of Beas.[7] Wherever I am, I will write to you as often as I find someone who will deliver a letter to you. In your charity, please pray for me.

12. May His Majesty repay you for the care you show the sisters there,[8] for you are showing great charity; they are not without their trials. I would be so happy to be there. But, since you are not located along the way to the next foundation, it would be very difficult for me to go there. Unless I were to receive a command, I wouldn't go; nor must I do anything without approval of the authorities. I think that since the nuns are offering him more, he will be satisfied, for the place is very good and there is room for expansion (the site you mention seems to me to be out of the way), and the church is nice. In sum, the location is what matters most. As for the rest, it wouldn't bother me much if anything of what has been constructed were lost. Your lordship, along with Father Rector, should consider the whole matter as a transaction to be made for our Lady, and we will act accordingly. Lest some change be introduced, I would like to see the plan delayed, in one way or another, until I return from Beas. If possible, I will return in April.

13. Your imperfections[9] do not shock me, for I see myself with so many. Here, I have had more time to be alone than I have had in a long while; it has been a great consolation for me. May our Lord give the consolation to your soul that I ask of him, amen. With regard to the one you told me to make a fuss over, I had already come to this awareness, and of all the rest, but both my obligation to be grateful and your great zeal enable me to endure more than with my temperament I could otherwise bear. Nonetheless, I am on my guard! The prioress relies greatly on your prayers. Now that she knows you, she is sorry about how little she understood of the great grace God gave her through your visit.

Today is 2 January.

Your lordship's unworthy servant,
Teresa of Jesus

Her Early Sixties

To Padre Luis de Granada, Lisbon
Beas, May 1575(?)

Teresa had never had the opportunity of meeting Fray Luis de Granada, a Dominican author of spiritual books that she prized. Now, a mutual friend, Teutonio de Braganza, gives her the chance to write him a letter of appreciation.

---

1. Jesus. May the grace of the Holy Spirit be always with your paternity, amen. Many persons love you in the Lord for having written such holy and beneficial doctrine, thanking His Majesty for giving it to you for the good of souls—and I am one of them.[1] And for my part I know that no amount of effort would have prevented me from seeing the one whose words console me so much, if my state in life and my being a woman had allowed it. Unable thus to see you, I had to search out persons like you for assurance against the fears in which my soul lived for some years. And since I have not merited to meet you, I am consoled that Señor Don Teutonio has ordered me to write this letter, something I wouldn't have dared to do on my own. But, trusting in obedience, I hope in our Lord that it will benefit me because you will at times remember to pray for me. I am in great need of prayers since I go about exposed to the eyes of the world and with little to show, nothing to verify in the least what they imagine about me.

2. If you understand these things, it will be enough that you grant me this favor and alms; for knowing so well what the world is, you can comprehend the great trial it is for someone who has lived a wretched life. This being so, I have often dared to ask our Lord to grant you a long life. May it please His Majesty to grant me this favor, and may you continue growing in holiness and in his love, amen.

Your paternity's unworthy servant and subject,
Teresa of Jesus, Carmelite

3. Señor Don Teutonio, I believe, is one of those who are deceived in my regard.[2] He tells me he likes you very much. In recompense for this, you are obliged to visit his lordship; don't think it would be fruitless.

To Padre Juan Bautista Rubeo,[1] Piacenza
Seville, June 18, 1575

Teresa, who always had high esteem for the holiness of her Father General (Rubeo), now finds herself in a difficult situation in her relationship with him because of the discalced friars. They had founded three monasteries of friars in Andalusia without permission of the general and without notifying him, although they did have authorization from the visitator. The general chapter of Carmelites in Piacenza, Italy (May–June 1575), suppressed these monasteries under pain of excommunication. Teresa writes to explain the state of affairs in Andalusia to Rubeo and to intercede for Gracián and Mariano, who were mainly responsible for what had been done. She states her opinion about the decisions taken by the chapter at Piacenza and pleads with the general to look at things in a different light.

---

1. Jesus. The grace of the Holy Spirit be always with your lordship. Last week I wrote to you at length in the same vein in two letters, each sent in a different way, because I want the letter to reach you. Yesterday, 17 June, I received from you two letters, which I had eagerly desired, one sent in October, the other in January. Although they were not dated as recently as I would have desired, I was much consoled by them and the knowledge that you are in good health. May our Lord continue to give it to you as all your daughters in these your houses beseech him. Each day in choir we pray for you especially, and in addition all the nuns are concerned about you. Since they know of my love for you and they have no other father, they have great love for you. And this is not surprising, since we have no other good on earth. And since all the nuns are happy, they never cease being grateful to you for having encouraged us in the beginning.

2. I wrote you about the foundation in Beas and how another was being requested in Caravaca, and that the license for the latter contained so many unsuitable requirements that I did not want to proceed with it. Now they have given another license similar to that of Beas, in which the nuns are subject to you, and this will be so, God willing, for all the houses. I also wrote you about the reasons for which I came here to Seville to make a foundation.

May our Lord be pleased to bring about my purpose in coming here, which is to rid the discalced friars of the things that provoke you. May God grant me this favor. You should know that before coming to Beas I made many inquiries to make sure it was not Andalusia. In no way would I have otherwise considered coming here, for I do not fare well with these people. And it is true that Beas is not Andalusia, but it is in the province of Andalusia. This I learned only a month after the foundation was made.[2] Since I was here with the nuns, it seemed to me that I should not abandon the monastery. It was one of the reasons for my coming here. But my main desire is the one I wrote about to you, to understand the complicated situation of these fathers, for although they justify their cause (and indeed I don't gather from them anything else than the desire to be your true sons and not displease you), I cannot help but blame them. Now it seems they are beginning to understand that it would have been better for them to have proceeded otherwise so as not to have been troublesome to you. Mariano and I especially argued a great deal, for he is very impetuous.[3] Gracián is like an angel, and were he alone he would have done otherwise. His coming here was by order of Fray Baltasar,[4] who was at the time prior of Pastrana. I tell you that if you knew Gracián you would rejoice to have him as your son, and I know truly that he is, and Mariano is too.

3. This Mariano is a virtuous and penitential man and is known by all for his inventive talents, and you can be sure that he has been moved solely by zeal for God and the good of the order; but as I say, he has gone to extremes and been imprudent. I don't think there is any ambition in him, but he says many things he doesn't mean, and the devil, as you say, stirs up trouble. I have suffered very much from him at times, but since I see that he is virtuous, I pass over it. If you could hear the excuses he makes for himself, you would be satisfied. Today he told me that he wouldn't be at peace until he could prostrate at your feet. I already wrote to you how both of them have asked me to write to you and present their excuses, for they don't dare do so themselves. So I will say nothing here but what seems to me necessary, since I have already written you about it.

4. First you should understand for love of our Lord that I would not give a thing for all the discalced friars together if they dared

even so much as to brush against your robes. This is a fact, because to cause you the least displeasure would be like striking me in the pupil of the eye. They have not seen and will not see these letters, although I have told Mariano that I know you will show them mercy if they are obedient. Gracián is not here, for the nuncio sent for him, as I wrote to you, and believe me if I saw they were disobedient, I would not either see them or listen to them; but I couldn't be any more devoted to you than they show themselves to be.

5. I will now give you my opinion and if it amounts to foolishness, please forgive me. With regard to the excommunication,[5] this is what Gracián has now written to Mariano from Madrid: Father Provincial, Fray Angel, told him that he could not stay in the monastery because he had been excommunicated. So he stayed in his father's house. When the nuncio found out, he sent for Padre Fray Angel and scolded him very much, saying that it was an affront to say that those who were in Andalusia through his orders were excommunicated and that anyone saying this should be punished. Gracián then went to the monastery, where he is now residing, and he is preaching in the city.

6. *Mi padre* and lord, this is not a time for excommunications. Gracián has a brother close to the king who serves as his secretary and of whom the king is very fond. And the king from what I have learned might side with the reform. The calced[6] friars say they don't know why you treat such virtuous men in this way, and that they would like to communicate with the contemplative friars[7] and witness their virtue, and that you by this excommunication prevent them from so doing. They say one thing to you, and here they say something else. They go to the archbishop[8] and say they do not dare punish them because they will immediately have recourse to you. They are a strange lot. I see the one group and the other, and our Lord knows that I speak the truth, for I believe that the most obedient are the discalced friars, and they will continue to be so. Over there you don't see what is going on here. I see it and feel responsible for it all, for I truly know of your holiness and how fond you are of virtue. The things of the order are going so badly here, on account of our sins; and now that I have seen what is going on here, the friars in Castile seem to me to be very good. Even since

I have been here something very distressing happened—in broad daylight the police found two friars in a house of ill-fame and publicly brought them to jail. This was handled badly. I am not surprised by human weaknesses, but I would expect that more consideration be given to avoiding scandal. This happened after I wrote to you. Nonetheless, people are saying that it is good they were arrested.

7. Some friars have come to see me. They seem to be good, the prior especially, who is an excellent man. He came that I might show him the patent letters authorizing me to make the foundation. He wanted to have a copy. I asked him not to start a litigation, for he saw that I had the authority to make the foundation. For the last patent letter you sent me in Latin, after the visitators came, gives permission and says that I can make foundations everywhere.[9] And this is the way learned men understand it, for you do not designate any house or kingdom, nor are any limits indicated; rather foundations are to be made everywhere. And it even issues a command, which made me push myself to do more than I was able, for I am old and worn out; but this all seems to me to be nothing, including the fatigue I underwent at the Incarnation. I never have good health, nor do I have any desire for it; but yes, I do have a great desire to depart from this exile, even though God gives me greater favors every day. May he be blessed for everything.

8. With regard to the calced friars who were received by the discalced friars, I have already spoken to Mariano about it. He says that Peñuela[10] took the habit deceitfully, for he went to Pastrana and said that the visitator here, Vargas, had given it to him, but it was found out that he had taken it on his own. For some days they have been trying to send him away, and they will certainly do so. The other friar is no longer with them. The monasteries of the discalced friars were founded by orders of the visitator, Vargas, who has the apostolic authority to do so. He holds that for this region the main tool for reform is to have houses of discalced friars. And so the nuncio sending Fray Antonio de Jesús as visitator gave him the license to be a reformer so that he could found monasteries. But he went about it in a better way, for he made no foundation without asking you.[11] And if Teresa of Jesus had been here, perhaps this would have been

carried out more carefully, for if they even considered founding a house without your permission they would have been fiercely opposed by me. And in this matter Fray Pedro Fernández, the visitator in Castile, proceeded well, and I owe him much because he was always careful not to displease you. The visitator here has given so many licenses and faculties to these fathers, asking them to make use of them, that if you saw the powers they were given you wouldn't think they were so much at fault. Thus they say that they never wanted to accept Fray Gaspar[12] or have his friendship—who begged them for it—or others; and the house[13] they took over from the order they later abandoned. And so they say many things in their defense, from which I see that they have not proceeded with any malice. And when I see the great trials they have undergone and the penance they do—for I really believe they are servants of God—it pains me to learn that you disapprove of them.

9. The monasteries were founded by the visitator, and he ordered the friars with grave precepts not to abandon them. And the nuncio gave patent letters of reformer to Gracián and gave him care of the houses of the friars as well, and you say they ought to observe what the visitator commands; and as you know, the pope says the same in the brief that suppresses the faculties of the visitators. I don't know how everything can now be undone. Besides, they tell me there are constitutions in print prescribing that in every province there should be houses of reformed friars. Whether the whole order is reformed or not is not a concern here. These reformed friars are considered to be saints, whatever may be the case. Truly they are good and live with great recollection and practice prayer. Among them are some distinguished persons, and more than twenty have taken courses—or I don't know what they call them—some in canon law and others in theology, and they are very talented. And in this house together with those of Granada and La Peñuela they say there are more than seventy friars, or so it seems to me I heard. I don't know what would become of all of them or how it would appear now to everybody, considering the opinion they have of them. Perhaps we would all have to pay. They are highly regarded by the king, and this archbishop says that they are the only real friars. Now to make them leave the reform (since you don't want any

reformed friars)—believe me that even though you had every reason in the world, it wouldn't seem that you did. Well, if you were to remove them from your protection, they wouldn't want this, nor would you be right in doing so, nor would it please our Lord.

I commend you to His Majesty; as a true father, forget the past and remember that you are a servant of the Blessed Virgin and that she would be displeased if you were to forsake those who by the sweat of their brow desire to bring increase to her order. Matters are now such that much careful thought . . . [14]

To King Don Philip II, Madrid
Seville, July 19, 1575

While Teresa was taken up with the foundation in Seville, the Carmelites held a chapter at Piacenza in Italy (May 22, 1575), the results of which were unfavorable toward Teresa and her work. She foresees many difficulties in the making and proposes to the king that he erect a separate province for the discalced friars and nuns. She also asks that Gracián be made its superior.

1. Jesus. The grace of the Holy Spirit be always with your majesty. While much afflicted and praying to our Lord about the affairs of this holy order of our Lady and considering the great need there is that these initiatives God has taken in its regard not crumble, it occurred to me that the best safeguard for us would be that you realize what giving a solid foundation to this edifice entails;[1] even the calced friars would benefit from the increase in numbers.

2. I have lived among them for forty years,[2] and, considering everything, I know clearly that if a separate province is not made for the discalced friars—and soon—great harm will be done, and I think it will be impossible for them to move ahead. Since this lies in your hands and I see that the Blessed Virgin, our Lady, has chosen you to support and protect her order, I have dared to write and beg you that for the love of our Lord and his glorious Mother you give orders that this separate province be formed.[3] It is so important for the devil to hinder this project that he will raise many objections, without any of them being valid, for only blessings of every kind can come from doing this.

3. It would be most beneficial to us in our situation if you would appoint a discalced *padre*, named Gracián, whom I have recently come to know, to be in charge of us in our beginnings. Although he is young, I was moved to praise our Lord greatly for what he has given to that soul and for the great works he has done through him for the salvation of many souls. And so I believe that the Lord has chosen this friar to bring many blessings to our order.[4] May our Lord so direct things that you will want to render him this service and issue the necessary commands.

4. I kiss your hands many times for the favor you granted me in regard to the license for founding a monastery in Caravaca.[5] For the love of God I beg you to pardon me, for I recognize that I am being very bold. But in reflecting that the Lord listens to the poor and that you stand in his place, I don't think you will become annoyed.

5. May God give you peace and a long life, as I beg him continually and as is needed by Christendom.

Today 19 July.

Your majesty's unworthy servant and subject,
Teresa of Jesus, Carmelite

To Padre Baltasar Alvarez, Salamanca
Seville, October 9, 1575

Teresa has been in Seville four months, but the nuns still do not have their own house. On the other hand, neither do the nuns in Salamanca, who have been there for five years. Teresa continues to have the interests of that Carmel at heart and enlists the help of Julián de Avila, Gaspar Daza, and probably Baltasar Alvarez, S.J.

1. Jesus. The grace of the Holy Spirit be with your honor, *padre* and *señor mio*. Padre Julián de Avila and also Señor Maestro wrote me about the house of Juan de Avila de la Vega which is for sale.[1] It is just right for us, both the price (which Padre Julián de Avila says will be little more than 1,000 ducats) and the location, which for our purpose is excellent. That it is close to you is sufficient.

2. I really think that it will be so old that there will be immediate need for repairs. That matters little if there is ample space and a well. I beg you to begin at once to confer about buying it, but without looking too eager because then they will raise the price.

3. My brother[2] is going to Madrid and you can notify him there to send you the authorization. May the Lord direct matters, for it would be a great thing to have our own house. Because I have many letters to write I cannot go on at length. May God preserve you for me for many years and give me the opportunity to see you.

4. I think there is so much to do down here that I will have to stay a long while. I am well, and my brother kisses your hands many times.

Today is 9 October.

Your honor's unworthy servant and true friend,
Teresa of Jesus

To Padre Jerónimo Gracián, Toledo
Seville, October 1575(?)

Teresa had received letters from John of the Cross, praising Gracián, and from Gracián, asking her advice concerning his first visitation to the Carmels in Castile.

---

1. If she wants, you would be doing much good for the house by leaving her there; if she doesn't, let her come down here and she can go with the nuns as far as Malagón.[1] But truthfully, I hope no one ever does me this favor. There is no house more in need of talented persons than Toledo. The prioress there will soon end her term of office, but I don't think there is another who would be better for that house.[2] Although she is very ill, she is careful, and even though she is friendly with "the cats," she has many virtues.[3] If you think it a good thing, she could resign, giving as a reason the hot weather of that region that is killing her, which is evident, and another election could be held. But I don't know who could go there as prioress, for almost all of them love her so much that they wouldn't adapt easily to another, in my opinion, although there will never be lacking someone who is contentious—that's for sure.

2. You should be careful, *padre mio*, in this matter, and believe that I understand women's nature better than you. In no way is it fitting that you let a prioress or subject think it is possible to transfer someone from her house except in the case of making a new foundation. And truly, even for this reason I see that this expectation does so much harm. I have often desired that the time for making foundations were to end so that all the nuns could settle down. And believe me when I tell you this truth— and if I die, don't forget it—that for people who are enclosed, the devil doesn't want anything else except to foster the opinion that something like a transfer is possible. There is much to say about this, for I have the permission from our Father General,[4] which I asked for, since sometimes the weather will be bad for a nun and she can then be transferred to another region. Nonetheless I have afterward seen so many disadvantages in this that unless

a transfer is for the good of the order I don't think it should be allowed. It is better that some die than that all be harmed.

3. There isn't any monastery that has the full number of nuns; rather some are far short of the full number, and in Segovia I believe they are three or four short, for I paid close attention to this. In Malagón I gave the prioress I don't know how many permissions to receive different nuns, warning her to be very careful, for we took some nuns away from there and left only a few. You should revoke these permissions, for it is better that they have recourse to you.[5] And believe me, *mi padre*, now that I don't feel obliged, for I know the care with which you consider things, it will be a great consolation for me to be relieved of that obligation. As things stand now we can proceed with more order, but the one who had to make foundations with nothing but air at her disposal needed help from all sides and had to be obliging.

And you should believe that they gain a great deal from being attached to the Society of Jesus—even though some mistakes might be made in this respect—as time will tell and I will show you. At least these fathers have been my main help and I would never fail to recognize this. I wouldn't want you to impede the nuns in Valladolid from sending something from the garden, for they have a surplus and the others are poor. And believe me, *mi padre*, being gracious even in trifling matters cannot be avoided with some persons. This is the only thing that seemed to me a little rigorous in the visitations, even though—since they were made by you—there must have been a reason.

4. Seneca is delighted and says that he has found more in his superior than he could have desired; he is giving great thanks to God.[6] I wouldn't want to do anything else. May His Majesty keep you for many years.

5. I tell you I am angry about those falls you have; it would be good if they tied you to the saddle so that you couldn't fall.[7] I don't know what kind of donkey that is, nor why you have to go ten leagues in a day, which on a pack saddle is killing. I am worried about whether you have thought of putting on more clothes, for it is now getting colder. Please God the fall didn't do you any harm. Since you are fond of helping souls, consider

the harm that many would suffer by your loss of health and, for love of God, take care of yourself.

6. Elías now has less fear.[8] The rector and Rodrigo Alvarez are very hopeful that everything will work out well. As for me, all the fear I previously had has left me, for I cannot feel it even were this my desire. My health has been wretched recently. They have purged me and I am well, better than I have been in four or five months; I got to the point where I couldn't go on.

Your paternity's unworthy servant,
Teresa of Jesus

To Madre María Bautista, Valladolid
Seville, December 30, 1575

Two letters from María Bautista have arrived filled with advice for Teresa, which makes her laugh. Teresa gives news about her family. The work of the reform is going badly in Andalusia. Teresa is given orders to choose a monastery for herself and stay there.

1. Jesus be with you, my daughter, and may he give you as many good years as I ask of him. I tell you that you make me laugh when you say that on another day you will say what you think about some things. As usual you have advice to give! On the last day of the Christmas feasts, they gave me the letter that came by way of Medina, and before that the other containing one from *mi padre*.[1] I have found no one through whom I could send a reply. I was overjoyed to receive the news about Señora Doña María, for since the bishop wrote that she was sick with fever, I have been very worried, and so we all have been praying much for her. Tell her this and give her my best regards. May God be blessed who has made her well. My regards also to her daughter and all the others.

2. The letter was written more out of devotion than a desire to fulfill an obligation. I would like to be so disposed toward him that whatever I say will be courteous. It is a strange thing that the affection I have for this other *padre* of ours[2] causes me no embarrassment as though he were no person. Actually, he doesn't know that I am now writing to you. He is doing well. Oh, what trials we undergo with these reforms! There's no obedience; he has excommunicated them; there is another uproar. I tell you I have had much more suffering than happiness since he has been here; things were going much better before.

3. Were I allowed I would already be there with you, for they have notified me of the mandate of our most Reverend *Padre*.[3] That is, I must choose a house and remain there permanently and make no more foundations, for I can no longer go out, because of the Council.[4] Clearly this is due to annoyance over my having come down here. I have reached the conclusion that the mandate came at the request of the friars of the cloth.[5] They think it will do

me much harm. And it so pleases me that I doubt whether it will be granted. I would like to choose your house for some reasons that cannot be mentioned in a letter, except for one, which is that you and *mi padre*[6] are there. Father Visitator has not allowed me to leave here because for now he has more authority over me than our most Reverend Father General. I don't know where it will all end up.

4. It would be very good for me now not to be involved in all the turmoil of these reforms. But the Lord does not wish to free me from these kinds of trials; they are most displeasing to me. Our *padre*[7] tells me I may leave when summer comes. As for what pertains to this house—I mean his foundation—there is no longer any need of my presence. As for my health, clearly this region is better for my health and even in a way for my quiet since here they do not have that inflated opinion of me that they do up there. But there are other reasons why I believe it will be better for me to settle down up there; being closer to our other houses is one of them. May our Lord guide matters, for I don't think I have a personal opinion; wherever they send me I will be happy.

5. My brother[8] has returned—and very sick; the fever, however, is now gone. He didn't meet with success in any of his business affairs, but since his possessions here are now safe, he has more than enough to live on. In the summer he will return to Castile, for this was not the right season. He is delighted with his sister and with Juan de Ovalle—they seek to please him and show him every courtesy—and they are delighted with him. He stopped by here for only a moment and so I didn't say anything about that other matter, but I believe it will be necessary to do no more than mention it and he will do it. As for the children's needs, one page will be more than enough.

6. My brother says that, if the page comes here, his mother can feel assured that he will be treated as though she were with him, and if he is capable and virtuous he can study with them at San Gil,[9] and he'll be better off than elsewhere. And as soon as I said that you desire this, Juan de Ovalle said he would take care of the matter, which made me laugh, for whatever he imagines I want, he is pleased to do. And thus I have succeeded in promoting so close a bond of friendship between my brother-in-law, his wife,

and my brother that I hope in God they will gain much. My brother will not lose thereby, for he is at peace.

7. Juan de Ovalle has been extremely kind to him; the children never stop praising him. I say this because that boy, if he comes—I mean here—in the event that they will not be in Avila by April, there will be no one to teach him anything else but virtue. If I were able to arrange everything, I would be delighted to remove any worry from *mi padre*,[10] for considering his character, I am amazed at how much he takes this to heart; God must have inspired him since the parents of the boy had no other solution. I would be very sorry if he went to Toledo. I don't know why he would rather stay there than in Madrid. I fear it won't come about. May God ordain whatever will be for his service, which is what is important. I am sorry for you,[11] and my desire to stay in your house has greatly diminished. I indeed believe, as I have said, they will send me to the place where there is most need.

8. With regard to his sister, there is no use speaking about it until our *padre* goes there, and indeed I am afraid that in trying to free them from one expense we will get them involved in a greater one. Since she was reared there for her whole life, I don't know how she would get along here, and from what I have been half given to understand, she doesn't get along well with her sisters. What I mean is that she must be somewhat bent on having her own way. May it not be a sanctity made of melancholy! Well, our *padre* will look into everything and until then, nothing should be said.

9. By now you will have received my letter in which I told you that I sent a nun from here as prioress for Caravaca. The nun from your house accepted it with much joy, and so the prioress of Malagón, where she has remained, writes me that she is happy. I tell you she must be a good soul. She wrote me wanting to know about you, and she speaks much about what she owes you and speaks of you with much love. The house was founded before Christmas, as far as I know; I haven't heard anything.[12]

10. I believe it will be good if you say nothing about the page to *mi padre* until I speak to my brother. Write and tell me how old he is and if he knows how to read, because it's necessary that he go with them to school. My best regards to María de la Cruz[13] and to

all, and to Dorotea. And why don't you say anything about how the chaplain is? Look after him, for he is a good man. And how is the arrangement of the room working out and do you find it satisfactory both in winter and summer? As usual, despite what you say about the subprioress, you are not more submissive.[14] O Jesus, how we do not know ourselves! May His Majesty give us light and watch over you for me.

11. With regard to matters concerning the Incarnation, you can write to Isabel de la Cruz,[15] for I can help much more from down here than from up there, and this I am doing. And I hope in God that he will give life to the pope, the king, the nuncio, and our *padre* for one or two years,[16] and everything will be settled. If any of them should die we would be lost, since our most Reverend Father General is of the present mind; yet God would resolve the matter in another way. Now I am thinking of writing to him and offer to serve him more so than before, for I am very fond of him and owe him much. It grieves me greatly to see what he is doing because of bad information. Everyone here sends you their best regards.

12. The situation here is not suited to composing songs. Do you think things are going so well? Pray much for our *padre*, for a serious person told the archbishop[17] today that perhaps they will kill him. They are in a state that arouses pity, and even more when one sees the offenses committed against God in this region on the part of nuns and friars. May His Majesty provide a remedy and free me from every offense, for up there I don't know. . . . But if God is to make some use of me, my life matters little; I would like to have many lives.

Tomorrow is New Year's Eve.

Yours, Teresa of Jesus

13. The weather is such here that I would have to go in search were I to want cold weather at night. May the Lord be praised for this. At least for my health, it is a good region, and nonetheless I do not desire to be here. My brother's becoming a friar[18] has gone nowhere nor will it.

To Padre Juan Bautista Rubeo, Cremona
Seville, January–February(?) 1576

Gracián has returned to Seville with new powers from the nuncio. The Andalusian and Castilian friars who were present at the chapter of Piacenza have returned to Spain. Teresa learns in a twisted version the decision made in her regard. In Avila, Fray John of the Cross is arrested for the first time. Teresa has written a number of letters to her Father General but doesn't know whether he has received them. She tries to clear the air and get the general and Gracián to enter into direct dialogue. She manifests her sad conviction that the general no longer pays any attention to what she has to say.

1. Jesus. The grace of the Holy Spirit be always with your lordship, amen. After I arrived here in Seville, I wrote to you three or four times,[1] and I did not write any more because the fathers who returned from the chapter told me that you would not be in Rome, that you had gone to visit the Mantuans.[2] May God be blessed that the chapter is over. In those letters I also gave you an account of the monasteries that were founded this year, which are three: Beas, Caravaca, and this one here. You have in them subjects who are great servants of God. Two of the houses were founded with an income; the one in this city was founded in poverty.[3] We still do not have our own house; but I hope in the Lord that we will. Because I am certain that one of these letters must have reached you, I am not going to give a detailed account of everything in this one.

2. I also mentioned how different speaking with these discalced fathers—I mean Padre Maestro Gracián and Mariano—is from what one would imagine through what I heard in Castile. Certainly they are your true sons, and I would dare say that, substantially, none of those who insist they are your true sons would surpass them. Since they have asked me to be an intermediary so that you may look favorably toward them again, for they did not dare write to you, I begged you in those letters as earnestly as I could, and so I beg you now, for the love of our Lord, that you do me this favor and believe my words. There is no reason for me to say anything but the complete truth, aside from the fact that I

would consider it an offense against God not to speak the truth. And even if it were not an offense against God, I would consider it a great evil and betrayal with respect to a father I so love.

3. When we stand before the judgment throne, you will see what you owe your true daughter Teresa of Jesus. This alone consoles me in these matters; for I well know there must be some who say the contrary. And so, in every way that I can I will try to make all understand, I mean all those who are not prejudiced, that I am your true daughter and will continue to be this as long as I live.

4. I have already written to you about the commission Padre Gracián received from the nuncio and how he was called to Madrid. You must know by now how he was again given the task of visitator to the discalced friars and nuns and to the province of Andalusia. I know very definitely that with regard to the latter, he tried to refuse in every way he could—although this is not being mentioned, it is true—and that his brother, the secretary,[4] was also opposed because nothing would come of it but a great trial.

5. But if these fathers would have listened to me after it had become a fact, everything would have been done quietly and as though among brothers. And I did all I could to foster this attitude.[5] For, apart from the fact of it being the correct attitude, these fathers have helped us in every way since we have been here. And, as I wrote to you, I find gifted and learned persons here of the kind that I would love to have in our province of Castile.

6. I am always fond of making a virtue out of necessity, as they say, and so I would have wished that when they decided to resist they would have considered whether or not they would be able to win out. On the other hand, I am not surprised that they are tired of so many visitations and innovations that, for our sins, have been taking place for a good number of years. May it please the Lord that we know how to profit from this, since His Majesty is waking us up. Yet, since the visitator is from the same order, there is less humiliation. And I hope in God that if you show favor to this *padre* in such a way that he understands that he is in your good graces, everything will proceed very well. He is

writing to you and has a great desire for what I said and not to displease you, for he considers himself your obedient son.

7. What I again want to ask you, for love of our Lord and his glorious Mother (whom you so love, and this *padre* does also since he entered the order through his devotion to her), is that you answer him and do so with gentleness and leave aside the things of the past, even though he may have been somewhat at fault, and receive him as your son and subject, for he truly is. And poor Mariano is also, although sometimes it is not evident. I am not surprised that what he wrote to you differed from what he intended, since he doesn't know how to express himself. He confesses in fact that he never intended either in word or in deed to offend you.[6] Since the devil gains so much when things are interpreted according to his own wishes, he must have pushed these fathers to conduct their affairs badly without their meaning to do so.

8. But note, it is characteristic of sons to make mistakes and of fathers to forgive and overlook faults. For the love of our Lord, I beg you to do me this favor. See how this would be appropriate for many reasons that perhaps you would not understand over there as I do here. And even though we women are not good for giving counsel, we sometimes hit the mark. I don't know what harm could come of it and, as I say, there can be many advantages. And I don't see that any harm could come from your being receptive to those who would very willingly cast themselves at your feet, if you were present, for God never fails to forgive. And no harm can come from your making it known that you are pleased that the reform be carried out by one of your subjects and sons, and, as though in exchange for this, you are happy to forgive him.

9. Would that there were many to whom this task could be entrusted! But apparently there are none with the talents of this *padre* (for I am certain that if you were to see him you would agree). Why don't you show that you are pleased to have him as your subject and let everyone understand that this reform, if carried out correctly, is being done with your approval and with your advice and counsel? And were others to understand that you are pleased with this work of reform, everything would proceed more smoothly. There are many more things I would

like to say in this regard, but I think it will be more to the point for me to beg our Lord to give you understanding of what is appropriate for you to do; because for some time now you have paid no attention to my words. I am fully certain that if I am mistaken in my words, my will does not intend to be.

10. Padre Fray Antonio de Jesús is here, for he couldn't get out of coming.[7] Nonetheless, he also has begun to defend himself as have the other fathers. He is writing to you. Perhaps he will be more fortunate than I in getting you to believe us, as would be fitting, with regard to all I am saying. May our Lord provide, as he can, in keeping with our need.

11. I learned of the general chapter act in which I am ordered to remain in one house and not go out. Father Provincial, Fray Angel, had sent it here to Padre Ulloa with orders that he notify me.[8] He thought that it would cause me much grief, which was the intention of these fathers in procuring it, so it was kept from me. It must have been little less than a month ago that I was able to get them to give it to me, for I had heard of it from elsewhere.

12. I assure you that from what I understand of myself, it would have been a great gift and happiness for me if you had sent it to me with a letter to let me know that you were feeling sorry about the great trials I was undergoing in making these foundations— for I am not much for suffering—and that as a reward you were ordering me to rest. For even taking into consideration the way it did come, it consoled me greatly to know I could live in peace.

13. Since I have such great love for you, I could not help, sensitive as I am, feeling hurt that the order should come as though to someone very disobedient and in such a way that Padre Fray Angel could publish it in Madrid before I knew anything about it, as though they were using force with me. And so he wrote me that I could have recourse to the papal chamber, as though that would bring me great relief. Indeed, even if the work of making foundations, a task you had given me, had not cost me such great trials, it wouldn't enter my mind not to obey, nor would God allow me to find any happiness in going against your will. For I can truthfully say—and our Lord knows this—that if I experienced some relief in the trials and anxieties and afflictions and slander that I have suffered, it was in the thought that I was

doing your will and making you happy. And now, too, it will bring me relief to do what you command.

14. I wanted to carry out the orders at once. It was close to Christmas and since the journey is so long, they wouldn't allow me, knowing that you would not want to put my health at risk. So, I am still here, but with the intention of remaining in this house only until after the winter passes. I have little in common with the people of Andalusia. And what I beseech you is that you don't forget to write to me wherever I may be. Since I will no longer have business to attend to—which will certainly bring me great happiness—I am afraid you will forget me, although I will not give you the chance to do so. Even though it may tire you, I will not fail to write to you for the sake of my own peace of mind.

15. In these parts they have never understood, nor do they understand, the Council or *Motu proprio*[9] as having taken away from prelates the authority to allow nuns to go outside to do things for the good of the order, for many reasons for doing so may occur. I do not say this in regard to myself, but so that you will not have any scruple about the past, for I am not good for anything (and not only am I ready to stay in one house, for this will give me some relief and rest, but even stay in a prison cell if that would make you happy—and gladly for the rest of my life). For even though I had the patent letters, I never went anywhere to make a foundation—for otherwise, clearly, I could not have gone—without a written order or license from the prelate. And so Padre Fray Angel gave it to me for Beas and Caravaca, and Padre Gracián for here, for he had the same commission from the nuncio then that he has now, but he wasn't using it. Yet, Padre Fray Angel said that I was an apostate and excommunicated.[10] May God pardon him for you are a witness to how I strove that you would always be on good terms with him and to make him happy—I mean in matters that would not be displeasing to God—but he has never managed to act kindly toward me.

16. It would be much more to his advantage if he were as ill-disposed to Valdemoro.[11] Being prior in Avila, the latter removed the discalced friars from the Incarnation causing great scandal to the people, and he has so greatly disturbed the nuns—the spirit of the house had been something to praise God for—that it is heart-breaking to see. I have received word that to excuse

him they are blaming themselves. Now the discalced friars have returned and, according to what has been written to me, the nuncio has given orders that none of the friars of the observance be confessor to the nuns there.

17. The grief of those nuns has deeply afflicted me, for they are given no more than bread and, on the other hand, so much disturbance that it rouses me to great pity. May God provide a remedy for everything, and may he preserve you for many years to come. Today they told me that the general of the Dominicans is coming here. If only God would give me the grace of providing an occasion for you to come, although, on the other hand, I would regret the fatigue it would cost you. And so my rest will have to wait for that eternity that has no end, where you will see what you owe me. Please God through his mercy that I will be worthy of it.

18. I commend myself to the prayers of the reverend fathers who are your companions. These subjects and daughters of yours ask for your blessing, and I ask the same for myself.

To María de San José, Seville
Malagón, June 15, 1576

Teresa has been in Malagón four days, after a pleasant journey from Seville provided by her brother Lorenzo. In Malagón, the prioress is seriously ill and the house is in a dilapidated condition. Doña Luisa is putting off providing for the needed repairs. The nuns in Seville have financial problems and are involved in a lawsuit. Gracián is about to resume his visitation.

For Mother Prioress María de San José, Seville.

1. Jesus. The grace of the Holy Spirit be with your reverence, my daughter. Oh, how I would like to write a long letter, but since I have other letters to write, I don't have time. I told Padre Fray Gregorio[1] to write a long letter about the whole trip. The fact is that there are not many things to report because we journeyed very well; it wasn't hot, and we arrived in good health, glory to God, the second day after Pentecost. I found Mother Prioress's condition improved, although she is not completely well. Take great care to pray for her. I've spent some enjoyable moments with her. I have kept very much in mind the change that you must still make. Please God, you will not be lacking anything.

2. For charity's sake, I beg you to write me through every means you can so that I may always know how you all are. Don't fail to write by way of Toledo, for I will inform the prioress to send the letters in due time, and perhaps I may have to stay in Toledo for a few days, for I fear that this business with Doña Luisa[2] will demand much effort before being concluded. Pray for this. My regards to Mother Subprioress[3] and the other sisters. Take good care of San Gabriel[4] for me, for she was beside herself the day I left. Many regards to Garciálvarez[5] and tell us about the lawsuit[6] and everything else, and give us even more news about our *padre* if he has arrived.[7] I am writing him with much insistence that he not allow anyone to eat in the monastery parlor—see that you don't start something—except for himself since he is in such need, and if this can be done without it becoming known. And even if it becomes known, there is a difference between a superior and a subject, and his health is so important to us

that whatever we can do amounts to little. Mother Prioress will send some money with Padre Fray Gregorio for this and for any other need that may arise, for she is fond of him and so does this gladly. And it would be good for him to know about this, for I tell you that since you receive little in alms it could happen that you would be depriving yourselves of food so as to give it to others. I desire very much that the sisters not be troubled about anything; that they serve our Lord generously. May it please His Majesty that this be so, as I beg of him.

3. Tell Sister San Francisco[8] to be a good historian of all that happens concerning the friars.[9] Since I've just come from the house down there, this house now strikes me as even worse. These sisters here suffer many hardships. Teresa[10] was a little sad on the journey, especially the first day. She said it was caused by having to leave the sisters behind.[11] On arriving here, she felt as though she had been living with these sisters all her life. She was so happy she could hardly eat supper the day we arrived. I was delighted because I believe her affection for them is deeply rooted. I will write again through Padre Fray Gregorio. I have nothing more to say now other than ask the Lord to watch over you and make you holy so that all the nuns will be so likewise, amen.

Today is the Friday after Pentecost.

4. Give this enclosed letter to our *padre* personally, and if he is not there, do not send it to him unless through a very trustworthy person, which is important.

Yours, Teresa of Jesus

Teresa is not writing to you because she is busy. She says she is prioress and sends you her best regards.

To María de San José, Seville
Malagón, June 18, 1576

Teresa knows how much the nuns in Seville miss her and wants to help them in their financial difficulties. She is preparing for her trip to Toledo to meet with Doña Luisa, who has been lukewarm about the needed repairs for the house in Malagón.

For Mother María de San José, Carmelite and prioress of St. Joseph's in Seville.

1. May Jesus be with your reverence, my daughter. I tell you that if you experience some sadness over my absence, mine is greater. May the Lord make use of the many trials and the pain it cost me to leave daughters who are so dear to me. I hope that you are all well; I am in good health, glory be to God.

2. You will have already received the letters that the muleteer brought. This one will be short. I thought I would be here for some days yet, but since Sunday is the feast of St. John the Baptist, I have advanced the day of my departure, and so I have little time. Since Padre Fray Gregorio[1] will be my messenger, I am not bothered by this.

3. I am worried that you will be pressed this year into paying the annuity,[2] for by next year the Lord will have provided someone to pay it for you. Santángel[3] has a sister whom Mother Prioress here praises highly and would prefer her to the one who entered. She says a dowry of 300 ducats will be given for the one who has entered (who will have completed a year in August), and that the other sister will give the same amount, with which you would be able to pay the annuity for this year. It is a small amount. But if what they say about her is true, she deserves to be accepted for nothing, so much the more because she is from this region. Speak about this to our *padre*,[4] and if there is no other solution, you could accept her. The trouble is that she is only fourteen years old; for this reason I say she shouldn't be accepted unless nothing else can be done. Think about it.

4. It seems to me for many reasons that it would be good if our *padre* gave orders that Beatriz[5] make her profession at once. One

reason is that it would put an end to her temptations. Give my regards to her and to her mother[6] and to all whom you see and to everyone and to Mother Subprioress and all the sisters, especially my nurse. May God watch over you for me, my daughter, and make you very holy, amen.

5. My brother[7] wrote to all of you the other day and commends himself much to your prayers. He is more measured than Teresa,[8] who cannot manage to love any others as much as she loves all of you. Because Mother Prioress (with whom I am definitely delighted) will be writing and Fray Gregorio will tell you the news, I'll say no more. I believe I'll be in Toledo for some days. Write to me there.

Yesterday was the feast of the Most Holy Trinity.

6. Try to get a letter from our *padre* for me or send a lot of news about him, for I haven't received any word about him. May God make you all saints.

Yours, Teresa of Jesus

7. With regard to the nun,[9] I have found out more; for the time being she shouldn't be considered.

To Don Lorenzo de Cepeda, Avila
Toledo, July 24, 1576

In the peaceful surroundings of Toledo, Teresa takes up once more some of her writing tasks. She will continue her work on The Book of Her Foundations *and later* The Interior Castle. *She asks Lorenzo to send back from Avila some of the things she had already written.*

1. Jesus. The grace of the Holy Spirit be always with your honor. Oh, what a long fifteen days these have been![1] Blessed be God that you are well; I was greatly consoled. From what you tell me about your servants and the house, I don't think there is anything excessive. I had a good laugh over the master of ceremonies,[2] and I assure you I found it very amusing. You can really trust her since she is a good and wise person. Give her my fond regards when you see her, for I owe her much, and also to Francisco de Salcedo.

2. I am very sorry about your ailment. The cold will soon begin to bother you. I am better than I have been in years, in my opinion. I have a very lovely little cell, well set apart and with a window looking out into the garden, and not many visitors to take up my time. If I didn't have to write these letters and if there were not so many, I would be so well-off that the condition wouldn't last, for that is what usually happens when things go well for me. If you were here I would lack nothing, but if God favors me by granting you health, the separation can be easily endured. May God reward you for your concern about my health, for my sorrow was relieved when I saw that you are also suffering because of my staying here. I hope in God that I will not have to stay so long and that I can get to Avila by the time the cold weather starts there.[3] Despite the harm the cold can do me, I would not avoid it or delay here one day, for when God so wills he can give us good health anywhere. Oh, how much more for my own happiness do I desire that you be in good health! May God grant it to you, as he can.

3. Juan de Ovalle has written me a long letter in which he insists on how fond he is of you and what he would do to serve you. His only fault was to believe that you favored Cimbrón who he

thought had complete control over you; and that was the reason my sister didn't come. Those were feelings of jealousy, I certainly think, for he has a jealous temperament and I suffered much from him because of my friendship with Doña Guiomar.[4] All his complaining is about Cimbrón. In certain matters, he's very childish. He behaved much better in Seville where he showed you much love, and so you should bear up with him for love of God.

4. I wrote to him telling him what I thought and that I saw how much you loved him and that he ought rather to rejoice that Cimbrón was looking after your concerns; and I strongly urged him to try to please you and send you the money if you ask for it, and I added that each one is better off in his own house, that God perhaps had so ordained, and I blamed him and excused Perálvarez.[5] The trouble is that I think he has to come here and that all my efforts to prevent him from coming will have served for naught. Certainly I feel very sorry for my sister, and so we have to suffer much. With regard to you, I swear his desire to please you and serve you is great. God has not given him more. But he has endowed others with the good dispositions needed to put up with him, and this is what you will have to do.

5. The *agnusdei* is in the little chest, I think; if not, it is in the trunk with the rings.[6] I am telling the subprioress to send the chest to you so that you might take out the papers on the *Foundations* and send them back to the subprioress in a sealed wrapping. They have to send us I don't know what for my companion and also my mantle, which we had sent them in a hurry. I don't know what other papers are in there, but I wouldn't want anyone to see them, and so I would like you to take them out (for it doesn't matter to me if you see them), and the same holds true for the *Foundations*.

6. The key for the little chest broke. Force the chest open and keep it in another larger chest until a key is made for it. In the little chest is a key for a mail pouch that I am sending you, for also in it are some papers, I think, on matters concerning prayer. Feel free to read them and take out the paper on which some details about the foundation of Alba are written. Send it to me with the other papers because Father Visitator has asked me to finish writing the *Foundations*, and I need these papers to know

what I have already written and about Alba.[7] It's hard for me
to have to take up this task, for the time that I have left after
tending to letter-writing, I would like to spend in solitude and
rest. It doesn't seem God wants this. May the Lord be pleased
to make use of this work.

7. You ought to know that the prioress of Valladolid has written
me that Doña María de Mendoza had a copy made of the book
the bishop once had, and that he has the copy in his possession.[8]
I was delighted for your sake, because when I come we can
arrange to have you see it. Don't tell anyone. If he should happen
to go there, you could feel free to ask him for it.

8. I will write what you say to Seville, for I don't know if the letter was received. Why bother about four *reales*? Either they were
not enclosed in the letter, or the carrier knowing that something
was enclosed did not deliver it to them. The prioress here is in
much better health than usual; she and all the sisters kiss your
hands. We have prayed much for your health. I am sending you
some quinces so that your housekeeper may make them into
preserves and you can eat them after your meal, and also a box of
marmalade, and another for the subprioress at St. Joseph's who,
they tell me, is very weak. Tell her to eat it, and I beg you not to
give any of yours to anyone but eat it for love of me. And when
you finish it, let me know, for it is inexpensive here and I'm not
using money from the monastery. Padre Gracián gave me orders
under obedience to continue doing as I usually do,[9] for what I
had was not for me but for the order. On the one hand I have
regretted this; on the other, since there are so many expenses to
meet here, even if it involve no more than postage, I rejoiced. It
pains me that postage costs so much, and there are many other
things to pay for . . .

To Padre Jerónimo Gracián, Almodóvar
Toledo, September 5, 1576

Teresa is undergoing mystical suffering over a sense of God's absence. No priest was available with whom she could consult. Through a special favor from God, the situation was remedied. She confides this to Gracián.

1. Now I want to tell your paternity something, because the messenger is a person I can trust. You already know how Angela took for her confessor the prior of La Sisla,[1] for she believes that in many matters one cannot be without someone to consult. She wouldn't feel sure she was doing right nor would she be at peace. The said person began to see her often, but afterward he almost never came. The prioress and I could not discover the reason for this. Once while the unhappy Angela was speaking to Joseph,[2] He told her that He was the one who held him back, that Doctor Velázquez was better for her since he was learned in canon law and highly educated and that in this way she would find some relief, that He would move him to listen to her and understand (for he hesitated since he is very busy). And since Joseph is so serious a person as you well know, and he counseled her in similar ways before, she didn't know what to do, having already begun with someone else to whom she owed so much. On the other hand she feared displeasing Joseph.

2. She remained thus undecided for several days, and it was a trial for her not to be able to get your opinion, fearing she might lose her peace by consulting with so many. Padre Salazar[3] then came and she decided to do whatever he might say however much the change would cost her, and she almost complained to Joseph for not having informed her earlier. She told Padre Salazar about everything that was happening. He had been the one who had previously counseled her about the prior of La Sisla. She can discuss everything with Padre Salazar, as you are aware, because he already knows about it all. He told her to do what Joseph said. And this was done, and what Joseph said is being realized. First, that the prior came here and that when the prioress[4] asked him why he was acting in this way, he answered that

he did not know, that there was nothing he desired more than to come and that he saw clearly that afterward he would regret not coming. He was not master of himself in this regard nor could he do anything else and he was astonished at his powerlessness.

3. Second, that hardly was it mentioned one day to the other person[5] when he said that no matter how busy he was, he would come every week, and was as happy as if he had been offered the archbishopric of Toledo (although I don't think he would be so happy over the latter since he is so good). Fray Hernando de Medina[6] will tell you about him; don't forget to ask him. That you may see how he is accepting the task, I am sending you this note,[7] for I had contacted him over some doubts I had, which I will not mention since it would take too long; they did not concern prayer.

4. So it is, *mi padre*, that Angela is very happy to have him as her confessor, so much the more since after having met Paul,[8] her soul was unable to find comfort or happiness with anyone. Now, although not as much as with Paul, she feels settled and satisfied, and her soul is disposed to obey him. It is the greatest relief for her. For accustomed all her life to obeying, and being without Paul, nothing she did satisfied her, nor did she think she was doing right; and even if she wanted to she was not able to submit to another. Believe me, he who was at work in the first instance was so also in the second. For she is as amazed by this new condition as was the prior at feeling himself prevented from doing what he wanted.

5. I tell you that you can rejoice if you desire to give some comfort to Angela. It's enough that she is not as happy as with Paul, for her soul has no other comfort. He[9] was not ignorant of the friendship Joseph had with her, for he had heard a great deal, nor was he surprised. Since he is so learned, he backs everything up with sacred scripture. This affords the poor soul the greatest comfort, for in all ways God has banished from her everything she loves. May he be blessed forever.

6. What we must be careful about now is to prevent the prior[10] from finding out. We can let him think that because of his delays about coming I also at times confess with the other person and that you have informed me that I should do what I am told as

though it were being told to me by you for the good of my soul. For I assure you that the desires and impulses this woman has to do something for God are so great that now that she cannot do great works, she needs to find out how she can please God more in what she can do.

Your paternity's unworthy servant and daughter,
Teresa of Jesus

To Padre Jerónimo Gracián, Almodóvar
Toledo, September 5, 1576

Having the same date as the previous letter to Gracián, this one has a clearly different thrust. Gracián had convoked a chapter for the discalced Carmelite friars and planned to use his powers to form a separate province for them. Teresa sees the difficulties in such a plan and makes some suggestions. She is becoming more concerned that their correspondence be sent through safe channels.

1. Jesus. The grace of the Holy Spirit be with your paternity. Today I sent you some letters through the chief courier. You must not forget to tell me whether you receive them. I believe they will surely arrive in Seville, for he is a brother of one of our nuns.[1]

2. I told you that Tostado[2] left for Portugal the day you arrived here. Infante[3] and another preacher from Andalusia were waiting for him and sent a messenger to Madrid who brought them back this news. Blessed be the Lord who has so ordained.

3. You should know that the members of the Council say that if they are to give the license on the basis of the usual procedure, they cannot do so, for we need to have more convincing reasons. If they see a letter from the nuncio saying that he grants it, they will give it without further discussion. This information was given by a magistrate friend to Don Pedro González.[4] Write to me through those returning from the chapter about what we can do and whether it would be good to seek counsel from someone in Madrid, like the duke[5] or others.

4. I have begun to suspect they have impeded him with letters from Rome from giving these permissions, for he gave them to Padre Fray Antonio[6] easily, it seems to me. I have also been thinking that if they give this false information to the pope, and there is no one there to counter it, they will get as many briefs as they want against us, and that it is most important that we have some of our friars there. When it is seen how our own live, the prejudice of the others will become obvious. I don't think we ought to do anything until that moment comes. Then our friars can bring back the authorization to found a few houses.[7] Believe me, it's very important to be prepared for what may come about.

5. I am writing this in a hurry and so cannot say any more than that everyone recommends themselves to your prayers; and I to the prayers of all the fathers there, especially Father Prior of Los Remedios, although I'm angry with him. I want to know if Padre Mariano came. May God watch over you and lead you by his hand, amen.

6. I am overjoyed to see what nice weather it is for traveling. I am waiting for Antonio.[8] Don't forget to write to tell me the name of the man to whom I must send the letters going to Madrid, that servant of your father's. Be careful not to forget, and tell me how to address the envelope and if he is someone who should be reimbursed for the postage.

Today is 5 September.

7. We are well, and it seems I'm feeling somewhat relieved to see that it is easier to write to you from here.

Your paternity's unworthy daughter and subject,
Teresa of Jesus

8. Be careful, *mi padre*, not to lose the paper I gave you, for you said you would place it in the lining but you did not do so. I would like you to keep a copy of it in your little coffer, for many complications would arise if it were lost.

To Madre María de San José, Seville
Toledo, September 20, 1576

Once the chapter in Almodóvar was finished, Gracián and some of the other chapter fathers visited Teresa in Toledo. Gracián has returned to Seville, and Teresa is concerned for his well-being.

For Mother Prioress of St. Joseph's, Seville.

1. Jesus. The grace of the Holy Spirit be with your reverence, my daughter. I wrote at length to our *padre*[1] and so I have nothing more to say except that I desire news about you and that the prioress of Malagón[2] is a bit better.

2. My brother[3] wants to know if you received his letters, one of which contained four *reales* to be given to the pharmacist who lives near your house. They are for some ointment my brother received from him when, I think, he had the sore leg. If they didn't arrive, pay for this yourself and don't neglect to write to him, for I think he expects this even though I send him your greetings. My best regards to all the nuns; the prioress[4] sends her regards to you. She will write through the muleteer. I didn't permit her to do so now hoping to pay less postage. More letters have arrived than I expected, and so the cost for postage will be high.

3. I would like to have news about *mi padre*, about the prior of Las Cuevas,[5] and about what has been done in regard to the water.[6] May God in his power provide and watch over all the sisters for me; give them my regards. For goodness' sake, remember to tell our *padre* to be careful, and to show him every attention; and add what you spend to the forty ducats[7] and don't be foolish. Do what I'm telling you, and also pay the postage, for I will verify it here. I am asking all the nuns to pray hard for you, although I see there is no need to do so.

Today is the vigil of St. Matthew, and I am yours,
Teresa of Jesus

To Padre Jerónimo Gracián, Seville
Toledo, October 5, 1576

In a cell apart, Teresa is enjoying some solitude and has time now for things other than writing letters, such as reading the story of Moses and working on The Book of Her Foundations. *She still worries about Gracián's visitation in Andalusia and uses some unknown code names.*

---

1. The grace of the Holy Spirit be with your paternity, *mi padre*. If the letter you sent by way of Madrid had not arrived, I would have been in a fine state, for today is the day after the feast of St. Francis and Fray Antonio[1] has not come; nor did I know whether you had arrived in good health until I saw your letter.

2. May God be blessed that you are well and that Paul[2] is too and interiorly at rest. Surely so complete an improvement seems supernatural. All of that must be necessary for this nature of ours, for such things serve well to humiliate and give us self-knowledge. I prayed earnestly here that the Lord would give him a period of calm, for it seems to me he has enough other trials. Tell him this for me.

3. Right now I am without any trials. I don't know where this will end up. They have given me a cell set apart like a hermitage and very cheerful, and my health is good, and I am away from relatives, although they reach me through their letters. Only my worries about what is going on down there trouble me.[3] I tell you that as far as what pleases me goes you had a good idea in choosing to let me stay here. And even regarding the worries I mentioned, I feel more confident than usual.

4. Last night I was reading the story of Moses and about the troubles he brought on the king and his whole kingdom with those plagues and how they never touched him. In fact, I was amazed and happy to see that no one has the power to cause harm if the Lord does not wish it. I enjoyed the account of the crossing of the Red Sea, thinking of how much less it is that we are asking for. It pleased me to see that saint in the midst of those conflicts by order of God. I was feeling joy at seeing my Eliseo[4] in

the same situation and I offered him again to God. I remembered the favors Joseph[5] has granted me and what he has said about him: "Still much more has to be endured for the honor and glory of God." I was consumed with the desire to find myself amid a thousand perils in order to serve him. With these and similar thoughts, my life is passing. I've also written the foolish things you will find enclosed.

5. Now I am going to begin writing the story of the *Foundations*, which Joseph told me will be for the benefit of many souls.[6] If God helps, I believe this will be so. But even apart from this locution, I had already decided to write the account since you had ordered me to do it. I was delighted that you gave such a long report at the chapter.[7] I don't know how those who have written contrary to what you reported are not ashamed. It is fortunate that those who perhaps would have had to leave against their will are leaving of their own accord.[8] It seems to me our Lord is straightening out our affairs. May it please His Majesty that what we are doing will bring him glory and be of benefit to those souls. You will be doing well if you give orders from your own monastery[9] about what should be done. Then they won't have to be observing whether you go to choir or not; I tell you everything will go better. Here, our prayers are not lacking; they are better weapons than the ones used by those fathers.

6. I wrote to you at length through the chief courier, and while waiting to know if you have received those letters, I have been writing by way of Madrid. About the matter concerning David, I think he will hoodwink Padre Esperanza,[10] as he usually does, for they are together and his brother has left. Although the presence of Fray Buenaventura[11] can accomplish much, I fear that it will do no more than create obstacles, for the two know about the matter. This is fortunate because, God forgive me, I wish David would return to his first calling. I have learned nothing more since I've been here.

Your paternity's daughter and servant,
Teresa of Jesus

To Madre María de San José, Seville
Toledo, October 5, 1576

Because Teresa is worried about the visitation being conducted by Gracián in Andalusia, she reproaches Madre María for not writing. She then comments on a number of other topics: the excise, her brother's purchase of property, the loss of some articles, relations with the Jesuits, negotiations with the Franciscans over water, and other Carmels in the South.

For Mother Prioress of St. Joseph's in Seville.

1. Jesus be with your reverence. I don't know how it is you let the muleteer leave without sending a letter, especially since our *padre*[1] is down there and we would like to get news about him every day. I greatly envy all of you that you have him with you there. For goodness' sake, don't do this any more; and don't fail to write to me about everything that is happening. Our *padre*'s letters are short, and when he doesn't have time to write, you should be sure to do so. I've already written to you about the means you can use to send me frequent letters.[2]

2. I was delighted to learn, through the letter that Padre Mariano[3] brought—Fray Antonio[4] has not come—that you and all the nuns are well and that an agreement has been reached concerning the excise.[5]

3. My brother[6] is now well. He is always happy to receive news about you. I've already told you not to fail to write to him now and again. He bought some property—which he was already considering when he was down there—near Avila, I think a league and a half away, or not quite that. It has pasture lands, grain fields, and woods. It cost him 14,000 ducats, but the papers have not yet been drawn up. He says that what has happened down there has taught him a lesson not to close the purchase unless everything is very safe and clear, for he doesn't want any problems. Pray for him and his sons (who already have opportunities for marriage) that they will serve God.

4. You should know that as soon as I arrived here, thinking that we would leave immediately, the trunk and all the packages

were sent ahead with a muleteer. And I don't know if it was in unpacking or how, but Teresa's large *agnusdei* and the two emerald rings are missing, nor do I remember where I put them or if they were given to me. Really, I felt sad to see how everything happened so as to contradict the joy she had in the thought that I would be there with her; she needs me in many ways. Try to remember if these objects were in the house when we left, and ask Gabriela[7] if she remembers where I might have put them, and pray that they may be found.

5. I was very surprised by what you told me about the fathers in the Society.[8] As that other person told you, they are almost as rigorous as we are. It would be good if Padre Garciálvarez[9] were to speak to them. My regards to him and to all my daughters and to Father Prior of Las Cuevas.[10] We are praying hard for his return to health. May it please God to give it to him, for his illness distresses me and I am not going to write to him until I know that he is better. Keep me informed of his condition as often as you have a messenger.

6. It would be good, despite all this, if you were to arrange at times to have someone from the Society hear the nuns' confessions. This would help toward removing the fear they have in our regard. Padre Acosta[11] would be very good, if you could get him. May God forgive them, for if she is so rich, her entry would bring an end to their problems; yet, since His Majesty didn't bring her to us, he will provide. Perhaps there was a greater need for her in the community she entered.

7. I thought that since Fray Buenaventura was there the negotiations about the water would improve, but it doesn't seem there is any easing off. May God permit us to pay for the house; then, having money, you will be able to obtain everything. Let things go for now, since you have good wells. We would pay highly here for one of them, for this matter of getting water is a real problem.

8. Tell me how the visitation of Fray Buenaventura is going, and what is being done about the monastery they abolished near Córdoba, for I know nothing. I am feeling well and am at your service, as they say. Tell me also whether our *padre* comes to your monastery to eat sometimes and how you cater to him, for he

cannot be catered to in his own monastery, nor would it appear right. Send me news about everything, and remain with God, for now we will be able to write often, as is fitting.

9. I was amused by the account of the old woman you have there and how she used the stairs. Tell me if the boy is still there and if you have anyone to do your errands. Mother Prioress in Malagón wrote to me that she is doing better; but that illness is such that a little improvement is not enough to make me happy. Keep her always in your prayers. May His Majesty watch over you, my daughter, and make you a saint, and all your daughters as well. Amen.

10. In the enclosed letter from Sister Alberta you will see how things are going in Caravaca. I was delighted with the letter from Beas (for I hadn't received any news from them in some time) and that that nun who is very rich entered there. Everything is working out well, glory to God. Always pray hard for our *padre*, and for me too, for I am in need.

Yesterday was the feast of St. Francis.

11. Enclosed is the postage, for it's expensive, and be careful to let me know if you do not have the money to take good care of our *padre* when the occasion arises; and don't be proud, for that's foolish. I can send it to you. And take care of your health, if for no other reason than not to kill me, for I tell you the sickness of the prioress in Malagón is costing me dearly. May God provide by restoring her health, amen.

Your reverence's,
Teresa of Jesus, Carmelite

12. When letters are entrusted to the muleteer, you can enclose the postage. When they are not, you know what usually happens if you enclose it; the letters are at risk of never arriving. I tell you this so that you will never do it.

To Padre Ambrosio Mariano, Madrid
Toledo, October 21, 1576

Mariano has sent Teresa some weighty recommendations for the accep-
tance of both a novice and an aspirant into Carmel. In her response,
Teresa also discusses his projects for foundations of discalced friars in
Madrid, Salamanca, and Ciudad Real. She doesn't show much confi-
dence in either Mariano or Don Teutonio as negotiators. The letter is
a good example of her dealings with the impetuous Mariano.

1. Jesus. The grace of the Holy Spirit be with your reverence. It's
quite clear that you have not understood all that I owe to Padre
Olea[1] and how much I care for him, for you have written me
about matters that he has discussed, or is discussing, with me.
I believe you now know that I am not an ungrateful person. So,
I tell you that if in this matter I should have to give up my rest
and health, it would already be done. But where a matter of conscience is involved, friendship doesn't suffice, for I owe more to
God than to anyone. Would to God the matter involved no more
than a lack of dowry, for you already know—and if you don't
you should inquire for yourself—that there are many nuns in
these monasteries who have brought no dowry, while the dowry
of this person is a good one. They are giving 500 ducats, which
is enough for her to become a nun in any monastery.

2. Since Padre Olea doesn't know the nuns in these houses, I
am not surprised by his disbelief. I know what servants of God
they are and the innocence of their souls. I could never believe
they would refuse the habit to anyone without many reasons. I
know how scrupulous they usually are about these things, and
for them to make a decision like that, they would have had to
have good reasons.[2] And since we are few nuns, the disturbance
caused by those who are not suited for religious life is so great
that even someone with an unscrupulous conscience would
have a problem about accepting them; how much more would
someone who seeks not to displease the Lord in anything.

3. Would you tell me how I could get them by force to take a
nun if they do not vote in her favor—and they are not doing

so—and if no prelate is even capable of doing this? And don't think this matters to Padre Olea. He has written to me that he has no greater interest in her than in anyone else he may pass on the street. It's because of my sins that you have been inspired by charity toward something in which I cannot be of help, and I feel badly about it. Even if I were to help, it wouldn't benefit her to stay where she is not wanted.

4. I have done even more in this case than was reasonable. And I asked them to keep her for another year of trial, contrary to their will, so that if I pass by there when I go to Salamanca I can become better informed about the whole matter. I'm doing this as a favor to Padre Olea that he may feel more satisfied. I see clearly that the nuns are not lying, for you know how even in matters of little importance such a thing would be far from their minds. It is nothing new for nuns to leave our communities; it is common. And nothing is lost if they say they didn't have the health for so austere a life, nor have I seen anyone less esteemed on this account.

5. Having learned my lesson by this, I will have to be more careful about what I do from here on. So, the person proposed by Señor Nicolao will not be accepted, even if you are more satisfied with her. I have other information, and I don't want to make enemies in order to do a favor for my lords and friends. It is strange that you would wonder why there is a discussion about this. Were we to behave otherwise, no nun would ever be accepted. I wanted to do him a favor, but I had received new information different from what I had first received, and I know Señor Nicolao desires what is good for these houses over anyone's particular good. So he was at peace with this.

6. For love of God don't speak any more about this. She has a good dowry and can enter some other community—not one in which the numbers are so small that the nuns have to be extremely careful about whom they choose. And if up until now we were not so cautious in some cases—although these are rare—things turned out so badly that from now on we will be. And do not put us at odds with Señor Nicolao, which would happen if we had to send her away again.

7. I was amused by your saying that just by seeing her you will be able to recognize the kind of person she is. We women are not so easy to get to know. After many years of hearing confessions, confessors themselves are amazed at how little they have understood. And it is because women cannot express their faults clearly, and the confessors judge by what they are told. *Padre*, when you desire that one of these houses do you the favor of accepting somebody, send us those who are gifted for this life, and you will see that we will not make an issue over the dowry. When such talent is lacking, I can by no means be obliging.

8. You should know that I thought it would be easy to have a house in Madrid where the friars could stay. And even though the house were not a monastery, it wouldn't be unusual for them to have permission for Mass; it is given to *caballeros* for Mass in their homes. So, I informed our *padre*[3] about this. He told me that it wouldn't be opportune since this could do harm to our cause, and I think he was right. And knowing his will in this matter, you shouldn't have decided to bring so many friars together and set up a church as though you had permission, which has made me laugh. I never even bought a house until I had permission from the ordinary of the place. You know well what it cost me in Seville for not having gotten this permission.

9. I told you often that until you have a letter from the nuncio[4] granting permission, nothing should be done. When Don Jerónimo[5] told me that you asked the friars of the observance, I was dumbfounded. So as not to resemble all of you by trusting them so much, at least for the moment, I have no intention of speaking to Valdemoro.[6] I have a suspicion that any friendship he shows us is not intended for our good but only to catch us in something that he can report to his friends. And I wish you were as suspicious and would not trust him or make use of such friends for this affair. Leave the matter to the One to whom it belongs, that is to God, for His Majesty will take care of it in his time. Don't be in such a hurry, for that will ruin everything.

10. You should know that Don Diego Mejía[7] is a very good gentleman and that he will do what he says. Since he has decided to speak about the matter, he must have come to know that his cousin will act in our favor. You should realize as well that if

his cousin does not do it for him he will not do it for his aunt either. There's no reason to write to her or to anyone else. They are first cousins, and a relative and friend of Don Diego Mejía is to be highly esteemed. And it is also a good sign that the archdeacon[8] has said he will present a report about us, for if he hadn't thought of doing it in our favor, he wouldn't have taken on this task. The matter is moving along well. You should not be stirring things up; you may make matters worse. Let's see what Don Diego and the archdeacon do. I will try to find out if there is anyone here who may be able to intervene. And if the dean[9] can do anything, Doña Luisa[10] will be able to get him to do so.

11. All of this has pleased me greatly and made me believe that God will make good use of this foundation; nothing came about through what we ourselves did. It's very nice that you have the house, for sooner or later we will have the permission. If the nuncio had given it to us, everything would now be over. May it please our Lord to give him the health that he sees is necessary in our regard. I tell you that by no means does Tostado[11] lack confidence, nor am I sure that the One who began all this will give up working through him.

12. Regarding Salamanca, Padre Fray Juan de Jesús[12] is in such a state, because of his quartan fevers, that I don't know what he could do; nor do you say what services he might be able to render. As for the college there, let us begin with what matters most, which is that the nuncio grant his permission. Once he has given it, the main thing is done. If mistakes are made in the beginning everything will be wiped out. What the bishop[13] is requesting, in my opinion—since he knows that Señor Juan Díaz is in Madrid and what he is doing there—is to have someone in Salamanca who can do the same. And I don't know if our rule allows for your taking on the task of chaplains. It doesn't seem suitable to me, nor do I know what one could accomplish in two months, were the task to be accepted, other than annoy the bishop. Nor do I know how the fathers would manage that kind of governing (for they will perhaps want to set high standards of perfection for that community, and such standards will not be suitable for those people[14]). Nor do I know if the bishop would be pleased to have the friars.

13. I tell you there is more to do than you think and where we plan on gaining we will perhaps lose. Nor do I think our order will be seen as responsible if friars who are to be seen as contemplative hermits take on these chaplaincies—for the friars are not wanted for any other reason—and move about here and there with these kinds of women. I don't know how this will look, even though these women will be rescued from an evil way of life.

14. I raise these objections so that all of you there may consider them and then do what seems good to you, for I submit to that. You will arrive at a better decision. Read this passage to Señor Licentiate Padilla[15] and to Señor Juan Díaz, for I don't know anything more to say than this. Permission from the bishop will always be sure in coming. Otherwise, I don't have confidence in Señor Don Teutonio[16] as a great negotiator—in his good will, yes; in his abilities, no.

15. I have been looking forward to being there so as to move this project along, for I am good at bargaining (if you don't think so, my friend Valdemoro will tell you). I wouldn't want the project to fail from your not explaining it well, for I have greatly desired that you have a house in Salamanca and one in Madrid. That you set aside thoughts of a foundation in Ciudad Real[17] for a more opportune moment made me happy. I see no way in which it could have turned out well. All things considered, Malagón would be a much better place. Doña Luisa is eager to have you come and will provide well for your needs as time goes on, and there are many large towns in the surrounding area. I know you will not lack food.

16. And to have a justifiable pretext for abandoning the house in Madrid you could transfer it to Malagón. Let them think for now that you are not abandoning it definitively but only until the work on the house is completed. For you would appear irresponsible were you to start something one day and give it up the next.

17. I gave Don Jerónimo the letter for Don Diego Mejía. He will send it with another for the Count of Olivares. I will write him again when I see that it's necessary. Don't let the matter be forgotten. And I repeat that if he said clearly he would take it up

and has discussed it with the archdeacon and considers it as good as done, he is a man of his word.

18. Now he has written me in favor of an aspirant. Would to God the two we let go had possessed her gifts; we wouldn't have had to refuse them. Father Visitator's mother has inquired about her. In mentioning this, it occurs to me that it would be good, under the pretext of saying something to Don Diego about this nun, to speak to him about the other matter and entrust it to him again. That is what I will do. Send the letter on to him. And remain with God, for I've really been lengthy, as though I had nothing else to attend to.

19. I'm not writing to Father Prior,[18] because I have many other letters to write now, and he can consider this one as being for himself. Best regards to my Padre Padilla. I am giving much praise to our Lord because he is well. May His Majesty be with you always. I will strive to procure the document even if this means talking to Valdemoro—and that would be doing a lot, for I don't believe he would do anything for us.

Today is the feast of the Virgins.

Your reverence's unworthy servant,
Teresa of Jesus

20. Today they gave me other letters from you before Diego[19] arrived. Send this letter to our *padre* with the first messenger; it's for some permissions. I am not writing anything to him about those business matters. So don't fail to write to him yourself about them.

21. That you may see whether or not my nuns surpass yours, I am sending you a section of a letter from the prioress in Beas.[20] See the nice house she has found for the friars in La Peñuela;[21] it has indeed given me great satisfaction. Surely, you would not have found one so quickly. They have accepted a nun whose dowry is worth 7,000 ducats. Two others are ready to enter with just as much. And they have already accepted a woman of illustrious background. She is the niece of the Count of Tendilla.[22] The silver objects she has sent, the candelabra, cruets, and many other things, a reliquary, a crystal cross would all take too long to enumerate.

22. And now a lawsuit[23] has been initiated against the nuns there, as you will find out in these letters. See what you can do. It would be important to speak to Don Antonio about this. Mention how high the grates are and that having the window open is more important to us than trying not to bother them. Well, see what you can do.

To Padre Jerónimo Gracián, Seville
Toledo, November 1576(?)

In this fragment of uncertain date, Teresa in all confidence begs Gracián not to be so open with everyone and above all not to read her letters to him in public.

---

1. Time will bring you to lose a little of your simplicity, which I certainly understand to be that of a saint. But since the devil does not want everyone to be a saint, those who are wretched and malicious like myself would want to remove the occasions of sin. I can express and have much love for you for many reasons, but this cannot be so for all the nuns, nor will all superiors be like *mi padre* with whom one can speak so familiarly. God has entrusted this treasure[1] to you, but you mustn't think that all the others will care for it the way you do. I tell you truly I fear much more the fact that men can rob you than that demons can. And what the nuns see me say and do (because I know whom I'm addressing and my age allows it), they think they can do also, and they will be right. But this does not mean that you should stop loving them, rather that you should love them still more.

2. And the truth of it is that, despite my wretchedness, from the time I began to have daughters like these I have gone about with so much circumspection and vigilance, keeping a watch on how the devil might tempt them through me that, glory to God, I don't think there are any particularly serious things they have been able to note (for His Majesty has helped me). I confess that I have striven to hide my imperfections from them—although there are so many they must have seen a good number—as well as my love and concern for Paul.[2] I often point out to them how necessary he is for the order and that I am under an obligation— as if I could act otherwise if I didn't have this reason.

3. But how tiresome I am! May it not prove a burden to *mi padre* to have to hear these things, for you and I are weighed down with a very heavy load and we have to render an account to God and to the world. And since you understand the love with which I say this, you can pardon me and do me the favor I've asked of you: not to read in public the letters I write to you. Remember

that people interpret things differently and that superiors should never be so open about some matters. It may come to pass that I am writing about a third party or about myself and that it would not be well for such matters to be known. There is a great difference for me between speaking of certain things with you and speaking of them with others, even my own sister. Just as I would not want anyone to hear me when I speak with God, or hinder me from being alone with him, so it is with Paul . . .

To Padre Jerónimo Gracián, Seville
Toledo, November 1576

Surrounded by so many enemies and spies, Gracián was a victim of calumnies. Teresa warns him about his pastoral intervention in the delicate case of a woman of bad repute.

---

1. In a way, even though it deeply grieved me, it caused me profound devotion to observe, on the other hand, the tact you are using amid so many calumnies. I tell you, *padre*, God loves you very much and you are doing well in your imitation of him. Rejoice since he is giving you what you ask of him, which are trials, for which he will repay you because he is just. May he be blessed forever.

2. In what regards that girl or woman, I am convinced that it is due not so much to melancholy as to the devil. He is the one putting the woman up to those lies. He is trying to see if he can fool you in some way, now that he has fooled her. So you must proceed with great discretion in this matter and by no means go to her house. May what happened to Santa Marina (I believe it was) not happen to you, for they claimed a child was hers, and she suffered much.[1] Now is not the time for you to be suffering in a matter like this. In my poor opinion you should set this matter aside, for there are others who might win over this soul, and there are many others toward whom you can be helpful.

3. Remember, *padre*, that if she didn't give you that letter under the seal of confession or in confession, it is a matter for the Inquisition, and the devil has a thousand snares. I have learned that someone else died in the Inquisition prison for the same reason. Truly I don't believe she gave the letter to the devil—for he wouldn't have returned it so quickly—or all that she says. But I believe she must be lying in some way—God forgive me—and enjoys seeing you. Perhaps I am calumniating her, but I would like to see you far away from where she is so that you can more easily protect yourself.

4. How malicious I am! But everything is necessary in this life. Don't try to straighten out a matter that's been going on for

four months. Be careful, it's very dangerous. Let them fend for themselves. If there is anything to accuse her of in this regard (I mean outside of confession), be careful, because I fear there will be more publicity and they will blame you afterward, saying that you knew about it and were silent. But I'm aware that my saying this is foolish because you already know it . . .

To Madre María de San José, Seville
Toledo, November 19, 1576

In a humorous vein, Teresa notices that María de San José affects ignorance in writing to her, and erudition in writing to Mariano. She responds to many matters and comments on others that cross her mind, showing special concern for the welfare of Gracián.

For Madre María de San José, prioress in Seville.

1. Jesus. May the Holy Spirit be with you, my daughter. I received your letter written on 3 November. I tell you that your letters never tire me but give me rest from other tiring things. I was amused that you spelled out the date. Please God you didn't do so to avoid humbling yourself by putting it down in numbers.[1]

2. Before I forget, the letter to Padre Mariano is very good, if it were not for that Latin.[2] God deliver all my daughters from presuming to be Latinists. May you never try doing so again or permit other nuns to try. I desire much more that you dare to appear simple, which is very characteristic of saints, rather than so eloquent. This is what you get for sending me your letters open. But now since you have gone to confession to our *padre*, you will be more mortified. Tell him that I almost made a general confession the other day to the one I mentioned, and I didn't experience a twentieth of the sorrow I experienced when I had to confess to him. See what an ugly temptation this is![3]

3. Pray for my present confessor who has been a great consolation to me, for it is no small matter for me to be satisfied in this regard. Oh, how well you acted in not calling on the confessor who tormented me so much down there! I wasn't happy in that place with anything. If our *padre* was a source of happiness, you well know how many anxieties went along with it. And the happiness that you could have given me, if you had so wished, because I find your company delightful, you refused to offer. I am glad that you now understand my affection. As for the other one from Caravaca,[4] may God forgive her, she is sorry now also. Such is the power that truth has.

4. Today she sent me a habit made of coarse wool and it's the most suited to our purposes that I've worn—very light. I was deeply grateful to her, for my other one was too worn out to protect me from the cold. And they themselves made the material for the undertunics, although here there is no mention at all of undertunics during the whole summer, and they do much fasting. Now I am beginning to be a nun. Pray that this will last.

5. I sent word to my brother that you have the money. He'll send the muleteer from Avila to get it. You do well not to send it without a letter from him. Take care to remind our *padre* to take up the matter with the duke that he mentioned to me. With his having so much business to attend to and being so alone, I don't know where he finds the energy if not—through a miracle—from God. I don't think it even entered my mind to say that he not eat there at the monastery, for I see that the need is great. I only say that outside meal times he not go there often, lest this be noticed and he be prevented from ever going there. Rather you are doing me a great favor by the diligence you use to provide for his comfort. I will never be able to repay you. Tell this to the sisters, for also my Gabriela was happy to tell me about this in her letter. Give my regards to her and to all the sisters and all my friends. Give my special greetings to Padre Antonio de Jesús. We are praying that he will benefit from the treatment he is undergoing. I have been sorry for him and so has the prioress. Also give my regards to Fray Gregorio and Fray Bartolomé.

6. The prioress of Malagón is even worse than she usually is. Yet I am somewhat consoled, for I'm told that the source of the pain is not in the lungs and that she does not have tuberculosis. And Ana de la Madre de Dios, the nun who is here, says that she was in that same condition and that she got well. God can do it. I don't know what to say about all the trials that God has given them there. Besides the illnesses they are destitute; they have neither wheat nor money but a world of debts. Please God the 400 ducats that Salamanca owes them, and were reserved for this house—for I already spoke to our *padre* about it—will be enough to take care of the situation. I have already sent a part of the amount. Their expenses have been high and of many kinds. For this reason I would not want the prioresses of houses having

an income[5] to be very prodigal, nor any of the others either, for they will end up by losing everything.

7. The whole burden lies on poor Beatriz,[6] the only one who is well. And she has been entrusted by the prioress with charge of the house. For want of good men, as they say . . .[7] I am very happy that you are not in want of them there. Don't be foolish in not noting the cost of postage and everything else I tell you to note. You would be losing so much, and it's foolishness. I am sorry that his companion is Fray Andrés, for I don't believe he knows how to keep quiet, and I'm even more sorry that he eats at El Carmen.[8] For love of God tell him to be careful, and he would be tempting God to go elsewhere than Los Remedios on leaving there. May God watch over you and all the nuns and make you saints, for I have many more letters to write.

Today is 19 November.

Yours, Teresa of Jesus

8. Turn over. I have already mentioned that I received the letters among which were those from the Indies and Avila. I would like to know who gave them to you, so as to respond, and when the armada is leaving.

9. I am delighted that you bear poverty so well and that God so provides for your needs. May he be blessed forever. You did very well to give the tunics to our *padre*, for I have no need of them. What we all need most is that you not allow him to eat with those people, and that he be on his guard, for God is doing us such a favor by giving him health in the midst of so many trials. With regard to using linen and wool mixed together, I would prefer that you wear linen when necessary. Otherwise you would be opening the door to never observing the constitutions well. The material you would end up with would be almost as hot, and you would be observing neither one rule nor the other, and the custom will have begun.

10. I am troubled by what you say about how the rule stating that stockings be made of coarse cloth or rough tow is not observed. Tell our *padre* some time that where the rule speaks of stockings no indication should be given about the material other than that it be poor, and let me know what he says; or better, that

nothing be said at all about the material, but that it simply mention stockings. And don't forget. Get him to delay his visitation of the province as much as you can, until it is seen where some things will end up. Have you noticed how charming his letter to Teresita is?[9] There is no end to the talk about her and her virtue. Julián[10] speaks wonders of her, which is no small matter. Read the letter that Isabel[11] wrote to his paternity.

To Padre Jerónimo Gracián, Seville
Toledo, Around December 1576

Teresa refers to Padre Antonio's jealousy.

I am happy that Padre Fray Antonio[1] is not with you, for according to what they tell me, when he sees so many letters of mine and none for him, he becomes disturbed. O Jesus, what a wonderful thing it is for two souls to understand each other, for they neither lack something to say, nor grow tired.

To Lorenzo de Cepeda, Avila
Toledo, Christmas Season 1576–77

We don't know whether this represents a short note or a postscript to a lost letter. It accompanied a little song Teresa sent to Lorenzo.

. . . is a little song for Fray John of the Cross they sent me from the Incarnation. Tell him that I told you I greatly enjoyed it. I would like Francisco to sing it for you.[1]

To Don Lorenzo de Cepeda, Avila
Toledo, January 2, 1577

Written during the Christmas feast days, this letter reflects the spirit of those days of gift giving in which the nuns composed verses for one another. Teresa, as Lorenzo's spiritual director, replies to the questions he had put to her. She asks him to send her a chest, which contains some of her important papers, and for some information for the nuncio. Comments are made about some responses submitted for her Satirical Critique.

---

1. Jesus be with your honor. Serna allows me so little time that I did not want to go on at length, but when I begin writing to you—and since Serna comes so seldom—I need time.

2. Do not read the letters I write to Francisco, for I fear that he is somewhat melancholic and is doing a lot by being open with me. Perhaps God gives him those scruples to detach him from other things. Fortunately, for his good, he is able to believe me.

3. Clearly, I didn't send the paper, although I was wrong in not telling you. I gave it to a sister to copy, and I have not been able to find it. Until they send another copy from Seville, there is no way I can send it to you.[1]

4. I think by now they will have given you a letter I sent by way of Madrid, but in case it has been lost I will have to repeat what I said there. I regret having to spend time doing so. First, look over that house you have rented belonging to Hernán Alvarez de Peralta. I think I have heard it mentioned that in one of the rooms the walls are ready to cave in. Be very careful.

5. Second, send the small chest and any other of my papers that may have been in the bundles, for it seems to me there was a bag containing papers. Have them sent to me well sewn. If Doña Quiteria through Serna sends a parcel that she needs to send, they will easily fit inside. Add my seal also, for I can't bear using this seal with the skull. I prefer the one with the monogram of him whom I would like to have engraved on my heart as had St. Ignatius.[2] Don't let anyone open the chest, unless it's yourself, for I think the writing on prayer is in there, and don't tell anyone

what you find in it. Be on guard, for I don't give you permission to do this, nor would it be fitting. Even though it may seem to you that this would render service to God, I forbid it because of other disadvantages that would result. Enough said, for were I to learn that you tell someone, I would never let you read anything again.

6. The nuncio has asked me to send him copies of the patent letters authorizing me to found these houses, and an account of how many there are, and where, and how many nuns, and from where, their ages, and how many I think have the qualities for being prioress. The lists of these things are in the chest, or maybe in the bag. Well, I need everything that is there. They say he wants it so as to set up the province.[3] I fear, instead, that he may want our nuns to reform other monasteries, for he has spoken of this previously, and such a thing would not be good for us, except for monasteries of our order. Tell this to the subprioress, and tell her to send me the names of those who are in that house, the ages of those who are there now, and how long they have been nuns. This should be done with good handwriting in a small notebook, and signed with her name.

7. Now it occurs to me that I am prioress there and that I can do it, and so it is not necessary that she sign it but only send me the information, even if in her handwriting, for I can copy it. There is no reason for the nuns to know about this. You take care of how this is to be sent so that the papers aren't in danger of getting wet, and send the key.[4]

8. That which I said is in the book is in the one where I treat of the *Paternoster*. There you will find much about the prayer you are experiencing, although not to the extent in which it is explained in the other book. It seems to me it is found in the section on *Adveniat regnum tuum*.[5] Read it again, at least the part on the *Paternoster*. Perhaps you will find something that satisfies you.

9. Before I forget, how could you make a vow without telling me? That's a nice kind of obedience![6] This troubled me, although your determination pleased me. But what you did seemed to be dangerous. Inquire about this, for that which is a venial sin could become a mortal sin on account of the promise. I will also ask my confessor, who is a most learned man. And it seems to me

foolish, for what I promised carried with it certain conditions.[7] I would not dare promise what you did, for I know that even the apostles committed venial sins. Only our Lady was free from them. I am sure that God accepted your intention, but it would seem to me wise for you to have the vow commuted at once for something else. If it can be done by means of a bull, do so immediately. This jubilee year would be a good occasion for doing so.[8] God deliver us from committing ourselves to something in which it is so easy to fail without our hardly even being aware of it. If God hasn't charged you with a greater fault, it is because he knows our nature well. In my opinion you should correct this situation at once, and don't make any more vows, for it's a dangerous thing. It doesn't seem to me to be inappropriate to speak at times about your prayer with your confessors, for, after all, they are close at hand and they can give you better counsel about everything, and nothing would be lost.

10. Your being sorry that you have bought La Serna is the work of the devil, who doesn't want you to be grateful to God for the favor he granted you in this regard, which was great.[9] Be convinced that it is the best you could do from many viewpoints, and you are providing your children with something more than property, which is honor. Nobody hears about your purchase without thinking that you were most fortunate. And do you think there is no work in collecting rent? You would be spending all your time in property seizures. Consider this a temptation; don't pay any heed to it, but praise God for what you bought, and don't think that if you had more time your prayer would go better. Make no mistake about this, for time well spent, like looking after your children's property, does not hurt prayer. God often gives more in a short moment than in a long time. His works are not measured by time.

11. Try, then, after these feast days are over to devote some time to getting all the records in suitable order. And what you spend on La Serna will be well spent, and when summer comes you will be happy to go and spend some days there. Jacob did not become less a saint for tending his flock, nor Abraham, nor St. Joachim. When we try to avoid work, everything tires us. That's the way it goes for me, and for this reason God wills that I be always loaded down with many things to do. Discuss all these

things with Francisco de Salcedo, for in these temporal matters I willingly let him stand in my stead.[10]

12. It is a great favor from God that you tire of what others find restful, but not for this reason should you renounce it. We have to serve God as he wishes and not as we wish. The livestock business is what in my opinion you can disregard. For this reason I am somewhat happy that you have given up the business with Antonio Ruiz that was based on profit. For even in the eyes of the world one suffers some little loss through such dealings. I think it would be better for you to be moderate in almsgiving, for God has given you food and what you need to give alms, but not a lot. I do not call what you want to do at La Serna the livestock business, for it is something very good; it is not what I call a business. I've already told you that in all these matters you should follow the opinion of Francisco de Salcedo, and you will no longer have such ideas. And always give my best regards to him and anyone else you choose, and to Pedro de Ahumada, to whom I would like to have time to write so that he might answer, for his letters are a delight to me.

13. Tell Teresa not to fear that I love anyone as much as I do her and that she should distribute the holy pictures, except those I put aside for myself, and that she give some to her brothers. I long to see her. I was moved by what you wrote about her to Seville. They sent me your letters, which filled the sisters with joy when I read them in recreation, and me too. Whoever would take away gallantry from my brother would be taking away his life. Everything seems to him good, since his gallantry is put into practice for saints, for I believe these nuns are saints. In every instance they put me to shame.

14. We had a great feast yesterday for the Holy Name of Jesus; may God reward you. I don't know what to send you for all you do for me except these carols I composed, for my confessor gave me orders to bring some happiness to the sisters. I spent the past evenings with them, and I didn't know how to bring them joy except with these. They have a delightful sound—it would be nice if Francisquito[11] could sing them. See if I'm not making good progress! Nonetheless, the Lord has granted me many favors during these days.

15. I am amazed by those he is granting you. May he be blessed forever. I understand why devotion is desired, which is good. It is one thing to desire it and another to ask for it. But I believe that what you are doing is the best. Leave it all to God and leave your interests in his hands. He knows what is fitting for us, but always strive to journey along the path I wrote you about. Realize that it is more important than you think.

16. It wouldn't be bad when at times you wake up with those impulses of love of God to sit up in bed for a while; always being careful, though, that you get the sleep your head needs (for unawares you could end up incapable of prayer). And be careful and try not to suffer much cold, for the cold is not good for the pains in your side. I don't know why you want those terrors and fears, for God is leading you by love. They were necessary back then. Don't think it is always the devil who impedes prayer, for God in his mercy sometimes takes it away. And I am inclined to say that this is almost as great a favor as when he bestows much prayer; and this for many reasons that I do not have time to tell you now. The prayer God gives you is incomparably greater than thinking about hell, and you wouldn't be able to do so even if you desired. And don't desire to do so, for there is no reason for it.

17. Some of the responses of the sisters[12] made me laugh. Others were excellent, for they gave me light on the subject, for don't think that I know the meaning. I didn't do any more than mention to you haphazardly what I will speak to you about the next time I see you, God willing.

18. I was amused by good Francisco de Salcedo's response. His humility is in a sense strange. God so leads him with fear that it could even seem to him wrong to speak of these matters in this way.[13] We have to accommodate ourselves to what we see in souls. I tell you he is a holy man, but God is not leading him along the road he is leading you. Indeed, he is leading him as he does the strong, and us as he does the weak. The response was long for someone of Francisco's temperament.

19. I just now read your letter again. I hadn't understood that you wanted to get up during the night, as you say, but thought you just wanted to sit up in the bed. I thought that was already a

lot, for it is important not to go without sleep. In no way should you get up no matter how much fervor you feel, and even less so if you can sleep. Don't be afraid of sleep. If you could hear what Fray Peter of Alcántara said in this regard, you wouldn't be afraid of going to sleep, even if you had become wide awake.

20. Your letters do not tire me, for they console me greatly, and I would be consoled if I were able to write more frequently. But I have so much correspondence that I cannot write more often, and even tonight my prayer has been impeded by this work. This doesn't cause me any scruple, only regret at not having time. God gives it to us that we might always spend it in his service, amen.

21. Different kinds of fish in this town are so scarce that it is a pity for the sisters, and so I was delighted with those sea bream. I think considering the weather they could have been sent without bread.[14] If you manage to have some when Serna comes, or some fresh sardines, give the subprioress the means for sending them, for her package was very well wrapped. This is a terrible place for having to go without eating meat, for there is never even a fresh egg around. Nonetheless, I was thinking today that I haven't felt so well in years, and I am keeping all the observance that the other nuns do, which is a great consolation for me.[15]

22. The enclosed verses that are not in my handwriting are not my work, but they seem to me good for Francisco. In the way the nuns at St. Joseph's compose theirs, one of the sisters here did these. During these Christmas festivities we did a lot of this in recreation. Today is the second day of the year.

Your honor's unworthy servant,
Teresa of Jesus

23. I thought that you would send us your carol, for these have neither rhyme nor reason to them, and the sisters sing everything. I now recall one that I once composed while in deep prayer, and it seemed I entered into even greater quiet. Here it is, but I don't remember if the verses went just like this. See how even from here I want to provide you with some recreation.

Oh Beauty exceeding
All other beauties!
Paining, but You wound not,
Free of pain You destroy
The love of creatures.
Oh, knot that binds
Two so different,
Why do You become unbound
For when held fast You strengthen
Making injuries seem good.
You bind the one without being
With Being unending;
Finish, without finishing,
You love, without having to love,
Magnify our nothingness.

24. I don't remember any more. What a brain for a foundress! But I tell you I thought I had a great one when I composed this. God forgive you for making me waste time, but I think these stanzas will touch you and inspire you with devotion, but don't tell anyone. Doña Guiomar[16] and I were together at that time. Give her my regards.

To Padre Ambrosio Mariano de San Benito, Madrid
Toledo, February 28, 1577

Teresa gives advice to Mariano, urging him to obey the nuncio, keep his temper in check, and not go directly to the king with his requests. She informs him about the calumnies in Andalusia and her own recent illness.

1. Jesus be with your reverence, *mi padre*. Today Señor Don Teutonio,[1] who is in Madrid, wrote me that the nuncio[2] is not going to leave. If this is true—unless you stay in Alcalá under the pretext of being ill—you must in no way give the impression that you are disobedient.[3]

2. You should know, *padre*, from what I understand, that these fathers[4] would now like to be our friends; and until we see what God ordains, it is good to be compliant, as you have been. Certainly I do not cast blame on the nuncio, but the devil's battery is of the kind that nothing would surprise me. You shouldn't fear that no one will dare defend you, for the Lord is your keeper. Since up to the present he has granted us the favor of helping you hold your temper in check, may you continue doing so. Let this be your cross for now, certainly no small one. If the Lord had not helped you in a special way, I don't believe you would have been able to put up with so much.

3. As for the Council's response,[5] there is nothing to hope for. Don't you see that these are all polite words? What need is there to have this directive sent from here so that it can be annulled, since they have a copy of it there and know that it is authentic? Now is not the time. Let us wait a little, for the Lord knows what it is he is doing better than we know what it is we want.

4. What do you think of how they make us appear in this piece of writing? I don't know why one tries to refute these things. Our *padre*[6] is making a mistake, for this is something utterly base. For the love of God, don't show it to anyone, for they would think it imprudent to pay any attention to such foolishness or talk about it. I think it would be very imperfect to do anything about it, except laugh.[7]

5. You should know, *mi padre*, that my heavy correspondence and many other duties that I tried to handle all alone have caused a noise and weakness in my head.[8] And I have been given orders that unless it's very necessary I should not be writing letters in my own hand, and so I will not be long. I only say that as regards what you said you want to procure from the king, don't think about doing it until you have considered it most carefully, for in my opinion we would lose much of our credibility. God will do what is necessary by another means. May he watch over you for me.

Your reverence's servant,
Teresa of Jesus

To María de San José, Seville
Toledo, March 1–2, 1577

Though not yet well enough to be writing her own letters, Teresa dispenses herself and sends a four-page letter in her own hand to María de San José. Also there is an urgent matter concerning one of the discalced nuns in Paterna who was publicly manifesting some unusual prayer experiences. Such publicity could incur criticism for the nuns and trouble with the Inquisition. Finally, she sends along her little work A Satirical Critique *together with the writings that were the object of her satire.*

For Mother Prioress of San José in Seville.

1. Jesus. The grace of the Holy Spirit be with your reverence, my daughter. After so much good news and the many gifts you have sent me, I have every reason to write a long letter; at least doing this would make me very happy. But I wrote you yesterday and the labor this winter of letter-writing has so weakened my head that I have been truly sick.[1] I am much better, but nevertheless, I almost never write in my own hand, for they say I must not do so if I want to recover completely.

2. Oh, how delighted I was with the beautiful things you sent me through the administrator.[2] You wouldn't believe how much work he takes on for the monastery in Malagón and how ready he is to help me. And don't think it takes little effort to keep the construction work going well, for there are a thousand things that have to be attended to with the workmen. I gave him the small reliquary. Both are very lovely, but the large one is still better; especially the way it was embellished here, for it arrived with the glass broken as I wrote you. New glass was put in that looks very nice. The base was twisted, so we had an iron one cast. This should have been done in the first place. I also gave him the jar, I mean the little cup, which was the most charming I've ever seen. Don't think that because I have to wear a habit of finer material, things have got so bad that I need to drink from something as nice as that! I also gave him the bottle just as it was. He greatly appreciated this. He is a man of integrity. Well, from down there you have helped your house in Malagón.[3] They

wouldn't let me give away the orange-flower water, because it gives life to the prioress and is beneficial for me too, and we didn't have any. Ask for some, on my part, from the mother of the Portuguese nun[4] and have it sent to us. Do this out of charity—that is the condition.

3. Oh, how happy I am that you have paid off the debt on the house. But until that nun is professed we ought not rejoice too much. It is true, though, that if that should not happen, God will provide in another way. Pray hard that he might be pleased to take away this trouble I have with my head. Today, by the mail carrier, I sent you an account of what in part brought it on.

4. Your manner of prayer makes me happy. Recognizing that you have it and that God is doing you a favor is not a lack of humility since you understand that it is not your doing but his. That is how we know that the prayer is from God. I greatly praise him that you are faring so well, and I will try to give him joyful thanks as you ask me. Ask God that I might be the kind of person whose prayers he will answer.

5. In regard to Beatriz,[5] her prayer is good, but insofar as possible avoid paying attention to these things in conversations or any other way. You know this depends very much on the prioress. San Jerónimo[6] did not speak of that here, because the prioress[7] immediately interrupted and scolded her, and so she kept quiet. And you saw that when I was there she never carried on in this way. I don't know whether we were wrong in letting her leave our midst. Please God things will turn out well.

6. Think what would have happened if the others rather than the prioress had found the page![8] May God pardon the one who has told her to write. Our *padre*[9] would like me to write to her in a severe manner with respect to this. Read the enclosed letter that I am writing her, and if it seems all right to you, send it to her. You are doing extremely well in not allowing anyone to talk about it to others. The prioress in Beas[10] writes me that the nuns speak only of their sins with their confessor and that they are all finished within a half hour. She tells me that it should be like this everywhere, that they are all very much at peace, and that they have a great love for their prioress, in whom they confide. Since I have some experience in this matter, you could ask them why

they don't write to me but go and ask someone who perhaps doesn't have as much as I do. And in a matter like this it would be fitting more than in any other. And tell San Francisco[11] to make her eat meat after Lent is over and not let her fast.

7. I would like to know what she means when, without explaining, she speaks of the great force that God uses over her. What a trial it is that she now goes around weeping all the time in front of others and is seen as ready to write at any moment. Get what she wrote and send it to me. And remove any hope she has of speaking about this with anyone other than our *padre*, because those conversations have ruined her. Be aware that this language is understood there less than you think. However, if it is used in confession and with Padre Acosta[12] no harm can come. But I know well that it is less fitting for her than for anyone. It is a good thing the order was given that in Paterna more leeway could be allowed to the nuns, although it would have been better if from the start they had required only what was obligatory.[13] In these matters of reform, if the nuns obtain something by shouting, it seems to them at once that they will obtain everything else in the same way. You did very well in advising them to live in community.

8. I have not given the letters or reliquary to Doña Luisa[14] because she was away and returned the day before yesterday. I am waiting for all the visits to die down. Pray for her and for Doña Guiomar, for they have many trials.

9. Since I am not writing this letter all at once, I don't know whether I may have forgotten to answer any of the things you asked about. Since these bolts I am sending are similar to the ones that are here on the grille in the choir, I don't think it's necessary that they be more attractive, although I suppose you won't be satisfied with them. But do as they do here, for the nuns here don't consider themselves less refined than you, and a little bolt is better than something else, for I don't know what kind of locks you want. The crucifixes are being made. I believe they will cost a ducat.

10. All the nuns ask for your prayers, and Isabel[15] was delighted with the sweets and the coarse woolen cloth. May God reward you. As for myself, I have plenty of clothes. Do you think it

doesn't sadden me to have nothing to send you? It certainly does. But the barrenness of this region is incredible except for the quinces when they are in season, and even then, the quinces down there are much better. The nuns were delighted with the spices and the *catamaca*.[16] They didn't allow me to send any to anyone—I very much would have liked to—for many have great need for it.

11. Enclosed are the responses[17] to the question I posed to my brother. The respondents had decided to submit their answers to the judgment of the nuns at St. Joseph's in Avila. The bishop was present and told them to send the answers to me so that I might judge them, just when my head was in too miserable a state even to read them. Show them to Father Prior and to Nicolao,[18] but you must explain to them what was being done, and don't let them read the judgments before reading the answers they submitted. And if you can, send them back so that our *padre* can enjoy them—for that is why they sent them to me from Avila—even though this may not be along the muleteer's way.

12. I am sending you this letter that my brother[19] wrote me (he writes many about the favors that God grants him and this one was near at hand). I think it will make you happy since you are fond of him. Tear it up right away, and remain with God, for I'll never end this and writing is bad for me. May His Majesty make you a saint.

13. Now they have just given me a letter written by our *padre* from Málaga fifteen days ago, I mean from tomorrow. He is well, glory to God. Today is 2 March.

My regards to all, and let me know about Fray Bartolomé's health.

Your reverence's servant,
Teresa of Jesus

14. Be grateful that I wrote this out myself, for I haven't been writing my own letters even to St. Joseph's in Avila.[20] Yesterday I wrote to you and to our *padre* through the mail carrier. Thus, I'm not doing so now.

To Lorenzo de Cepeda, Avila
Toledo, January 17, 1577

Teresa answers Lorenzo's questions about prayer and gives him advice regarding his contemplative experiences. In doing so, she manifests something about her own extraordinary experiences at the time and speaks of her secret writings. She also gives attention to the more ordinary things of life: sardines, sweets, money, repairs on a house, health remedies, and a hand warmer.

1. Jesus be with your honor. I already mentioned in the letter sent through the mail carrier from Alba that the sardines arrived in good condition and the sweets at a good time, although I would have preferred that you had kept the best for yourself. May God reward you. Now don't send me anything else, for when I want something I'll ask for it. Congratulations for having moved to our area. Nevertheless, look over carefully the room I mentioned, for if repairs are not made it will be dangerous; it was in such a state that the danger was great. Anyway, be careful.[1]

2. With respect to the secret[2] in my regard, I don't mean that you should feel obliged under pain of sin, for I am very much opposed to that sort of thing and one can slip if not careful. It's enough that you know it would cause me distress. As for the promise, my confessor has told me that it was not valid, which made me very happy, for I was worried about it. I also told him about the obedience you promised to me, which seemed to me inopportune. He says that obedience is good, but that you shouldn't promise it to me or to anyone else. And so I don't want you to do so, and even without the promise I accept your wish only reluctantly. I do so for the sake of your consolation on the condition that you don't make a promise of it to anyone. I rejoiced that you feel that Fray John understands you, for he has experience. And even Francisco has a little, but not of what God is granting you. May he be blessed forever without end. With both of them you are now well cared for.[3]

3. How good God is! It seems to me he wants to show his greatness by raising up miserable people, and with so many favors, for I don't know any who are more wretched than the two of us.

You ought to know that for more than eight days I have been in such a state that were it to last I would not be able to attend to so many business matters. From the time before I last wrote you, I've begun to have raptures again, and this distresses me because they happen in public sometimes. One came upon me at Matins. Trying to resist them doesn't help, nor can they be disguised. I'm so terribly embarrassed that I want to hide I don't know where. I plead with God not to let this happen to me in public. Beg this of God for me, because there are many disadvantages to experiencing them, and it doesn't seem to me that the prayer is better. I've been going around these days as though I were partially drunk; at least I am well aware that the soul is in a good place. Since the faculties are not free, it is a difficult thing to have to attend to more than what the soul wishes.

4. Prior to this, for about eight days I often found it impossible even to have a good thought, but was left in extreme aridity. In a certain way this highly pleased me, for I had spent some other days before those like the ones I am having now, and it is a great pleasure to see so clearly the little that we can do of ourselves. May he be blessed who can do everything, amen. I have said a great deal. The rest is not meant to be written or even spoken. It's good that we praise the Lord, each for the other; at least you should do so for me, for I am incapable of giving him the thanks I owe him, and so I need much help.

5. As for what you told me you experienced, I don't know what to say, for it is certainly beyond what you can understand and the beginning of many blessings, if you do not lose them through your own fault. I have already passed through this kind of prayer, and the soul afterward usually finds rest, and sometimes undertakes some penances. Especially, if the impulse is very strong, it doesn't seem the soul can endure it without doing something for God. It is a touch of love that is given to the soul in which you will understand, if it goes on increasing, what you say you do not understand in the poem;[4] for it is a great affliction and pain that comes without one's knowing how, and most delightful. And although, as a matter of fact, it is a wound caused by the love of God in the soul, one doesn't know where it comes from or how, or whether it is a wound or what it is, but it feels this delightful pain that makes it complain, and so it says:

Sin herir, dolor hacéis
y sin dolor deshacéis
el amor de las criaturas[5]

6. For when the soul is truly touched by this love of God, the love it has for creatures is taken away without any pain, I mean in such a way that the soul is no longer attached to any love. This doesn't come about without this love of God, for whatever regards creatures, if we love them greatly, causes pain; and separation from them causes much more. As God takes hold of a soul, he gives it dominion over all creatures. And even if that presence and delight is taken away (which is what you are complaining of), as if nothing had been experienced in the bodily senses, to which God wanted to give some share in the soul's joy, God doesn't abandon it. Neither does he fail to leave it enriched with favors, as is seen by the effects afterward with the passing of time.

7. As for the lascivious feelings that you tell me about, don't pay any attention to them. For although I have never experienced this—for God in his goodness has always delivered me from those passions—I think it must happen because the delight of the soul is so great that it arouses these natural feelings. They will die away with the help of God if you pay no attention to them. Other people have spoken to me about this.

8. The shaking will also go away, for since it is something new the soul grows frightened, and it has reason to be frightened. As the experience repeats itself you will become more capable of receiving favors. Do all that you can to resist this shaking and any exterior thing so that none of this becomes a habit, for it is a hindrance more than a help.

9. As for the heat you say you feel, it has little importance; it could be somewhat harmful to one's health if excessive, but it will also perhaps go away as will the shaking. These things, in my opinion, have to do with one's physical constitution. Since you have a sanguine temperament, the intense movement of the spirit along with one's natural heat, which is gathered in the superior part and touches the heart, can give rise to this. But, as I say, the quality of the prayer isn't any greater on this account.

10. I think I've answered what you said about "feeling afterward as though nothing happened." I think it may be St. Augustine who says that the spirit of God passes without leaving a trace just as an arrow passes through the air without leaving one. Now I recall that I answered this question. A huge amount of mail has arrived since I received your letters, and I still have many letters to write so that I don't have much time for this one.

11. At other times the soul is left in such a condition that it cannot return to itself for many days, but it seems like the sun that cannot be seen although its rays can be felt. So the soul seems to have its seat far off somewhere, and it animates the body, not being in it, since one or other of its faculties is suspended.

12. You are doing very well with your style of meditation, glory to God; I mean when you don't have the prayer of quiet. I don't know if I have answered everything; I always reread your letters, which requires a bit of time, and now I haven't had time to reread your last one except in bits and pieces. You shouldn't make the effort to read over those you send me. I never reread mine. If some word is missing, put it in, and I will do the same here with yours. The meaning is at once clear, and it is a waste of time to reread them unnecessarily.

13. For those days when you are unable to be recollected during the time of prayer, or have a desire to do something for the Lord, I am sending you this hairshirt, for it is a great help in awakening love, provided that you don't wear it when fully dressed or when sleeping. You can wear it anywhere on the body and adjust it so that you feel discomfort.

14. I am fearful of doing this, for you are so sanguine that anything could alter your blood. But doing something for God (even a trifle like this) when one has this love brings about so much happiness that I wouldn't want us to neglect trying it. When winter is over, you will do some other little thing, for I am not forgetting you. Write to let me know how you are faring with this trinket. I tell you that whatever may be the punishment we desire to impose on ourselves, it does become a trinket when we remember what our Lord suffered. I am laughing to myself to think how you send me sweets, presents, and money, and I send you hairshirts.

15. Give my regards to Aranda. Tell him to throw some of these enclosed pastilles around your room or close to the brazier, for they are very healthy and pure, and were given to me by the discalced nuns, who don't use anything out of the ordinary. However mortified you want to be, you can use them. They are excellent for rheumatism and headaches. Would you have this little package delivered to Doña María de Cepeda at the Incarnation.[6]

16. You should know that everything is agreed on for a very good nun to enter the monastery in Seville. She has 6,000 ducats free of any ties, and before entering she has given some gold ingots worth two thousand. She insists so much that they begin to pay for the house with them that the prioress is doing so and has written me that she will pay three thousand now. This made me very happy, for they were carrying a great burden. Well, as soon as the nun makes profession, the prioress will pay off everything, and perhaps even before. Pray for this and give God thanks, for in this way the work you began is coming to its conclusion.[7]

17. Our Father Visitator is busy organizing different things; he is well and making his visitation of the houses. It is amazing how calm the province is and how they love him. The prayers are having their good effect, as well as the virtue and talents God gives him.

18. May God be with you and keep you, for I don't know how to stop when I speak to you. All send their best regards, and I do too. Give Francisco de Salcedo my best. You are right to be fond of him, for he is a holy man. My health is very good.

Today is 17 January.

Your honor's unworthy servant,
Teresa of Jesus

19. I wrote to the bishop to ask him to send the book,[8] for perhaps I will be stirred to finish it by writing about what the Lord has given me since. Or another large one could be written, if the Lord should desire that I be able to express myself; and if I can't, there would be no great loss.

20. There were some little things belonging to Teresa in the small chest; I'm sending them back. The little round brazier is

for Pedro de Ahumada, for since he spends much time in church, his hands must get cold. I don't need any money now. May our Lord reward you for your care and watch over you for me, amen. You can entrust the matter about the money to the prioress of Valladolid, for she will take care of it very well. She knows a merchant who is a great friend of the house, and a friend of mine and a good Christian.[9]

To Don Lorenzo de Cepeda, Avila
Toledo, February 27–28, 1577

Lorenzo had written Teresa in concern about her health, but he also took the opportunity to seek further spiritual guidance. She responds, assuring him that she is better and giving him the guidance he seeks. Some of the other topics deal with their relatives, the Inquisition, Tostado, and the goodness of some of the prioresses toward her.

1. Jesus be with your honor. Before I forget, as I have at other times, tell Francisco[1] to send me some well-cut pens. There aren't any good ones around here, they are a nuisance and make my task harder. Never prevent him from writing to me, for perhaps he may have a need to. He is satisfied with a few words for an answer and they don't cost me anything.

2. I think this illness will end up serving a good purpose, for I am beginning to get accustomed to having another do my writing for me. I could have already done so in matters of little importance; I will continue doing this now. I am much better, for I have taken some pills. I think it did me harm to start fasting during Lent, for it wasn't only my head but my heart as well that was affected. The heart is much better, and even the head has improved the last couple of days, for that is what caused the most pain—which wasn't little. I was afraid I might become incapacitated for everything. It would have been a serious imprudence to try to practice prayer. And our Lord sees clearly the harm this would have done me. I don't experience any more supernatural recollection. It is as though I had never received any, which truly surprises me, for it wasn't possible for me to resist.[2] Don't be troubled, for little by little my head will become stronger. I take all the care of myself that I see is necessary, and even a little more than is the custom here. Otherwise I wouldn't be able to practice prayer.

3. I have a strong desire to get well. My illness is at a cost to you. For this reason I think my desire is good. I am in such a condition that I need to get better so as not to be a burden. Since mutton does not agree with me, I always have to eat fowl. The root of the whole problem is weakness from my having fasted since the

feast of the Exaltation of the Cross in September along with all my work and at my age. Well, to see myself capable of so little is bothersome, for this body of mine has always done me harm and prevented me from good. I'm not so bad off that I cannot write to you myself. I will not inflict this mortification on you for now, which would be a great one judging from myself.

4. As regards the mortification of not being able to use the hairshirt, you will have to pardon me for imposing it on you, for you must not be doing what you choose to do. You should know that the discipline ought to be taken for only a short duration. In that way, you feel it more and it is less likely to do harm. Don't hit yourself too hard; this won't matter even though you may think it is a great imperfection. That you might do something of what you would wish, I am sending you this hairshirt you can wear on two days during the week, by which I mean from the time you get up until you go to bed; don't wear it while sleeping. I was amused by the precision with which you count the days. This is a new practice, and I don't believe the discalced Carmelite nuns have attained to such resourcefulness. See that you never wear the other one; store it away for now.

5. I am sending one to Teresa[3] and also a discipline that she requested of me, a very hard one. Have it sent to her with my best regards. Julián de Avila[4] in writing me has many good things to say about her, which moves me to praise the Lord. May he guide her always, for he has granted a great favor to her, and to us who love her dearly.

6. In a certain way I had desired that you experience some aridity during these days, and so I was delighted when I saw your letter, although what you mentioned cannot be called aridity. Think that what you experience is beneficial for many reasons. If this hairshirt fits all around the waist, place a little linen cloth between it and the stomach. And be careful so that if you feel any discomfort around the kidneys you do not wear it or take the discipline, for you will suffer harm. God desires your health more than your penance, and that you obey. Remember about Saul, and don't do otherwise.[5] You will be doing no small thing if you learn how to put up with that person's disposition, for I hold that the source of all those troubles and sorrows is melancholy, which has a tight control on him. So, there is no fault or

anything for us to be surprised about; we should praise the Lord that he does not give us this torment.

7. Take great care not to give up sleep and to eat enough at your collation, for with your desire to do something for God you will not notice anything until the harm is done. And I tell you that I had to learn my lesson for the sake of myself and others. In a certain sense the daily use of the hairshirt is less of a burden because through habit the novelty of which you speak wears off. You shouldn't tighten it around the shoulders the way you usually do. Be careful that none of these things do you any harm. God is granting you a great favor by your being able to bear so well the lack of prayer, for this is a sign that you are resigned to his will. This I believe is the greatest good that prayer brings about.

8. There is good news about my papers. The Grand Inquisitor himself read them, which is something new—he must have heard some praise of them—and told Doña Luisa that they contained nothing the Inquisition would have to deal with, and that there were good things in them rather than bad.[6] And he asked her why I hadn't founded a monastery in Madrid. He is very favorable toward the discalced friars. He is the one who has now been made Archbishop of Toledo. I believe Doña Luisa went to see him there where he is, and recommended this matter strongly, for they are great friends, and she wrote to me about it. She will be coming soon and I will find out the rest.[7] You may tell this to the bishop, the subprioress, and Isabel de San Pablo (in secret, so that they don't tell anyone but pray for this matter),[8] and to no other person. This is very good news. My stay here has been beneficial for everything, except for my head because I have had more letters to write than elsewhere.

9. In the letter from the prioress you will see how they have paid half of the amount on the house, without touching the dowry of Beatriz and her mother.[9] They will soon pay everything with the Lord's help. I was delighted with it, as also with that letter from Agustín and to know that he is not going down there.[10] I was sorry that you had already sent a letter without mine. I will have one from the Marchioness of Villena for the viceroy—she is his beloved niece—when they can be sent safely. It grieves me to see him still involved in these things.[11] Pray for him, which is what I am doing.

10. Regarding what you say about holy water, I don't know the reason but only what I experience. I have mentioned this to some learned men and they did not object to it. It's enough that the Church uses it, as you say.

Despite all the difficulties that the nun reformers are having, many sins are being prevented by them.[12]

11. There is a lot of truth in what Francisco de Salcedo says regarding Señora Ospedal—at least that in this instance I am like her.[13] Give my best regards to him, and to Pedro de Ahumada also. I do not want to write any more except that you look to see if you could give Juan de Ovalle what he needs to buy some sheep. This would be most helpful to him and a great act of charity, if you can do it without a loss to yourself.

12. I have changed pens so often in this letter that my handwriting will seem worse than usual; it is due to this and not to my being sick. I wrote this yesterday, and today when I got up I felt better, glory to God. The fear of remaining incapacitated is worse than the illness.

13. My companion has been charming in her words about the stone paver. She told me such wonderful things about him that I told her to write to you. Nonetheless, I think that since the prioress says he is reputable, she ought to know. I don't think he would do a bad job, seeing that she knows both workers; although I always thought that Vitoria would be best suited. Please God the work will be done well, and may he keep you, as I beg him, for his service, amen. Today is 28 February.

14. Father Visitator is well. Now Tostado is returning, according to what they say. From the way all these affairs of ours are going one learns what the world is, for it seems to be nothing but a farce. Nonetheless, I long to see him freed of all those affairs. May the Lord do as he sees is necessary. The prioress and all the nuns send their regards. The prioress of Seville pampers me as does also the prioress of Salamanca. And even those of Beas and Caravaca have not failed to do what they can; in short, they show their concern.

15. I would like to be near you so that you could see all of this, and also, that I could have the pleasure of sending some of it to you. Even just now some very tasty shad arrived from Seville

wrapped in bread. I was delighted, for there is a great scarcity of fish in this town. Seeing the affection with which they do it is what pleases me.

Your honor's unworthy servant,
Teresa of Jesus

To Madre María de San José, Seville
Toledo, July 11, 1577

Madre María has again sent gifts, among which were some coconuts. She was having a number of difficulties: her own poor health, a nun gravely ill, a melancholic aspirant proposed to the community by the archbishop, and some other problematic candidates. Teresa gives advice and sympathizes with her.

For Mother Prioress, María de San José.

1. Jesus be with you, my daughter. By the fact that you tell me you are somewhat better, it seems I am capable of bearing everything willingly. May it please the Lord that you continue to improve and may he repay the doctor, for I am dutifully grateful to him.

2. It's amazing that the subprioress[1] is still alive. He who made her can easily give her health, for he gave her being from nothing. He is truly exercising her in suffering as he is all of you. Enduring something like this makes one ready for anything, even going to Guinea[2] or beyond. Nonetheless, I would like to see it over with, for it causes me much grief.

3. Since I told Madre Brianda[3] to write about what is happening here, I will only mention the things I need to. Neither the pictures intended for Doña Luisa nor the letter arrived, nor did you mention whether you received the cloth and the crucifixes. Let me know in the next letter and pray for Brianda, for I am happy to see her so much better.

4. Accept the nun gladly, for the dowry you say she has is not a bad one. I wish that that widow had already entered. The other day I wrote to you to take the little black girl gladly, for she will not do you any harm, and her sister as well. Neither did you mention whether you received that letter. I was sorry about Garciálvarez's illness. Don't forget to tell me how he is and whether your improvement is continuing. I received the coconuts; and they are something to behold. I will send them to Doña Luisa. The one for me is beautifully decorated. Our *padre*[4] says he will break it open tomorrow.

5. Regarding Paterna, he says not to talk about it until he goes there—we spoke to him a lot about that today—for everyone would be disturbed at the thought that he is not the visitator,[5] and he is right.

6. May God repay you for all the gifts you give me—you must dream of being a queen—and for even sending the portage. For goodness' sake take care of yourself and take it easy, for I would be receiving a great gift by your doing that. The sisters were delighted to see the coconuts, and I too. May he be blessed who created it, for it is certainly something to behold. It pleased me how with all your trials you have the vitality to think of things like this. The Lord well knows whom he gives trials to.

7. Just now I have spoken to our *padre* about the aspirant proposed by the archbishop.[6] I am very displeased to see how persistent they are in their entreaties while he does not favor it. Our *padre* says that he thinks she is a melancholic *beata*—and with such we should have learned our lesson—and it would be worse to send her away afterward. Try to speak to her a few times to see what she is like. And if you see that she is not for us, it wouldn't seem to me a bad idea for Padre Nicolao[7] to speak to the archbishop and tell him about the bad luck we have with these *beatas*; or try to delay the decision.

8. It has been a long while since I wrote the enclosed letter to Fray Gregorio[8] and sent it to our *padre* to send on to him, and now he returned it to me. It's dated, but don't fail to read it so that the foolish temptation you've had to leave the house you are in doesn't return. I am sorry about the great trial you will have with that sister, and I pity the poor little soul for what she suffers. May God provide a remedy. Give everyone my regards. It would be a great consolation for me to see you, for I find few nuns so pleasing to me, and I love you greatly. The Lord can do all.

9. Best regards to Padre Garciálvarez and to Beatriz, her mother,[9] and the others, to whom I say that they need to be very perfect. The reason is that the Lord is beginning this foundation with them and has deprived them of their support.[10] I don't know how you are able to manage everything. It's true that it would have been worse for you if you had to deal with calced nuns as was the case elsewhere.[11] For, after all, your nuns will follow the

path you point out to them. The worse thing is that you have to undergo everything with poor health. My experience is that when one's health is good, everything is bearable. May God grant it to you, my daughter, as I desire and beg of him, amen.

Today is 11 July.

Your reverence's,
Teresa of Jesus

10. Since our *padre* was here, he opened the package and gave me the letters, but kept the pictures and must have forgotten. I accidentally found this out today, for he and Padre Antonio[12] were arguing over them. I saw two and they were beautiful.

To Padre Jerónimo Gracián, Madrid(?)
Toledo/Avila, July 1577(?)

Teresa warns against allowing situations that would give rise to small-town gossip.

1. If some friar should have to stay there, your paternity ought to advise him strongly not to spend much time talking to the nuns. Look, *mi padre*, this is very necessary. And I wouldn't even want the licentiate to do so, for even though he is so good, such goodness can give rise to bad judgments in people with malicious minds, especially in small towns, and everywhere else as well.

2. Believe me, the more you see that your daughters are cut off from such very special relationships, even though they are very holy ones, the better it is, even for the peace of the house. And I wouldn't want this to be forgotten . . .

To King Don Philip II, Madrid
Avila, September 18, 1577

This letter was motivated by a libelous document being circulated against Gracián and the discalced nuns. It was the work of the notorious Baltasar de Nieto and signed by a lay brother, Miguel de la Columna, who had accompanied Gracián in his travels as visitor. In it Gracián is accused of grossly immoral conduct at some of the Carmels. Tomás Gracián, secretary to the king, wrote a defense of his brother and presented it along with Teresa's letter to Philip II. By the end of the month, the confused Miguel de la Columna retracted what was contained in the letter he had signed.

---

1. Jesus. The grace of the Holy Spirit be always with your majesty, amen. News has reached me that a memorandum was delivered to your majesty against Padre Maestro Gracián. I am astonished at the intrigues of the devil and these calced fathers. They're not satisfied with defaming this servant of God (for he truly is and has so edified us that the monasteries he has visited[1] always write to me about how he has left them with a new spirit), but they are striving now to discredit these monasteries where God is so well served. For this purpose they have made use of two discalced friars.[2] The one had been a servant in these monasteries before becoming a friar and did things that made it obvious he often lacked good judgment. The friars of the cloth[3] have availed themselves of this discalced friar and others antagonistic toward Padre Maestro Gracián—for he is the one who must punish them—and had them sign things that were absurd. I would laugh at what is said about the discalced nuns if I didn't fear the harm the devil can do with it, for in our communities such things would be horrendous.

2. For love of God I beg your majesty not to allow such infamous testimony to be presented to tribunals. The world is such that some suspicion can remain—however well the opposite is proven—if we provide the opportunity. It is not helpful for the general reform that aspersions be cast on an order that by the goodness of God has been so well reformed. Your majesty could, if you care to, acquaint yourself with this reality through some

testimonies that were gathered by order of Padre Gracián. They concern certain facts about these monasteries taken from some serious and saintly persons who have dealings with these nuns.

3. Since the motives of those who wrote the memorandum can be investigated, consider, your majesty, for love of our Lord, that this matter is something concerning God's honor and glory. If those of the cloth see that you are paying attention to their testimonies, they will accuse the visitator of heresy to prevent any further visitations, and where there is little fear of God this will be easy to prove.

4. I feel sorry for all that this servant of God suffers, despite the rectitude and perfection with which he proceeds in everything. This obliges me to beg your majesty to favor him or give orders that he be removed from this situation so full of perils, for he is the son of parents who are in your majesty's service,[4] besides his own good qualities. Truly, I think he is a man sent by God and his Blessed Mother. His devotion to her—and it is great—is what led him to the order and to helping me. For more than seventeen years I suffered alone from these fathers of the cloth, and I no longer knew how to bear it; my own weak efforts were insufficient.

5. I beg your majesty to pardon me for being so lengthy. The great love I bear you has made me bold, and I reflect that since the Lord puts up with my indiscreet complaints, you will also.

6. May it please him to hear all the prayers of the discalced friars and nuns that he preserve your majesty for many years, for we have no other support on earth.

Written in St. Joseph's in Avila on 13 September 1577.

Your majesty's unworthy servant and subject,
Teresa of Jesus

7. I suspect that since Tostado[5] will remain in his present position, the visitation will be of no benefit, but rather very harmful, especially since that preacher[6] who was previously a calced friar, and about whose life I beg your majesty to inquire, has linked up with him. And if it is necessary, all of us discalced nuns will swear that we never heard Padre Gracián speak a word—nor did we see anything in him—that was not edifying. And he was

so extremely cautious about not entering the enclosure of the monasteries that even in conducting the chapters, when entering would seem unavoidable, he usually did so at the grille.[7]

To Madre María de San José, Seville
Avila, October 22, 1577

The new nuncio, Felipe Sega, resistant to Teresa and her endeavor, has arrived in Madrid. Libelous statements against Gracián had been circulated and sent to the king, but the calumniators were made to retract. Yet the false reports against Gracián, María de San José, and the discalced nuns kept reappearing. Many nuns at the Incarnation in Avila have been excommunicated for electing Teresa as prioress against the provincial's orders.

For Mother Prioress in Seville.

1. Jesus be always with your reverence, my daughter. Last month I wrote to you by way of a muleteer from this city, and my brother also wrote. In the letter I mentioned that our business matters had gotten complicated. You will have learned this from Padre Fray Gregorio in a more complete way than I could have then put in writing. Now, God be blessed, they are proceeding very well, better each day. Our *padre*[1] is well, and he still retains his commission, although I would very much like to see him liberated from those people.[2] They make up so many things that it would be impossible to put them all in writing. But the good part is that everything ends up raining down on their own backs and turns out to our benefit.

2. You will have already learned how Fray Miguel and Fray Baltasar[3] retracted. Fray Miguel swears that he wrote nothing in the memorandum and that they made him sign it, with force and threats. He said this and other things in the presence of witnesses and a notary, and before the Blessed Sacrament. The king[4] understood that this is evil and so they do nothing but harm themselves. My head is in a wretched state. Pray for me and for these brothers that God will enlighten them for the salvation of their souls.

3. I tell you that what is going on at the Incarnation[5] is of a kind, I think, never before seen. By orders of Tostado,[6] the provincial[7] of the calced friars came here fifteen days ago for the election with threats of great censures and excommunications for anyone who

might cast a vote for me. Despite this, they paid no heed, and as though he had said nothing to them at all, fifty-five nuns voted for me. As each vote for me was given to him, he excommunicated the nun, and he cursed and pounded and beat the ballots with his fist and burned them. He has left the nuns excommunicated for fifteen days now without their being allowed to hear Mass or enter the choir, even when the Divine Office is being said. And they cannot speak to anyone, not even their own confessors or parents. And what is most amusing is that the day after this pounding election the provincial returned and called them together for an election, but they answered that there was no need for another election because they had already had one. And seeing this, he excommunicated them again and called the remaining nuns, which numbered forty-four, and had them elect another prioress[8] and sent the result to Tostado for confirmation.

4. Now she has been confirmed in office, but the others are holding fast and say they will not obey her except as a vicaress. Learned men say that the nuns are not excommunicated and that the friars are acting contrary to the Council[9] in confirming a prioress who received an insufficient number of votes. The other nuns sent word to Tostado that they want me for prioress. His answer was no; if I wanted, I could go there to live in seclusion,[10] but it would be inadmissible for me to go as prioress. I don't know where it will all end up.

5. This, in sum, is what is happening now, for all are stunned to see something like this which offends everyone. I would gladly pardon the nuns if they would leave me in peace, for I have no desire to find myself in that Babylon[11]—and even less so because of my poor health. And it gets even worse when I'm in that house. May God do what serves him most and free me from them.

6. Teresa[12] is well and sends you her regards. She is a lovely child and has grown a great deal. Pray for her that God may make her his servant. Let me know whether the widow[13] has entered—as has been my wish—and whether her sister has returned to the Indies.

7. I have felt a longing to speak to you about many things, which would be consoling for me. But some day I will have more time

and a safer messenger than the one who is going to bring this. Señora Doña Luisa is a great help and favors us in every way. Pray for her and for the Archbishop of Toledo, and don't ever forget the king.[14]

To Padre Jerónimo Gracián
Avila, November 1577

Gracián used to confide everything about his interior life to Teresa, and at one point he made the same promise as Teresa did of always seeking to do whatever is the most pleasing to God. She here expresses her feelings about the promise he made.

---

1. I take it as a very great favor from God that in the midst of so many storms Paul[1] has the strength to make such great decisions. Just one hour of these troubles a month would be too much, for they present so many occasions for taking away one's peace. Glory be to the One who gives it.

2. If you carry out that promise, I will need nothing more for my consolation, for all other trials will finally come to an end. And if they did not, it would matter little. Tell him[2] that I must keep that written document so as to remind him of its words should he not have it.

3. His willingness came just at the right time because of the fears I experience. My great anxiety is that Paul might stray in some way from the will of God. In this regard Joseph[3] has greatly reassured Angela[4] that he is doing well and continuing to merit more and more.

To Padre Jerónimo Gracián
Avila, December 1577(?)

Teresa urges Gracián not to give up prayer time for the sake of his business matters.

I just read again the letter from Paul[1] in which he says he is giving up sleep so as to work on his projects. And I think he says this in reference to his absorption in prayer. He shouldn't get into the habit of abandoning so great a treasure—tell him this—unless it involves giving up the sleep that the body needs. For the blessings the Lord gives in prayer are most remarkable, and I am not surprised that the devil would like to take them away. And since this favor cannot be received whenever one wants, it must be prized when God gives it. In a moment His Majesty will present to us better plans for serving him—apart from so great a gain—than the intellect could ever search out. And believe me, what I'm saying is the truth—unless there is question of some important business matter that has to be concluded at the moment—even if then the sleep does not come because of worries. And if sleep does come, there will be other times for thinking about what the fitting thing to do is. A book I once read says that if we leave God when he wants to be with us, we will not find him when we want to be with him.

To King Don Philip II
Avila, December 4, 1577

During the previous night, Fray John of the Cross was taken prisoner, and no one knows his whereabouts. The city is scandalized; Teresa worries for his life. The situation is aggravated by the ongoing oppression of the nuns at the Incarnation. Fray John of the Cross is a saint "and has been one all his life."

---

1. The grace of the Holy Spirit be with your majesty, amen. I strongly believe that our Lady has chosen you to protect and help her order. So, I cannot fail to have recourse to you regarding her affairs. For the love of our Lord, I beg you to pardon me for so much boldness.

2. I am sure your majesty has received news of how the nuns at the Incarnation tried to have me go there,[1] thinking they would have some means to free themselves from the friars, who are certainly a great hindrance to the recollection and religious observance of the nuns. And the friars are entirely at fault for the lack of observance previously present in that house. The nuns are very much mistaken in their desire that I go there, for as long as they are subject to the friars as confessors and visitators, I would be of no help—at least not of any lasting help. I always said this to the Dominican visitator,[2] and he understood it well.

3. Since God allowed that situation to exist, I tried to provide a remedy and placed a discalced friar[3] in a house next to them, along with a companion friar.[4] He is so great a servant of our Lord that the nuns are truly edified, and this city is amazed by the remarkable amount of good he has done there, and so they consider him a saint; and in my opinion he is one and has been one all his life.

4. When the previous nuncio through a long report sent him by the inhabitants of the city was informed of the things that were happening and of the harm that the friars of the cloth were doing, he gave orders under pain of excommunication that the confessors be restored to their house (for the calced friars had driven them from the city, heaping abuse on them and giving

much scandal to everyone). And he also ordered that no friar of the cloth under pain of excommunication go to the Incarnation for business purposes, to say Mass, or hear confessions, but only the discalced friars and secular clergy. As a result, the house was in a good state until the nuncio died. Then the calced friars returned—and so too the disturbance—without demonstrating the grounds on which they could do so.

5. And now a friar[5] who came to absolve the nuns caused such a disturbance without any concern for what is reasonable and just that the nuns are deeply afflicted and still bound by the same penalties as before, according to what I have been told. And worst of all he has taken from them their confessors.[6] They say that he has been made vicar provincial, and this must be true because he is more capable than the others of making martyrs. And he is holding these confessors captive in his monastery after having forced his way into their cells and confiscating their papers.

6. The whole city is truly scandalized. He is not a prelate, nor did he show any evidence of the authority on which these things were done, for these confessors are subject to the apostolic commissary.[7] Those friars dared so much, even though this city is so close to where your majesty resides, that it doesn't seem they fear either justice or God. I feel very sad to see these confessors in the hands of those friars who for some days have been desiring to seize hold of them. I would consider the confessors better off if they were held by the Moors, who perhaps would show more compassion. And this one friar[8] who is so great a servant of God is so weak from all that he has suffered that I fear for his life.

7. I beg your majesty for the love of our Lord to issue orders for them to set him free at once and that these poor discalced friars not be subjected to so much suffering by the friars of the cloth. The former do no more than suffer and keep silent and gain a great deal. But the people are scandalized by what is being done to them. This past summer in Toledo, without any reason, the same superior took as prisoner Fray Antonio de Jesús—a holy and blessed man, who was the first discalced friar.[9] They go about saying that with orders from Tostado[10] they will destroy them all. May God be blessed! Those who were to be the means of removing offenses against God have become the cause of so

many sins. And each day matters will get worse if your majesty does not provide us with some help. Otherwise, I don't know where things will end up, because we have no other help on earth.

8. May it please our Lord that for our sakes you live many years. I hope in him that he will grant us this favor. He is so alone, for there are few who look after his honor. All these servants of your majesty's, and I, ask this of him continually.

Dated in St. Joseph's in Avila, 4 December 1577.

Your majesty's unworthy servant and subject,
Teresa of Jesus, Carmelite

To Don Juan de Ovalle and Doña Juana de Ahumada, Alba
Avila, December 10, 1577

Teresa is trying to help her brother-in-law but not receiving much assistance from her friends. What has been happening at the Incarnation is distressing for her, especially the capture of John of the Cross.

1. Jesus be with your honors. I don't have time to write. I only want to say that I am being very careful about that business matter.[1] I wrote twice to Señora Doña Luisa, and now I am thinking of writing her again. It seems to me she is slow in responding. Certainly I have done and am doing all that I can. May God do what is best for your salvation, for that is what is important. There is no need to send her anything, for I fear that all may be lost. Rather, I am sorry about what you spent to go to Toledo, without any results that I can see. It wouldn't do any harm to send some gift to her brother,[2] for after all he is the master, and nothing would be lost thereby. They are incapable of doing anything unless they think they are gaining something.

2. All gentlemen spend their winters in the country. I don't know why you are troubled about doing the same. Since you—I mean my sister—will have the company of Señora Doña Beatriz, to whom I send my best regards, I am not concerned.[3] I am no worse than usual, and that's already good.

3. The nuns have been absolved, although they are still as insistent as before and bear a greater trial, for the discalced friars have been taken away from them. I don't know where it will end up, for it is really distressing to me. Those fathers are carrying on as though out of their minds.[4]

4. My brothers are well. They don't know about this letter, I mean this messenger, unless they found out from elsewhere. Teresa no longer has a fever, but the head cold continues.[5]

May God be always with your honors.

Today is 10 December.

Your unworthy servant,
Teresa of Jesus

To Madre María de San José, Seville
Avila, December 10, 1577

Not receiving any letters from Madre María, Teresa has been receiving news through the prior of Las Cuevas. She fears for the three discalced nuns in Paterna. In Avila, St. John of the Cross and his companion have been taken prisoner.

1. Jesus be with you, my daughter. Oh, how long it's been since I've received a letter from you, and how far away it seems that I am up here. Even were I close, it would have been difficult to write you these past days because of all the turmoil going on, about which you will be informed in this letter. I tell you the Lord has not left me idle. Before I forget, with regard to the *agnusdei*, I would like to see it decorated with pearls. If something pleases you, you don't have to ask me about it, for I am happy if you are. May you enjoy much happiness.

2. I would have wanted that in the midst of those disturbances— for they tell me the province is getting stirred up again—the nuns in Paterna be brought back quickly; this is something I strongly desire. Our *padre* has written me that he wrote telling you to do this, with the consent of the archbishop. Try to obtain it before other hindrances arise.

3. Here they are reminding me to ask you for a little *caraña*[1] because it's very helpful to me. It must be of pure quality. Don't forget, for goodness' sake. You can send it well wrapped to Toledo, for they will send it on to me. Or it's enough to entrust it to the man from here when he returns.

4. Don't fail to be most diligent regarding the nuns in Paterna, for apart from the nuns themselves, I would like this for your sake. I don't know how you've been able to get along without them. Now my companion will tell you the story of our trials.

5. Write and tell me whether you have paid for that house or have any money left and why you are in a hurry to move. Tell me about it all, for the prior of Las Cuevas is writing me about it.

6. You should know that the nuns at the Incarnation have been absolved after almost two months of excommunication in which

they underwent much anguish. The king commanded that the nuncio give orders to absolve them. Tostado and his councillors sent a prior from Toledo for this purpose, and he absolved them with so many constrictions that it would take a long time to list them all, and he left them more disturbed and dejected than before. And all of this happened because they did not want the prioress the superiors wanted, but me. And the two discalced friars[2] that had been placed there by the apostolic commissary and the previous nuncio were taken away and imprisoned as though they were criminals. I am terribly distressed and will be so until I see them freed from the power of those people. I would rather see them in the land of the Moors.

7. It is said that on the day they were captured, they were flogged twice. They are receiving the worst treatment possible. Maldonado—the prior of Toledo—took Padre Fray John of the Cross to present him to Tostado. The prior here[3] took Fray Germán to San Pablo de la Moraleja.[4] And when he returned he told the nuns that were on his side that he left that traitor in good hands. They said that blood was coming from his mouth as he was taken away.

8. The nuns are suffering over this, more so than from all their other trials, which are heavy. For goodness' sake pray for them and for those saintly captives, for tomorrow it will be eight days since they were seized. The nuns say they are saints and that in all the years the friars were there they behaved in every way like apostles. I don't know where the crazy ideas of those people are going to end up. May God in his mercy provide the remedy he sees as necessary.

9. Give my best regards to Padre Fray Gregorio.[5] Tell him to have prayers said to God concerning all these trials, for it is a great pity to see what these nuns are suffering; they are martyrs. I am not writing to him, because I did so a short time ago. The letter for him went along with the one I sent you. My best regards to my Gabriela and to all the nuns. May God be with you all.

Today is 10 December.

10. I can't figure out how you are going to get the money to buy another house, for I don't even remember if the one you are in is paid for. It seems to me you told me the interest has been paid

off. But if this postulant doesn't want to become a nun, she will clearly want her money back, especially if her sister gets married. Keep me fully informed about everything, for goodness' sake, for through Padre Padilla the letters arrive safely as long as they are sent to the archbishop. Or send them through our *padre,* and then they arrive sooner than when sent by way of Toledo.

11. If you have so much money, don't forget what you owe my brother.[6] He is paying five hundred ducats interest on a property he bought. It would be a great help to him even if you sent only two hundred ducats, for he has received nothing from the Indies.

12. Let me know also how the uprising in the province is going and whom they made vicar, and give my regards to Padre Evangelista and tell him that God is giving him good opportunities for becoming a saint.[7] Tell me all about your health and give me news about the nuns. And if you don't have time, let my Gabriela write me about it.

13. Many greetings to Beatriz and to Señor Garciálvarez; I was very sorry about his illness. My greetings to all the nuns and to Padre Nicolao. May God watch over you for me.

Your servant,
Teresa of Jesus

14. Be careful to take good care of your health, for now you see how important that is. Perhaps you will move to a house where you will roast alive. Consider the great comfort you have in the one you now occupy; and it is new. It could be that you will become so stubborn that I will let you buy one. I surely want you to be at peace. But you saw all the boasting about how good the first one was.[8]

To Padre Jerónimo Gracián, Pastrana
Avila, February 16, 1578

Despite her broken arm, Teresa writes at length. The central topic is Padre Salazar and his proposal to transfer from the Jesuits to Teresa's discalced friars. She is enclosing the Jesuit provincial's letter to her and her own response as well as Salazar's to her and her response. She tries to give Gracián all the pertinent information as objectively as she can, as well as her own opinion.

1. Jesus. The grace of the Holy Spirit be with your honor, *mi padre*, and may he give you health this Lent for the work I see that you have ahead of you. I am wondering if you will have to be moving from place to place. For the love of God watch out lest you have a fall along the way. For since my arm has been in the state it is, I am very careful in this regard. It is still swollen, as is also my hand, and covered with plaster, which looks like armor, and so I get little use out of it.[1]

2. It's extremely cold here now, which it hasn't been except at the beginning of winter. In fact the weather has been so good that it was much colder, at least for me, in Toledo. This perhaps is due to the door you ordered us to have made for the little room next to the one you said should become the infirmary. After this was done, the little room is like a stove. Anyway, I have been getting along extremely well in this cold weather. You always meet with success in the orders you give. May it please the Lord that I meet with success in obeying you. I would love to know if Padre Fray Antonio de Jesús is continuing to improve and what has happened to Padre Mariano, who has so forgotten me. Give my regards to Padre Fray Bartolomé.[2]

3. I am sending along a letter that the provincial of the Society sent me about the Carillo matter, which displeased me so much that I wanted to send him a worse answer than I did.[3] For I know that they told him I had no part to play in this proposal, which is true.[4] When I heard about it, I got very upset, as I wrote you, and greatly desired that he not proceed any further. I wrote him a letter urging him as strongly as I could not to do so, as I swear in this response of mine to the provincial. Their attitude toward

me is such that if I do not use strong words, they will not believe me. And it is most important that they believe me so that they don't keep thinking that I received the revelations they speak of and used them to persuade him, which is a big lie.[5] But I tell you that I have so little fear of their threats that I am amazed at the freedom God gives me. So, I told the rector[6] that neither the entire Society nor the whole world could keep me from carrying out something I understand to be for the service of God, but that in this matter I neither did nor would intervene.

4. The rector nonetheless asked me to write to Padre Salazar and say what I said in the enclosed letter, that he cannot do what he proposes without incurring excommunication.

5. I asked the rector if Carillo knew of these briefs.[7] He replied that he understood them better than I. I then answered that I was certain he would not do anything that would offend God. He replied that because of his great attraction he could be fooled and rush ahead with his desire. So I sent him a letter by the means which he used to send his.

6. Well, *mi padre*, see their simplicity. From certain indications I understood clearly that my letter had been opened, but I didn't mention this to him. I told him in my letter (knowing that they would read it) not to trust his brothers, that Joseph, too, had brothers. In fact, his own friends must have revealed his plan, and I am not surprised, for his brothers are extremely disturbed. They must be afraid that this might set a precedent.

7. I asked him whether there were not some in the Society who had become discalced friars. He answered yes, that some had become Franciscans, but that the Society had first dismissed them and that afterward they received the permission to enter the Franciscans. I said that the Society could do the same thing in this case. But they are not thinking of doing this, nor am I thinking of telling him not to pursue his plans but only of cautioning him, as I do in this letter and leaving the matter to God. If it is God's will, they will give their consent. Otherwise (as I say here in this letter), a transfer would certainly not be possible—I have inquired about this. Those who are advising him must be basing themselves on the common law, as did another canonist who tried to persuade me at the time of the foundation in Pastrana

that I could accept an Augustinian nun,[8] but he was mistaken. The pope could give his permission, but I don't think that will come about, for they will block the way. Would you inquire about this and advise him, for I would be extremely disturbed if some offense were committed against God. I am sure that he would not knowingly do so.

8. I am very worried, for if he remains among them after they know of his desire to transfer, he will not have the credibility he is accustomed to. We couldn't allow him to join us save under the most favorable circumstances. And I am always aware of what we owe to the Society, and I don't think God would permit them to do us harm for a reason like this. But to refuse to receive Padre Salazar out of fear of the Society would be wrong and would be a poor recompense for his affection. May God direct everything; may he guide him. But I fear that Padre Salazar will let himself be prompted by some experiences in prayer that he mentions and to which he gives too much credit. I have very often mentioned this to him, but that's not enough.

9. I am also sorry that the nuns in Beas must have said something to him about this, so great was Catalina de Jesús' desire for him to transfer.[9] The good thing in all this is that he is definitely a servant of God and if he is mistaken it is in thinking that this is what God wants, and His Majesty will look after him. But he has got us into trouble, and if I hadn't heard from Joseph[10] what I wrote to you, believe me that I would have done all I could to prevent it. But even though I do not believe as much in those things, it costs me a great deal to try to dissuade him. Who can say that I would not be hindering some great good from coming to that soul? You should realize that in my opinion he does not have the spirit of the Society. I have always thought so.

10. Ardapilla[11] wrote me about this matter telling me to try to get the ravens to write to Joanes asking him to send someone here to inquire about it.[12] I would be delighted, as long as I didn't have to get involved, but so many difficulties came to mind that I excused myself as best I could. I realize that he did it for our good, but you know that if we don't get to the root of a thing there is no other way to provide a remedy, unless Paul[13] lends a hand. May the Lord bring this about, for I desire it very much. I worry about being the obstacle causing everyone to suffer. I have

at times said that it would perhaps be best for them to throw me into the sea, as was done with Jonah, that the storm might pass. Perhaps my sins have caused all this.

11. The prioress of Seville[14] wrote to ask me to petition you to give permission for her to accept another sister of the Portuguese nun, Blanca,[15] who is not old enough to enter, in fact must be far from it. This would provide a great help for them to pay the rent on the house. I don't recall how much it comes to. It wouldn't be a bad thing if the parents in paying the dowry for Blanca would lend the community what they would plan on giving for her sister, or pay the interest instead of providing for her food. The nuns never finish speaking of how much they owe this Portuguese woman. You can consider this and do what you think best.

12. I don't know when to stop when I write you. My brother[16] always tells me to give you his best wishes. Accept these now all together and along with them those of all the sisters. May our Lord watch over you and bring you here soon, for your presence is very necessary, both for my sake and for other reasons. I don't mean that there is any problem you do not know about. Doña Guiomar[17] is doing poorly. She rarely comes here, for that humor from which she suffers is completely destroying her.

13. As quickly as you can, send this letter for Padre Salazar by way of the prior of Granada,[18] and insist that the prior give it to him secretly. For I fear that through the Society he will write to me again or to some of our sisters, and his code language is easy to decipher. You could send it by way of Madrid, paying good postage, urgently entrusting it to Roque[19] and making use of this same muleteer; it will be safe. Be careful, *mi padre*, and don't forget, for it is important to send this letter to Padre Salazar and that he not take any further steps—if he hasn't already.[20] And you should delay giving permission, in my opinion, for all of this is for his greater good. May God also give you, *padre mio*, all the blessings I desire for you, amen.

It is the First Sunday of Lent.

14. This letter from Father Provincial[21] and the reply may be useful to us some day. Do not tear it up, if you so think.

Your paternity's unworthy servant and daughter,
Teresa of Jesus

To Roque de Huerta, Madrid
Avila, March 8–12, 1578

The nuns at the monastery of the Incarnation who voted for Teresa to be prioress, against the orders given them, were excommunicated. They appealed to the Royal Council against the provincial. Teresa here asks for help since the provincial was trying to force them to withdraw their appeal. She had received confidential notes about the whole matter.

To the very magnificent Señor Roque de Huerta, chief forest guard of the woods.

1. Jesus be ever with your honor, amen. Tomorrow, Monday, marks the eighth day since I wrote by way of the carrier from here informing you about what took place as regards the provincial Magdaleno,[1] and I sent you the ordinance and notification given him.[2] I don't know whether you have received these. I would very much appreciate your letting me know, for I am worried. What happened afterward you will see through these notes. I feel very sorry for these nuns, so much so that I don't know what to say, except that God must love them very much because he gives them so many and such long-lasting trials.

2. All these ten days since the provincial and Valdemoro[3] have been here, they have done nothing but busy themselves with schemes, threaten the nuns, and seek out persons who will tell them about the penalties reserved for them if they do not obey and cast a vote contrary to the previous one they signed in an appeal to the Royal Council. Now that he has accomplished all that he wanted, the provincial is in a great hurry to go to Madrid to present the nuns' signatures to the council. I beg your honor, for goodness' sake, to do what is required to make the truth known and tell about how the signatures were obtained by force. This would be a great help to these poor nuns so that the council doesn't think the information presented by the fathers is true, for all the things that were done added up to tyranny. If it is possible for Señor Padilla[4] to see these notes, show them to him.

3. Here Magdaleno has said that he definitely carries a royal ordinance to imprison Padilla if he should find him here, that

he was two leagues distant from Madrid when they called him back to give it to him, that Tostado[5] has full powers over both the calced and the discalced Carmelites, and that Padre Fray John of the Cross[6] has already been sent to Rome. May God in his power deliver him, and grant grace to your honor.

8 March

Your honor's unworthy servant,
Teresa of Jesus

4. For the love of God I beg you to strive to make known briefly to the members of the council the force that was used with the nuns, for this is a very important point of the entire affair. It is a great wrong that they can get away with doing whatever they want, carrying on without justice and without truth in everything they have done, and there is no one showing compassion for these martyrs.

5. This was written three days ago, and that provincial is still tormenting the nuns.

To Padre Jerónimo Gracián, Alcalá
Avila, March 10–11, 1578

Teresa communicates her feelings and thoughts about the problems at the Incarnation and the imprisonment of John of the Cross. She takes up some other matters concerning her nuns and new postulants.

---

1. Jesus be with *mi padre* and free him from this people of Egypt,[1] for I tell you they have frightened me by what they have done with these poor nuns.[2] I tried to get the nuns to obey because the scandal was already great. This seemed to be the best solution, especially to the Dominicans. From what I surmise, these fathers are helping one another and have united against this reform. I am tired of all their clamoring. To tell the truth, the nuns have been suffering for a long time. Nonetheless, if I hadn't told them that in my opinion they would not do harm to their cause by obeying, I don't think they would have obeyed.

2. Since the discalced friars are no longer present,[3] little progress has been made on their cause. In fact, I wrote to Roque and to Padilla[4] that if what concerned the discalced friars were not resolved and the calced friars remained as visitators, the nuns' cause would make no headway. Even if the council did favor the nuns, it would be foolish for me to go there. Yet it would look very bad if I did not go but abandoned them after they suffered so much. In addition, I don't think I can shirk my duty, especially since I don't see things going in the right direction and the Lord must find some way of helping these souls. I pity them so much, for they are in distress as you can see through those notes.

3. For goodness' sake send Padre Germán[5] to them that he might pray for them. He is now really out of prison. As for Fray John, I am very disturbed with the thought that they might find some other fault to accuse him of. God treats his friends terribly. Truly, he does them no wrong since that is the way he treated his Son.

4. Read this letter that a gentleman brought from Ciudad Rodrigo, for he came solely to speak about this nun.[6] He has many things to say about her. If they are true, she will be most suited for us. She is bringing 450 ducats and a good trousseau as

well. Alba is asking me for a nun. This aspirant would like to go to Salamanca, but she would go to Alba as well. In Salamanca, though, they are in greater need because of the bad state the house is in. She will be able to go wherever you decide to send her. I promised to beg you to admit her. She seems agreeable to going to either of the two houses.

5. Here in this house the talk is of two aspirants from Burgos with 1,500 ducats. They say they are very good and the dowry is needed for some work projects including what needs to be done on the enclosure wall. With another nun, everything can be completed. Will you give permission for this.

6. Look at all the confusion stirred up by a member of the Society over a sister of the prioress of Beas. I asked the prioress of Medina to inquire. She will find out what is being said. They must know much more than we do. You should be careful about what she might do, for I tell you there are persons whose nature doesn't change. Well, even though Anne of Jesus saw her two or three times for a short moment, she must have been told about it. I answered as if I knew everything that I do now. In my hurry I saw that neither she nor her brother spoke of her. The brother belongs to the Society, and it seems good that they help each other.

7. I regret having had to go so long without confessing to you, for here I don't find confessors as I did in Toledo. This is a great trial for me. I wrote this yesterday, and now I am being told of so many things about the injustices being done to the nuns at the Incarnation that I feel great pity for them. I think some of the nuns in this house are afraid of falling into their hands, and I am not surprised by their fear, for they have reason to fear.

8. May God provide a remedy and watch over you. The night is far advanced, and the messenger will be leaving in the morning.

Today is 11 March.

Your paternity's unworthy servant,
Teresa of Jesus

To Madre María de San José, Seville
Avila, March 28, 1578

Teresa responds to letters asking her opinion about the admission of postulants and keeping a journal on one's prayer.

1. Jesus be with you, my daughter, and grant you and all your daughters as happy an Easter as I beg him. For me it has been a great comfort to know that you are in good health. My health remains as usual, with my arm in bad shape and my head too; I don't even understand what prayers they are saying.[1] Truly, this must be the best thing for me. It would be a consolation if my head were such that I could write a long letter, and send many greetings for everyone. Do so for me, and especially to Sister San Francisco,[2] whose letters are a delight for us. Believe me, during the time she was prioress she grew wings. Oh, Jesus, how alone I feel when I see you all so far away. Please God, we will all be together in eternity. I find comfort in the thought that everything passes quickly.

2. What you say about the fault you find with Fray Bartolomé's sisters amused me. Even though you could finish paying off the house with their dowries, it would not be permissible to accept them. Under no circumstances should you take anyone who does not have good judgment. That would go against the constitutions and bring incurable harm. Thirteen years old is very young—I'm speaking of the other one; at that age they tend to change their minds a thousand times. You will have to see for yourself what is best. As for me, I believe that I want everything that is good for you.

3. Before I forget, I am not in favor of the sisters writing about prayer, for this has many drawbacks which I would like to tell you about. You should know that even though doing this amounts to nothing but a waste of time, it impedes freedom of soul and allows one to imagine all kinds of things. If I remember, I will mention this to our *padre*; and if I don't, you tell him. Important graces are never forgotten; and if they are forgotten, there is no reason to mention them. When they see our *padre*, it will be enough for them to mention what they remember. In my

opinion, they are on a safe path, and if something can do them harm, it would be for them to give importance to what they see and hear. If they experience some scruple, they can tell you, for I so esteem you that if they trust you, God will give you the light to guide them. I insist so much on this because I understand the trouble they will run into from thinking about what they should write and from what the devil can put into their heads. If it is something very serious, you could write it down, but without their knowing this. If I had paid attention to the experiences of San Jerónimo,[3] she would never have finished. And if some of them seemed true, I still was silent about them. Believe me, it is better to praise the Lord, who gives these graces, and when they have passed to get beyond them, for it is the soul that will experience the benefit.

4. What you tell me about Elías is good. But since I don't have your erudition, I don't know who the Assyrians are. My best regards to her for I love her very much, also to Beatriz and her mother. It makes me very happy when you tell me about yourself and the good news about everyone. God pardon those friars who harass us so much.

5. And don't believe everything they say down there; up here we are given more hope. And in this we rejoice, although in darkness, as Madre Isabel de San Francisco says. With this painful arm, my heart is very bad on some days. Send me a little orange-flower water, and pack it so that the container doesn't break. That is why I didn't ask you for it sooner. The angel water you sent was so exquisite that using it caused me scruples, so I gave it to the church for the celebration of the feast of the glorious St. Joseph.

6. Give the prior of Las Cuevas my best wishes, for I love this saint very much, and Padre Garciálvarez and my Gabriela—certainly there is a reason why our *madre* calls her "her Gabriela"—whose presence there I could easily envy if it were not for all the love we have for one another in the Lord and if I didn't understand that the affection she has for you and your daughters is so well deserved. And how Madre Isabel de San Francisco does so much to make us aware of this. Even if she had gone to your house for no other reason than to praise you and all your nuns to the skies, her journey there was worthwhile. But wherever

you are, *mi madre*, you will be praised. Blessed be God who gave you so many gifts, which you use so well.

7. I ask *mi madre* San Francisco for prayers—I cannot say more—and for prayers from all the nuns, especially Sister San Jerónimo. Teresa[4] asks for your prayers. Señor Lorenzo Cepeda is well.

8. Please God, *mi madre*, you will be able to read this, written so poorly and in great haste. What else could be expected?

Today is Friday of the Cross.[5]

Send me only a little orange-flower water, until we see how it arrives.

Your reverence's,
Teresa of Jesus

9. The secretary is Isabel de San Pablo, servant of your reverence and of all in your house. *Madre mía*, now I remember that I heard it said that in Seville there are some paintings that are large and well done, that Julián Dávila[6] was praising them. Our *madre* told me to ask you for one of St. Paul. Send me one that is very beautiful. And pardon me, but it must be one that I will enjoy looking at.

To Padre Jerónimo Gracián, Alcalá
Avila, May 7, 1578

Among the items that Teresa informs Gracián of is the effort to reset her arm. The woman from Medina, big and strong, with the help of another woman of similar size, pulled forcefully on Teresa's arm in an effort to reset it. The pain was agonizing.

---

1. Jesus be with your paternity, my good *padre*. The day before yesterday I learned that Señora Doña Juana arrived in Valladolid in good health. And on the vigil or feast of St. Angelus, they gave the habit to Señora Doña María. May it please God to direct this to his own honor and make her very holy. The prioress in Medina also wrote me that they would have gladly given her the habit if she had so desired, but I don't think she would care for that. As I wrote to you, the nuns in Valladolid were very sorry that you did not go there. I already told them that you will go soon, with God's help, and certainly the need for you there is great. Once Tostado leaves, there will be nothing to fear.

2. I am writing to Padre Mariano that if he comes with the Sicilian he should arrange to have you come with them. For if he wants to reach an agreement on what he says in his letter, your presence will be necessary. I assure you that if what this friar says is true and we take these means, the negotiations with our Father General will most likely be successful. All the other possibilities seem to entail endless delay, and if after we pursue this course we find that it didn't work out for us, we will still have time. May the Lord guide things well.

3. If this *padre* doesn't come here, I wish you would arrange to see him. I think that in everything it is necessary that we speak together, even if what you do is right. A short while ago I wrote you at length and so today I am being brief, for today they brought me letters from Caravaca, which I have to answer, and I am also writing to Madrid.

4. Oh, *mi padre*, I almost forgot! The woman came to cure my arm, for the prioress in Medina did very well in sending her.[1] The cure involved a real struggle both for the woman and for me. I had

lost the use of my wrist, for it has been a long time since I fell. So the pain and toil were terrible. Nonetheless, I rejoiced to feel some little part of what our Lord suffered. I think the effort was successful, although the tormenting pain is such that it is difficult to know if the cure is complete. I can move the hand well and lift the arm as far as my head, but it will still take time before everything is all right. Believe me, if this had been delayed just a bit more, I would have ended up crippled. In truth, I would not have been terribly distressed, if God so willed. There were so many people who came to see the woman in my brother's house that one didn't know how to manage them all.

5. I assure you, *mi padre*, that since your departure from here, sufferings of every kind have had their day. Sometimes it seems, when they come one upon the other, that the body grows tired and the soul fainthearted, although the will, in my opinion, fares well.

God be with you always. Pray for these daughters of yours. Today is the vigil of the Ascension. Doña Guiomar is doing better; she is here.

Your paternity's unworthy daughter,
Teresa of Jesus

To Padre Jerónimo Gracián, Alcalá
Avila, May 8, 1578

Teresa intended this letter to be torn up immediately once it was read. In fact, Teresa herself opened the envelope and crossed out a paragraph lest the letter go astray. It contained strong words against Padre Mariano. Gracián saved the letter, but the copy of the lost autograph includes nothing of the crossed-out part. Teresa is concerned about the community in Malagón and Padre Antonio's visitation there, and upset over Padre Mariano.

---

1. Jesus be with your paternity. After having written the letter enclosed with this one,[1] I received today, the feast of the Ascension, your letters that came by way of Toledo. They caused me much distress. I tell you, *mi padre*, that what you mention is a reckless thing. Tear this up right after you read it.

2. You can well imagine the consequences with all his complaining about me, of which I am getting mighty tired.[2] Although I love him much, very much so, and he is a holy man, I cannot fail to observe that God has not given him a talent for discernment. Don't you see how much trust he placed in the more unruly nuns.[3] And without further information he wants to do and undo. I am well aware that she doesn't have what it takes to govern. But her defects are not something that brings dishonor to the order, for it's an in-house affair. I had earlier written them that you would go there and resolve matters, and that they should speak about their temptations with their confessor and not with her.

3. To want Isabel de Jesús to rule over them and be their subprioress is sheer nonsense. During the few days that they did have her while Brianda was prioress there, these very same nuns were ever telling stories about her and laughing over it all. They will never respect her. She is good, but not suited for that charge. To take away the office from Ana de la Madre de Dios for only a couple of days is foolish, and judging by his hurry to have her, Brianda will be back there shortly. It would be hard for me to see her brought back, for with the exception of her being brought there for the purpose of moving on as soon as possible to a new

foundation, I greatly fear her being in that place because of *the one who is there*.[4]

4. That she does nothing for the discalced friars only means that she is following your orders.[5] As for the rest of the gossip, I don't think it has merit. Neither do I regret the way she behaves toward me, for I know her and she is by no means reserved but very straightforward. They must be telling him the opposite of what she says. You already know that Brianda wrote asking me to give her orders not to give anything to any discalced friar. Another nun wrote that they had spent more on the discalced friars than on all their sick nuns, and many of them were sick that year. It seems to me, *mi padre*, that even if St. Clare went there, they would find much to complain about because of the one who is there[6] and their own stubbornness.

5. As for her not caring for the sick, that is a calumny, for her charity is great.[7] I was very embarrassed, *mi padre*, by her predecessor,[8] for all those things matter little as long as the honor of the house is not involved, especially in Malagón where everybody is passing through.[9] What they are saying about honor is a pretext, for she went to Toledo for her health on the advice of her doctors. I truly don't know what you can do about this.

6. It pleases me to observe how Padre Fray Antonio took care to forbid any mention of Brianda, which was the best thing he could do. You should examine the situation carefully, for goodness' sake. The best thing to do would be to bring in someone like Isabel de Santo Domingo[10] along with a good subprioress and remove some of those who are there. You need to write briefly to Padre Fray Antonio not to make any changes until you have carefully considered everything. I will write to him that I cannot do anything until I see what orders you give, and I will disillusion him about certain things.

7. In regard to the house, I felt sorry, for it is a pity that there has been no one to lament this. They could have built some part by now, and I just wish they would finish two suites of rooms and the enclosure wall. That would prevent all from being lost if the entire work can't be finished now. For they will be better off there, however little there is, than where they are now. Please write to them about this.

8. I don't know how, *mi padre*, you assigned him to a task in Malagón without first briefing him thoroughly.[11] I admit I feel like a dunce; nonetheless, I think that to remove and replace the superior there and without rhyme or reason brings great discredit to the house. If I thought that N[12] could amend her ways, it would be better for her to resume her office as prioress and finish out her term. But I have lost hope in her ever making amends. And Padre Fray Bartolomé de Jesús, and Fray Francisco de la Concepción, and Antonio Ruiz[13] have so insisted that she not return there that I think it would be rash not to pay heed to them. Please look into this and do as the Lord enlightens you. That is what will be the best thing to do. I will beg him to give you light. But it's most necessary that you warn this father at once and see that Padre Fray Antonio does not make a martyr of that saint,[14] for she certainly is one.

May God be with you always.

Your paternity's unworthy servant,
Teresa of Jesus

9. I don't think it would be a mortification for Isabel de Santo Domingo to go there. She would bring order back into the house, and Brianda could go to Segovia, or María de San Jerónimo.[15] May God take care of this. As for Isabel de Santo Domingo's health, that region is hot, and since she is so esteemed, the sisters will not dare say anything about her. I reopened this letter to cross out what I said about Mariano lest the letter get lost. I'm very much tried by him.

To Madre Anne of Jesus, Beas
Avila, August 1578(?)

This fragment was passed on by Jerónimo de San José, St. John of the Cross's biographer. It probably corresponds with John's final days of imprisonment in Toledo before his escape during the octave of the Assumption in 1578. He was later to enter into a deep spiritual relationship with Anne of Jesus, which is revealed in his prologue to his Spiritual Canticle.

You will not believe, daughter, the pain I suffer because of the disappearance of *mi padre* Fray John of the Cross. We find no trace of him and have no light as to his whereabouts. These calced fathers are making every effort to put an end to this reform. For the love of God I beg you, since you and my daughter Catalina de Jesús[1] commune so familiarly with our good Jesus, to beg him to favor and help us. For this intention recite the litany in choir for fifteen days. And during these days, in addition to the hours of prayer you have, add another hour. And inform me, daughter, of how you are implementing this.

To Padre Jerónimo Gracián, Madrid
Avila, August 21–22, 1578

These are two fragments from one letter. They reflect Teresa's first impressions on learning of St. John of the Cross's escape from his prison cell in Toledo and of what he suffered there.

1. I tell you that ever present to me is what they did with Fray John of the Cross, for I don't know how God bears with things like that; even you don't know everything about it. For all these nine months[1] he was held in a little prison cell where small as he is he could hardly fit. In all that time he was given no change of tunic, even though he had come close to the point of death. Only three days before his escape the subprior gave him one of his shirts. He underwent harsh scourges, and no one was allowed to see him.

2. I experience the greatest envy. Surely our Lord found in him the resources for such a martyrdom. And it is good that this be known so that everyone will be all the more on guard against these people. May God forgive them, amen.

3. An investigation should be conducted to show the nuncio what those friars did to this saint, Fray John, without any fault on his part, for it is a pitiful thing. Tell this to Fray Germán;[2] he will do it because he's quite mad about this . . .

To Roque de Huerta, Madrid
Avila, October 24, 1578

The discalced friars held an emergency chapter in Almodóvar del Campo on October 9. Hardly had the meeting closed when the nuncio, Filippo Sega, annulled everything that had been done and placed the discalced Carmelites under the jurisdiction of the provincials of the Carmelites of the observance in Andalusia and Castile. On October 22, Teresa received a copy of the acts of the unsuccessful chapter. She clearly disapproves of the chapter but focuses on the good will of the chapter members. She sent the acts to Roque with this cover letter.

---

1. Jesus be with you, my lord. I received the letter you wrote to me on the feast of St. Luke. But in it you do not tell whether you received the supplicatory letters that I sent you. As a result, I am a little worried. In fact, that letter of yours addressed to me to obtain permissions from our Father General as well as from our Father Visitator, the Dominican Padre Fray Pedro Fernández, and finally from Fray Angel,[1] was certainly sent from here. But indeed it seems it ended up in the hands of the Bishop of Osma.[2] It would be regrettable if it was lost along with my previous letter. I ask you then to inform me in this regard. Now, however, I am not as worried over the fact that you might think you have been responsible, as though in this entire affair you committed or caused the commission of some fault. If there is anyone who has little reason to torment himself in this matter, it is certainly you.

2. The letters of convocation for the chapter held on 9 October were promulgated. I have read them. What the constitutions order to be observed is mentioned in them: let no one be guilty, neither in small matters nor in great, of a transgression or offense against God. Also promulgated is the injunction against going forward with the house of Santa Ana,[3] in effect until tranquility is restored to the province at the end of the visitation.

3. Padre Fray Antonio de Jesús has consulted learned men who affirmed that he was bound in conscience,[4] and he wrote me about this. I answered that if this was really the case, God would in no way be offended; he could do as he wished . . . insofar as otherwise they would cast us headlong into tribulation.

4. The Archbishop of Seville, whom it is right that we obey completely, is firm in these words, asserting that he did not do otherwise. Truly in this whole affair he has no reason for moving against those whose only intention was to please and serve God. It seems prudent nonetheless, taking into account the testimonies that were given and the information received, and in consideration of the persons implicated, not to become involved in the promotion of the cause. Rather one should remain silent until it is seen more clearly what the wiser thing to do might be.

5. They[5] were convinced that so things should be if his submission[6] won them over. But in this regard they were mistaken, for from that moment the nuncio seized the occasion to show that he paid little attention to all their efforts. They tried everything, but he[7] was deprived of the power to do anything. Nonetheless, it could be that things will turn out better for him. I cannot convince myself that he[8] had wanted to propose a superior for them chosen from among their own discalced friars, since, as I also made known to you, I cannot rid myself of this suspicion that stays with me as if I were an accomplice in the whole affair. I beg you to try to find out from the Count of Tendilla if he[9] ever mentioned a desire to appoint one of the discalced friars, those observing the primitive rule. What he says corresponds to the truth, but could be interpreted as referring as well to the other Carmelites. Perhaps I alone am the cause of this misfortune in that I called the other one provincial, providing the Bishop of Osma, who was the first to write to Rome, a good occasion for doing so.

6. O unfortunate friars, called by their superior to a chapter that became the sole reason for their imprisonment. Padre Antonio received much in writing against his convoking the chapter at this time. Now I am begging these unfortunate friars to be silent for the love of God and to wait and not do anything precipitously in this regard. There is no doubt that they have given the nuncio good reason for being angry. In the very beginning he was forewarned by the other Carmelites.

7. Now believe me, I was never able to bring myself to approve this chapter; it displeased me very much. As a result, I was not one of its promoters. However, others who weighed the matter better than I, made a judgment in its favor.

8. I beseech you for the love of our Lord that, to the best of your ability, you do all you can to avoid arriving at any settlement before the matter has been brought to the attention of Rome. I would be greatly displeased if anything took place without permission from our *padre*[10] and the others[11] who are there. Please send me at once news about these things. Tell our *padre* and Padre Fray Antonio that in the meantime they should have patience until God provides a remedy.

9. See how all of this is the work of God, who wills that his servants be exercised in patience and put you to the test so that you do not grow fainthearted in those things that pertain to the service of His Majesty. There is hope that Padre Antonio will depart soon—he is old and sick and our *padre*[12] would find it difficult to do without his presence and help. If the nuncio bases his judgments on the information and testimony coming from Andalusia, Padre Antonio would be at a loss on how to defend against this and the situation would go from bad to worse. As you yourself will see, this is a question of great importance.

10. Enclosed is a letter addressed to Padre Fray Diego de Chaves.[13] Also enclosed for you are the chapter acts transcribed by the one from whom I have received them. No one should read them except you and Padre Mariano, who would have an interest in them. Afterward let Padre Chaves present them to the king; or if he thinks it more prudent, give an account of all that took place while defending the whole affair and the persons involved and explaining that Padre Antonio used the greatest care in making known and energetically publishing the act of convocation and without any offense against God. The fact that he may not have acted entirely well in this matter does not mean he was purposely neglectful or had any bad intention; of this I am certain. Therefore I would like you to hold fast to this assertion and get the others to hold fast to it as well. If we are not united, or you with us, or we with the others, a great trial will come upon us. And people will think badly of you and so will Padre Mariano. I don't have time now to write to Padre Mariano. It is best that, in seeing that others had not wanted to follow his advice, he be led by charity and not think he has any reason to become angry with them. Many such adversities occur in the

life of men. I . . . Padre Fray Antonio, if you are informed about it, must be very dejected.

11. By that time the deed was done, nor you. . . . We are greatly indebted to the count. He impels me to praise God. Undoubtedly, our order owes him much; so we must pray always to the divine Majesty for him. May God protect him, and you as well. I beg you not to become discouraged. Few there are with a competence like yours. A good work will be done if you can obtain freedom for Padre Fray Antonio, Padre Mariano, and Padre Juan de Jesús. And may Jesus be always with you.

12. Don't torment yourself any further. God knows how to draw good from evil. And the good is all the greater in the measure that we diligently strive that he not be offended in anything.

Today is 24 October.

Your unworthy servant,
Teresa of Jesus

13. I kiss many times the hands of those ladies.[14] The rumor is going about in Avila that the pope has died. But there is no news about this here. It doesn't seem to be true. I am enclosing a letter to our *padre*, in which I inform him about everything that is taking place. Be very careful so that it reaches him safely.

14. Take care also that you get back the enclosed letter to Padre Chaves so that you can read it. He will be able to inform you well and tell you about all the trials we are undergoing. Don't forget to write frankly to Padre Mariano about all the other things that are going on. For lack of space I must close this letter.

To Madre Anne of Jesus and the Community in Beas
November–December 1578

It is not certain whether these two fragments (nos. 1 and 2) belong to the same letter. The text comes from the process for the beatification of St. John of the Cross. At the end of October, the saint began his ministry in Andalusia as prior of the monastery of El Calvario, not far from Beas.

---

1. I was amused, daughter, at how groundless is your complaining, for you have in your very midst *mi padre* Fray John of the Cross, a heavenly and divine man. I tell you, daughter, from the time he left and went down there I have not found anyone in all Castile like him, or anyone who communicates so much fervor for walking along the way to heaven. You will not believe the feeling of loneliness that his absence causes me. Realize what a great treasure you have there in that saint. All the nuns in your house should speak and communicate with him on matters concerning their souls, and they will see how beneficial it is. They will find themselves making much progress in all that pertains to spirituality and perfection, for our Lord has given him a special grace in this regard.

2. I declare to you that I would be most happy to have my father Fray John of the Cross here, who truly is the father of my soul and one from whom it benefited most in its conversations with him. Speak with him, my daughters, in total simplicity, for I assure you that you can do so as though you were speaking with me. This will bring you great satisfaction, for he is a very spiritual man with much experience and learning. Those here who were formed by his teaching miss him greatly. Give thanks to God, who has ordained that you have him there so close. I am writing to tell him to look after you, and I know from his great charity that he will do so, whatever be your need.

To the Discalced Carmelite Nuns, Seville
Avila, January 31, 1579

The community in Seville was going through a crisis. Stripped of his powers as visitator, Gracián underwent a trial initiated against him by the provincial of Andalusia. The trial was seconded by the community's former confessor, Garciálvarez. The objective of the scheme was to discredit Gracián and depose the prioress, María de San José. Then the provincial appointed one of the most inept nuns in the community, Beatriz de la Madre de Dios, to take the prioress's place. Teresa knew all about what was happening. Lest her letter be confiscated, she sent it to her good friend, the prior of the Carthusians, so that he might read or give it to the interested nuns.

1. The grace of the Holy Spirit be with your charities, my daughters and sisters. You should know that I have never loved you as much as I do now, nor have you ever been so obliged to serve the Lord, for he has given you the great favor of being able to taste something of his cross and share in the terrible abandonment that he endured on it. Happy the day you entered that house where such a fortunate event was reserved for you! I envy you very much, and indeed when I learned of all those changes—for everything was carefully communicated to me[1]—and that they wanted to expel you from that house and about other details, I felt the greatest interior joy. I saw that, without your having crossed the sea, our Lord revealed to you mines containing eternal treasures.[2] Through these, I hope in the Lord, you will be left very rich and able to share with those of us who are here. For I believe that he will enable you to bear all without your offending him in any way. Don't be afflicted that you feel it very much, for the Lord would want you to understand that you are not capable of as much as you thought when you were once so desirous of suffering.

2. Courage, courage, my daughters. Remember that God does not give anyone more trials than can be suffered and that His Majesty is with the afflicted.[3] For this is certain, there is no reason to fear but to hope in his mercy. He will reveal the whole truth; and some machinations, which the devil kept hidden so

as to create a disturbance, will be made known. This was more painful for me than all that is happening now. Prayer, prayer, my sisters, and now let humility shine forth—and obedience in such a way that no one, especially the former prioress, practices it more toward the appointed vicaress.

3. Oh, what a good time it is for gathering fruit from the resolutions you made to serve our Lord. Consider that often he desires to have proof that our works are in conformity with our resolutions and words. Bring honor to the daughters of the Blessed Virgin, your sisters, in this great persecution, for if you help one another, the good Jesus will help you. Even though he sleeps at sea, when the storm gathers strength he calms the winds.[4] He wants us to ask of him, and he loves us so much that he is always looking for ways to be of benefit to us. May his name be blessed forever, amen, amen, amen.

4. In all these houses they are urgently praying to God for you, and so I hope in his goodness that he will soon provide the remedy for everything. So strive to be joyful and reflect that, if carefully considered, all that is suffered for so good a God, who suffered so much for us, is small, for you have not reached the point of shedding your blood for him. You are among your sisters and not in Algiers.[5] Let your Spouse act and you will find that it won't be too long before the sea will swallow up those who wage war on us in the manner of King Pharaoh.[6] And he will set his people free, and everyone will be left with the desire to suffer again, so great will be the gain they feel from what they underwent.

5. I received your letter and I regret that you burned what you had written,[7] for it would have been useful. According to learned men here you could have refused to hand over my letters, but it doesn't matter. Would that the divine Majesty be pleased to let me bear the weight of all the blame, although the afflictions of those who have suffered without blame have weighed heavily upon me.

6. What distressed me very much was that in the investigative process[8] carried out by Father Provincial some things were asserted that I know to be completely false because I was there at the time. Out of love for our Lord, consider carefully whether

anyone said something out of fear or confusion, for when there is no offense against God, it all amounts to nothing. But lies, lies prejudicial to others, are what hurt me deeply; although I cannot bring myself to believe what was said, for everyone knows of the integrity and virtue with which our Padre Maestro Gracián[9] converses with us and how much he has benefited us and helped us go forward in the service of our Lord. And since this is so, even if the accusations are insignificant, it is a serious fault to make them. Inform the sisters of this, for goodness' sake, and remain with the Holy Trinity, in God's safekeeping, amen.

7. All the sisters here send their best regards. They are waiting for these clouds to pass so as to receive an account about everything from Sister San Francisco. My regards to good Gabriela, and I ask her to be happy, for I have ever present in my mind the affliction she must have suffered in seeing Madre San José treated the way she was. I do not feel sorry for San Jerónimo if her desires are genuine, and if they are not I would feel more sorry for her than for all the nuns.

Tomorrow is the vigil of Our Lady of Candlemas.

8. I would much rather speak to Señor Garciálvarez[10] than write. Since in a letter I cannot say what I would like to say, I am not writing to him. My regards to the other sisters to whom you dare make mention of this letter.

Your charities' unworthy servant,
Teresa of Jesus

To Padre Jerónimo Gracián, Alcalá
Avila, Mid-April 1579

Gracián had been allowed his freedom again, and so Teresa eagerly awaits a visit from him. The nuncio, Sega, withdrew his decree of October 16, 1578, in which he annulled the elections carried out by the discalced friars in the chapter of Almodóvar and placed them under the jurisdiction of the provincials of Andalusia and Castile. At this time he appointed Angel de Salazar, a Carmelite of the observance, as vicar general of all the discalced Carmelites.

---

1. Jesus. The grace of the Holy Spirit be with your reverence, *mi padre*, and reward you for the consolation you have given me through the hope I can have of seeing you, which will certainly be a great joy for me. And so I ask you for the love of our Lord to arrange for this to come about, for the loss of a joy is not as disturbing as it is when the lost joy is what one was hoping for. I think His Majesty will be served if you come.

2. This happiness has helped me receive well the election of a new superior. May it please our Lord that he hold the office for only a short time. I don't mean that he die,[1] for after all he is the most talented one among them; and with us, he will be very restrained, especially because he has the good sense to understand where a thing will end up. In a way those fathers were dealt with as badly as we. For persons seeking perfection, we couldn't desire anyone more befitting than the Señor Nuncio, for he has made us all gain merit.

3. I praise our Lord that Padre Fray Gregorio[2] has already arrived at his house. And I will do the same if you succeed in having the prioress of Seville reinstated, for it is certainly the right thing to do. And if not her, then Isabel de San Francisco,[3] for the present one is a mockery and will end up destroying the house. May the Lord direct everything for his greater service, and reward you for the care you take in looking after those poor foreigners.[4] Since the provincial of the fathers of the cloth[5] is not in command over them, they will feel greatly relieved, for they will be able to write and receive letters. I wrote to them through the prior of Las

Cuevas, and I wouldn't mind if the letter fell into the provincial's hands, for I wrote it with this intention.

4. The traveler[6] has everything ready now, and the more I deal with him, the more hope I have that he will do everything very well. We had an argument here because I wanted a copy made of the letter to the king so as to send it with the first shipment of mail to the canonist Montoya[7] along with a parcel of letters that I am now sending his mother for delivery to him. And I am writing him that this letter will be brought to him now, or if not, that two fathers will bring it who are going to Rome to render obedience to our Father Vicar General. And it seems to me that in a matter so serious it is good to proceed along two different paths, for we are not certain of the successful outcome of a particular path. And it would be a troublesome thing in our present situation to have to wait for another trip to be made. Also, since the canonist has already taken up this cause, it is better not to turn aside from his help—as time goes on, he will prove a good friend, and this business is no easy matter—for that would do harm. And I hold that it is better for him to do the negotiating and that those fathers go directly to Father Vicar General. I have little trust that their mission will remain a secret, and if they go about negotiating with this one and that and the vicar general finds out, he will perhaps be displeased that they did not come to him first, something that would not be so with the canonist.

5. Padre Fray Juan[8] says that if the canonist does the negotiating there is no reason for him to go, but there is so much to do that there will perhaps be need for both of them. Would to God that he would find that the negotiations were finished. It would still be no small matter if discalced friars got to be known there who had more religious spirit and substance than those seen before. And these friars could explain everything to Father Vicar General. It also seems to him that he would be spending . . .

To Don Teutonio de Braganza, Evora
Valladolid, July 22, 1579

Two reasons for this letter were the printing of The Way of Perfection *and the fear of a war between Spain and Portugal. Teresa begs Don Teutonio, uncle of one of the claimants, to do all he can to prevent it. She would rather die than see war break out.*

To the most illustrious and reverend Don Teutonio de Braganza, Archbishop of Evora, my lord.

1. Jesus. May the grace of the Holy Spirit be always with your most illustrious lordship, amen. Last week I wrote you a long letter and sent you the little book,[1] and so I will not be lengthy. I am only writing because I forgot to ask you to have printed along with it the life of our Father St. Albert, which is in a little notebook enclosed with the other book. This would be a great consolation for all of our sisters since it now only exists in Latin. This translation was done by a father from the order of St. Dominic[2] out of love for me. He is one of the most learned men around here and a real servant of God. He did not think this was meant to be printed, for he doesn't have, nor did he ask for, permission from his provincial. But if you are satisfied with it and have it printed, the other doesn't matter much.

2. In the letter I referred to, I give you an account of how well our affairs[3] are coming along and how I received orders to go to Salamanca from here, where I think I plan to stay for a number of days. I will write to you from there.

3. For the love of our Lord do not fail to let me know how your health is, if for no other reason than as a remedy for the loneliness I will feel in not finding you there in Salamanca. And let me know if you have any news about peace in that place, for I am very distressed over what I am hearing around here. If, for my sins, this affair leads to war, I fear a terrible disaster in that kingdom, and that great harm will necessarily come to ours as well.[4]

4. They tell me it is the Duke of Braganza who is fomenting it. And that he is actually a relative of yours pains me to the depths of my soul, apart from the many other reasons there are for such

pain. For love of our Lord—since in this regard you rightly have an important part to play in his lordship's decision—strive to bring about an agreement. According to what I am told, our king is doing all he can, and this greatly justifies his cause. They must keep in mind the terrible harm that can result, as I said, and you should look to the honor of God without respect to any other thing, as I believe you will.

5. May it please His Majesty to put his hand to this task as we are all beseeching him, for I tell you I suffer so deeply from what is happening that if God were to permit so great an evil, I would rather die than see it.

6. May He keep you for many years in the holiness that I beg of him for you and for the good of the Church, and give you so much grace that you will be able to work out a peaceful solution in his service.

7. Here everyone is saying that our king is in the right and that he has made every effort he can to find out. May the Lord give the light needed to understand the truth without the many deaths there would be by taking a risk. And in a time when Christians are so few it would be a great misfortune were they to start killing one another.

8. All these sisters, your servants whom you know, are well and in my opinion their souls are making good progress. All of them are being careful to pray for you. Although a wretched person, I do so always.

Today is the feast of the Magdalene.

From this house of the Conception of Our Lady of Mount Carmel in Valladolid.

Your illustrious lordship's unworthy servant and subject,
Teresa of Jesus

Her Final Three Years

(Ages Sixty-Five through Sixty-Seven)

To Madre María de San José, Seville
Toledo, April 3, 1580

Teresa is writing on Easter Sunday and has been seriously ill since Holy Thursday. On arrival in Toledo, she found that Madre Brianda, the former prioress of Malagón, was at the point of death. Her concerns cover a broad field: the danger of war between Portugal and Castile; the election of a new general for the Carmelite order; the negotiations for the establishment of a new province for discalced Carmelites; a new foundation in Palencia that will require a long journey; the purchase of a new house for the community in Seville; and her friend, the prior of the Carthusians, in his illness. Doria has brought her a written account of the troubles that took place in the Seville community as well as his own verbal account.

For Madre María de San José, prioress of the discalced Carmelite nuns.

1. Jesus. The grace of the Holy Spirit be with your reverence, my daughter. You can well believe that I would be happy to be in a condition to write you a long letter, but my health has been poor these days. It seems I am paying for having been well in Malagón and Villanueva and along the roads.[1] Not for many days or even years, I believe, had my health been so good. It was a great favor from our Lord, so now it doesn't matter that I'm not well.

2. Since Holy Thursday I have had one of the worst attacks ever of paralysis and heart pains. I've had a fever up until now—which still hasn't left—and I am in such a state of weakness that I accomplished a great deal in managing to stay at the grille with Padre Nicolao,[2] who has been here two days now and whose presence made me happy. At least you were not forgotten. I am amazed at how you have fooled him. I am helping you in that, for I see that this won't be a bad thing for that house. What is worse is that it seems his illusion is sticking to me. May it please God, my daughter, that you don't do anything to disillusion him, and may the Lord be your guide. I was very happy about the good things you told me concerning those sisters. I would very much like to meet them. Tell them that and give them my regards and ask them to pray for the negotiations going on over

Portugal[3] and that Doña Guiomar[4] may have children. It is a pity to see the state the mother and daughter are in because she doesn't have any. Take this very much to heart, for you owe it to her. She is a very good Christian, but this trial is costing them both dearly.

3. I have received some letters from you, although the one that Father Prior of Pastrana brought is the longest. I am delighted that he has left the affairs of that house in such a good state, and now with Padre Gracián[5] going there you will not lack anything. Make sure, my daughter—there may be someone who will exaggerate what you are doing—that you avoid occasions for criticism. In truth, I believe that he is well aware of this.

4. I was startled by some of the things Padre Nicolao told me. Today he gave me the reports,[6] which I will read little by little. That soul[7] frightens me. May God provide a remedy. The plan for dealing with her that he gave you seems fine to me. Don't get careless about the other nun either.

5. He told me how generous you were in contributing toward the cost of the negotiations for the order. God reward you, for I did not know what more to do here. Mostly everything is done. They are expecting the official communication to come any day, for it has arrived there, and the news is very good.[8] All of you thank our Lord. Because Father Prior will write at length, I am not saying anything more about this.

6. Regarding that house they are selling you, he praised it highly to me, and also for having an orchard and views. In our manner of life, this is an important matter, especially because of the income you are going to have. That it is so far from Los Remedios[9] presents a difficulty, I think, for the confessor. He doesn't say whether it is far from the city or adjacent to a section of it. Whatever be the case, you should not negotiate the purchase of anything without seeing it first, along with two other nuns from among those you think are more knowledgeable. Any superior will authorize your going out for this. Don't trust any friar, or anyone else; you well know the trick they tried to play on us. I wrote to you about this in another letter; I don't know if it arrived there.

7. My brother's response to your letter to him is enclosed. I opened it by mistake but did not read any more than the beginning words. As soon as I saw it was not for me, I closed it. Father Prior is leaving with me the documents for withdrawing the money here, but I lack the delegation to do so. Roque de Huerta has it and he has left for your region on official business.[10] Anyway, send it with the document Father Prior asked you to send for Valladolid and address it to the prioress of this house.[11] For if God gives me a little health, I won't be here much beyond the end of this month. They are giving me orders to go to Segovia and from there to Valladolid to found a house in Palencia, which is four leagues from there.

8. I told them to send you the account of the foundation in Villanueva, and so I am not saying anything more here except that they are doing very well and I believe that our Lord will be greatly served there. From here I brought as prioress a daughter of Beatriz de la Fuente.[12] She seems very good and as suited for the people there as you are for Andalusia. San Angel, from Malagón, is subprioress there in Villanueva. She handles the office very well, and the other two with her are truly saints. Ask our Lord that he may be served by these foundations. Remain with him, for I am in no condition to say more. Although the fever is slight, the pains in the heart and the uterus are severe. Perhaps it won't amount to anything. Pray for me, you and all the nuns. Beatriz de Jesús will tell you about Madre Brianda.[13]

Your reverence's servant,
Teresa of Jesus

9. Our *madre* arrived here on the eve of Palm Sunday, I along with her. We found Madre Brianda to be so sick from the blood she has spit up that they wanted to give her extreme unction. Now she is somewhat better, although some days she still spits blood and she has a continual fever. There are days when she gets up. Think what would have happened if they had brought her to Malagón. She—and the community—would have been lost, and the nuns would have undergone a real trial because of the needs of the house.

10. Our *madre* has taken away two other nuns now; please God that will be enough. Have the nuns pray for her and for me, for I have great need.

11. Pray for the election of the general, that they will elect someone who will be a good servant of His Majesty. I encountered Padre Gracián here; he is well. Concerning the stove, we want you to know that we spent almost one hundred *reales*, and it was worthless—so much so that we broke it apart. It used up more wood than any benefit that was coming from it.

12. Send someone to visit the prior of Las Cuevas[14] for me and give him my best regards, for—being in my present condition—I'm unable to write. And see to it that now you take more care to have someone visit him so that it doesn't appear that because he is not in a position to help us, we are forgetting him; it would seem bad . . .

To Doña Isabel Osorio, Madrid
Toledo, April 8, 1580

Isabel was sick but had not given up on her idea of becoming a Carmelite nun. Teresa promises to meet her secretly in Madrid.

---

1. Jesus. The grace of the Holy Spirit be with your honor, my lady. I arrived here in Toledo on the eve of Palm Sunday, and although I had traveled thirty leagues, I wasn't tired but felt healthier than usual. After arriving here, my good health has turned bad. I don't think it will amount to anything serious.

2. I was delighted with the news they gave me here about your improvement. I received your letter in which you tell me that the illness did not suffice to take away your good resolve. May God be praised for everything. I hope in His Majesty that when you are well enough to follow through on your plan, what I have mentioned[1] to you will be accomplished. And if it is not, an alternative will be provided so that your holy desire may surely be realized.

3. I am certain, if God gives me the health, that before long I will go on from here to Madrid, although I wouldn't want anyone to know about this. I am not sure how we will be able to meet, but I will inform you secretly of where I am staying. Write to me and do not forget to pray to our Lord for me and to give my regards to Padre Valentín,[2] although I don't want you to inform anyone of my plan to go there.

4. They tell me that a provincial[3] now appointed for this province of the Society will soon be there, if he hasn't already arrived. You should know that he is one of my best friends. He was my confessor for some years. Try to speak with him, for he is a saint, and do me the favor of hand delivering my enclosed letter to him when he arrives, for I don't know how I would get it to him in any better way. May our Lord guide you in all things, amen.

5. I found that our Sister Inés de la Encarnación[4] had gotten so chubby that I was surprised, and I was consoled to see what a

great servant of God she is. May he guide her. She excels in the obedience and in all the virtues.

Your unworthy servant,
Teresa of Jesus

6. Father Prior[5] has been well. I gave him your message. I owe him much. I ask you to get an answer to the enclosed letter and send it to me in a very safe way, for this is important to me.

Today is 8 April.

To Madre María de Cristo, Avila
Toledo, April 16, 1580

Teresa's brother Lorenzo has been waiting for some years for the repayment of money he lent to the Carmel in Seville. Nicolás Doria has arrived in Toledo with news that Lorenzo's money will arrive shortly. María de Cristo is being asked to deliver letters to Lorenzo and Padre Angel de Salazar.

1. Jesus be with your reverence. Yesterday I wrote to you and afterward the occasion arose to send some letters to Father Vicar.[1] You being so poor, it isn't right to make you pay so much postage, but this cannot be helped.

2. In your charity, please send this letter to my brother[2] along with the one addressed to him so that he will know that Padre Nicolao,[3] having arrived late today, is now here. I immediately asked him about the money for my brother. He tells me that he will leave me authorization so that the prioress[4] here may withdraw the money from the amount they will be sending and send it to you. He tells me that the one who has the money has assured him that he will give it to him at once. So from what I understand it will be collected soon. The money from Valladolid, it seems, was sent to Seville for some business transactions and will be recovered; if not, it will be paid back in some other way; that is certain.

3. Give my regards to María de San Jerónimo[5]—tell me how she is—to Isabel de San Pablo,[6] to Teresa,[7] and all the others; may God make them all saints. May he be with you.

4. In any case, try to send me the answers from Father Vicar and my brother, as I have already mentioned to you in other letters. If Father Vicar is gone, let me know where; and the letters for him return to me.

Today is 16 April.

Your reverence's servant,
Teresa of Jesus

To Padre Jerónimo Gracián, Madrid
Toledo, May 5, 1580

Teresa had suffered for a terrible month with influenza from which she thought she would die. She answers several of Gracián's letters dealing with a number of topics: a moral case being disputed in Alcalá, the improvement of her health, the possibility of a foundation in Madrid, the Carmel in which Velasco's sister should enter, news of the business in Rome, her orders to travel again, and Gracián's new commissions.

---

1. Jesus. The grace of the Holy Spirit be with your paternity. Yesterday I received your letters. They came after the one about the rector of Alcalá. I discussed this with Señora Doña Luisa and with the licentiate, Serrano. And he answered in the enclosed letter.

2. Regarding the clash of opinions[1] you mention, I was very happy to learn that your opinion prevailed; for even though the fathers must have enough reasons, it would have been worse not to do what was safest at that time, but to be thinking of points of honor. When honor of the world is lost by one's acting in this way, one begins to understand how important it is to look only to God's honor. It could be they feared that a greater harm might result from a change in approach toward the enmity. The truth is that God provides with his grace when we are determined to do something for him alone. You have nothing to feel distressed about in this case, but it would be good if you presented some reason for excusing those fathers. I feel more distressed to see you going around in the midst of those contagious fevers.[2]

3. Blessed be God that you are in good health, for my illness no longer amounts to anything, as I have written to you. Only weakness remains, for I went through a terrible month, which I spent mostly on my feet. Since I am used to dealing with chronic pain, I thought that in spite of feeling quite sick, it was possible to put up with it. Certainly, I thought I was dying, although I didn't completely believe this, nor did whether I die or live matter to me. God grants me this favor, which I consider a great one, for I remember the fear I used to have at other times.

4. I was delighted to see this letter from Rome; for although the dispatch[3] is not coming as soon as was thought, it seems certain it will come. I don't know what kinds of turmoil its arrival might cause, nor why. It is good that you wait for Father Vicar, Fray Angel,[4] even if for no other reason than to prevent the appearance that you cannot wait to set out on your mission as soon as you receive it; he will take note of everything.

5. You should know that I wrote to Beas and to Fray John of the Cross that you are going down there[5] and about the commission that you have. Fray Angel wrote to me of how he had given it to you. Although I thought for a while that I should be silent, it seemed to me that since Father Vicar told me about it there was no need to be silent. I would so much like not to lose time, but if our documents[6] are to arrive soon, it will undoubtedly be better to wait so that everything can be carried out with greater freedom, as you say.

6. Even if you don't come to see me, I considered it a great gift for you to say that if I want you will come. It would be a real joy for me, but I fear the remarks of our brothers and the fatigue it would cause you, for you still have a long way to travel. I must satisfy myself with the thought that you will have to come eventually out of necessity. I would then like some of your time one day to find relief in conferring with you about the things of my soul.

7. When I get a little more of my strength back, I will try to speak with the archbishop.[7] If he gives me permission for a foundation in Madrid, it will be undoubtedly much better for her to enter there than elsewhere. These nuns become so disappointed when what they want isn't done that they torment me. Since I am waiting to see whether the Madrid foundation is possible, I have not written to the prioress in Segovia,[8] nor have I spoken seriously about their receiving her. I believe that although the prioress doesn't like the idea, all the other nuns would accept her. But I don't have time to go into this because according to what Father Vicar wrote me, I cannot stay here any longer than is necessary for me to be strong enough to travel, and I am becoming scrupulous about not moving on.[9] There are many nuns in Segovia, and now they want to receive another. But since she would be going there only temporarily, it shouldn't matter to them.

8. If nonetheless you think it worthwhile, I will write to the prioress in Segovia. You too should tell her that you would be very pleased if they accepted her, that this is very important. That house has been of little help or almost no help in all our business matters. And when you tell her about all we owe to Velasco,[10] it will have a good effect. Here they just gave five hundred ducats at my request to St. Joseph's in Avila. A tangle of things happened there, which I will tell you about, that was no one's fault; otherwise I would have already dealt with the matter.

9. Truly, until I speak to the archbishop, I don't know if it would be good to bring this matter up in Segovia. Let me know soon what you want done, for there are many carriers who will come here, if you pay a good portage. To bring her to Segovia without the nuns' knowing about her and wanting her would be unacceptable. And the permission from Padre Fray Angel—which I already have—sets this acceptance down as a condition. I didn't mention to him who she was. I tell you that I desire to accept her much more than you do. I think it would be better to speak with the archbishop in his house, entering through a church where he says Mass. When I am well enough I will do this and inform you. I have no more to say for now except that may God watch over you and give you what I beg of him.

It is 5 May.

Your unworthy servant,
Teresa of Jesus

To Padre Jerónimo Gracián, Madrid
Toledo, June 3, 1580

Teresa is answering Padre Gracián's letter by return mail through a safe messenger, Madre Brianda's brother. Her trip to Madrid has been delayed because Archbishop Quiroga is not giving her permission for a foundation in Madrid, nor even an audience. In the meantime her health has improved as has Padre Antonio's, but Gracián has not come to Toledo to accompany them. Teresa is still trying to have an interview with the archbishop and also with Gracián and Angel de Salazar. In passing, she mentions some news about the Princess of Eboli.

---

1. Jesus. The grace of the Holy Spirit be with your paternity, *mi padre*. I don't know what our Lord intends by allowing so many obstacles to my departing and speaking with this angel.[1]

2. So as to be able to leave, I wrote him today in the form of a request—it was suggested that I do so, and we shall see what the result is. But another snag arose today, which is my fear that we will miss Padre Fray Angel[2] on the journey. He wrote that after the feast days he would come to Madrid. If we finish our business with the archbishop, however, I don't think waiting for him would be reason enough to delay; so we will set out next Tuesday.

3. Padre Fray Antonio is now much better. He is saying Mass. And so you can be at ease, for I will speak with you there; and if not, we shall see each other in heaven. Padre Fray Antonio was in such a condition that I was afraid to go alone with him, thinking that he might die along the way. And since it would have made me happy for you to come, I tried to bring this about, still failing to realize that when I myself try to get something in this life the opposite happens. Since he was so sick, you had the occasion for coming to see him—and it would have appeared right. It would be good to write to him and express your happiness over his recovery, for you have been cold toward him.

4. Padre Fray Hernando del Castillo[3] is here. They said the Princess of Eboli was back in her house in Madrid; now they say she is in Pastrana.[4] I don't know which is true; either of these is very

good for her. My health is good, glory to God. Let me know as soon as Padre Fray Angel arrives there. These carriers deliver the letters quicker and more reliably. I have already written you two in which I told you that I had received Padre Nicolao's letter and those that came with it. The one dated the Tuesday before Corpus Christi was given to me today, Friday, the day after this feast.

5. I am answering you through Madre Brianda's brother; she is doing all right. All the nuns ask for your prayers; I ask for those of Señor Velasco. Since I wrote to him recently, I am not doing so now. I really hope the letter was not lost, for it is important that his sister be there when I pass through.

6. Padre Nicolao told me that he left eight hundred ducats on deposit in Seville, since the prioress wanted to have them on reserve for any need that would arise regarding the negotiations. I tell you this so that the person who lent you the hundred ducats may be sure of receiving them back soon. It will be enough for me to write to Casademonte,[5] and he will send you the amount at once—I mean if you cannot obtain a loan there. May God direct everything as he sees necessary, and watch over you as I beg of him.

Your paternity's servant,
Teresa of Jesus

7. Have this letter sent to Padre Nicolao and find out from the Carmel what they know about Padre Vicario; and if possible let me know, although I believe we will be leaving here on Tuesday or Wednesday—unless something else comes up, for it seems a kind of spell has been cast over us.[6]

To the Discalced Carmelite Nuns, Malagón
Medina, August 1580

Here we have a fragment from a letter Teresa wrote on hearing of the death of her former spiritual director and confessor, the Jesuit Father Baltasar Alvarez.

My daughters, this is one of the chastisements that our Lord brings about on earth; he takes away its saints.

To Padre Jerónimo Gracián, Seville
Valladolid, November 20, 1580

It is night, after Matins, and Teresa is dictating hastily to her secretary. She has received no word from Gracián and is anxious to know how his trip to Seville went. Her nephew Francisco's visit after his having left the discalced Carmelite novitiate in Pastrana produced mixed feelings in her. And she has to begin thinking again of carrying out what was stipulated in her brother's will about building a new chapel for St. Joseph's.

---

1. Jesus. The grace of the Holy Spirit be with your paternity. This letter is not in my own hand because I wrote a great deal to Avila today and my head is tired out. Yesterday I wrote to you through Señora Doña Juana de Antisco,[1] and before that I wrote you another very long letter. Please God it arrived there better than yours are arriving here—if you wrote any—for I worry very much until I know whether you arrived there safely. I am writing now so that you will know about the mail delivery between here and there and not fail to use it to write to me. I am well, glory to God, and the fever has also left Sister María de San José.[2]

2. What I mentioned in yesterday's letter is the story of Don Francisco,[3] which has astonished us all. It would seem they undid him so as to remake him into a different person. I am not surprised about his behavior toward his relatives, but I am surprised that God so abandons a creature who was desiring to serve him. Great are God's judgments. I felt great pity when I saw him. He is now actively engaged in managing his property and is attached to it, and he is so afraid of speaking with either discalced friars or discalced nuns that I don't think he would want to see any of us, and least of all me. They say that he claims he is afraid that the desire he had will return.[4] In this is seen the great temptation to which he must be prey. I beg you to recommend him to God and show him compassion. He is looking to get married, but not outside Avila. It will be a poor marriage, for he is not without his regrets. The fact that you and Padre Nicolao[5] abandoned him so soon must have influenced his decision

very much. And that house in Pastrana isn't very enticing, in my opinion. A great burden has been lifted from me.

3. The chapel is again on track, for Padre Fray Angel wrote me about it yesterday. It all tires me out very much. He never did go to Madrid, for he is coming now to San Pablo de la Moraleja. He says that the general has sent him the acts of the chapter. Padre Pedro Fernández is not dead; he is doing very poorly. Here most of the sisters are well and want to know about you. And my secretary and Madre Inés de Jesús kiss your hands.

4. Since I think you will be concerned about what was paid to Godoy, you should know that I gave orders for it to appear to be a loan, and so as matters ended up he owed me more than I did him.

It is after Matins and the eve of Our Lady of the Presentation, a day I will not forget,[6] for that was the day the near riot broke out when you presented the brief to the Carmel there. May God watch over you and make you as holy as I beg of him, amen.

Your paternity's unworthy servant and daughter,
Teresa of Jesus

5. God willing, this letter will be legible considering the haste with which it was written.[7] Francisco is very disturbed, and I have learned that he suffers from stomachaches, headaches, and a weak heart. God granted me a great favor by his not taking the habit. He mentioned often in Avila that nobody forced him to do anything. I tell you, *mi padre*, that I always feared what I now see. I don't know why, but I have felt relief not to have to be responsible for him, even though he says that with regard to his marriage he will not do anything that I would not want. But I fear he will find little happiness. And so if it were not for the fact that I might appear to be displeased over what he has done, I wouldn't bother with what he is planning.

6. If you saw the letter that he wrote me from Alcalá and Pastrana you would be amazed by his happiness and the haste with which he wanted me to intervene on his behalf so that they give him the habit. He must have undergone a fierce temptation. But I did not speak to him about this, because he was very upset and a relative of his was with him. He must feel very embarrassed.

May God provide, and may he watch over you. In my opinion he would have been a holy man among holy men. I hope in God for his salvation, for he does have a fear of offending God.

7. Your companion, San Bartolomé,[8] sends her best regards, and she has a great concern and desire to know how you fared along those roads and without us, for here we do very poorly without you; it seems we have been left in a desert. Sister Casilda de la Concepción sends you her regards.

8. May our Lord keep you for us and allow us to see you soon, *padre mio*, amen. So as not to tire you, I'll say no more.

Your paternity's unworthy subject,
Ana de San Bartolomé.

9. If you learn anything about the good Fray Bartolomé de Jesús, let me know, for this would be very consoling to me.

To Doña Juana de Ahumada, Alba
Palencia, January 13, 1581

The Christmas season had stirred thoughts in Teresa of her family. Francisco de Cepeda on December 8, 1580, had married in Madrid without informing his relatives in Alba. Teresa is happy with the way the new foundation in Alba has turned out.

---

1. Jesus. The grace of the Holy Spirit be with your honor, my sister. I have had the strongest desire to know how you are and how your Christmas was. Believe me, many a Christmas has gone by in which I never have had you and your household so much in mind as this year, recommending you all to our Lord and even grieving over your trials. May he be blessed who did not come into this world for any other reason than to suffer. And since I understand that whoever best follows his example in suffering, keeping his commandments, will have the more glory, I feel greatly consoled; although I would prefer to suffer your trials myself and let you have the reward, or be where I could more easily spend time with you. But, since the Lord ordains otherwise, may he be blessed for everything.

2. On the feast of the Holy Innocents, I set out from Valladolid with my companions in the midst of harsh weather for this city of Palencia. But my health is no worse, although the usual ailments are not lacking. When there is no fever, however, one can put up with them.[1]

3. Two days after our arrival, I installed the bell at night, and a monastery of the glorious St. Joseph was founded. The happiness of all the people here was so great I was amazed. I think this is partly due to the fact that they see they are thereby pleasing the bishop, for he is much loved here and he favors us. Things are proceeding in such a way that I have hope in God this will be among the best of our houses.

4. I have no other news of Don Francisco than that his mother-in-law wrote a little while ago saying he had to be bled twice. She is very happy with him, and he with both of them. Pedro de Ahumada must be the least happy, according to what he has

written to me.[2] For Don Francisco seems to want to live with his mother-in-law, and it is not possible for Pedro de Ahumada to join them. It's a pity that he cannot be at rest anywhere. He wrote to me that he was now well and that he was going to Avila for the Epiphany to find out how to collect the money from Seville, since they are not giving him anything. The more those in Madrid inform me about this marriage,[3] the more reason I see for us to be happy, especially over all they say of the discretion and pleasing manner of Doña Orofrisia. May God protect them and give them the grace to serve him, for all earthly consolations pass away quickly.

5. If you send the letter to Mother Prioress in Alba to forward to Salamanca it will surely arrive here, for there is a regular mail delivery. For goodness' sake don't neglect to write to me; you owe it to me these days, for I have had you all on my mind more than I would like.

6. Let Señor Juan de Ovalle consider this letter as addressed also to him—I would like to know how he is getting along. Regards to Señora Doña Beatriz. May God watch over you all and make you as holy as I beg of him, amen.

Today is 13 January.

7. Don't fail to write to Don Francisco, which would be appropriate. He is not to blame for having failed to inform you of his marriage; it came about in such a way that there wasn't time. Madre Inés de Jesús[4] is well and sends her best regards to all of you.

Your honor's servant,
Teresa of Jesus

To Padre Jerónimo Gracián, Alcalá
Palencia, February 1581

Teresa continues to give her suggestions for the coming chapter in Alcalá. She has eight points to make concerning the nuns' constitutions. As for who might be elected provincial, she also has suggestions and urges Gracián not to withdraw his name.

1. I consider it very important that vicars[1] not also be confessors to the nuns, and this should be always so. It is imperative for these houses that the nuns have the friars as confessors, as you say and I myself see. I would support having things remain as they are rather than grant that each confessor be also the vicar. There are so many drawbacks to this, as I will explain to you when I see you. I beg you to trust me in this matter, for when St. Joseph's was founded much attention was given to it. And one of the reasons it seemed to some persons, myself included, that it was good that the monastery be subject to the bishop was to avoid this practice. There are serious disadvantages that result from it, as I have learned. And for me one is enough: I have seen clearly that if the vicar likes some nun, the prioress cannot prevent him from talking to her as much as he wants, for he is the superior. This can result in a thousand woes.

2. For this reason, and for many others, it is also necessary that they not be subject to the priors. It will happen that someone who doesn't know much will give orders that are disturbing to all the nuns. There won't be anyone like *mi padre* Gracián, and since we have so much experience, we have to look ahead and remove the risks. The greatest good that can be done for these nuns is that no talking with the confessor take place other than what is necessary for the confession of sins. As for safeguarding the recollection of the monastery, it is enough that the confessor inform the provincial.

3. I have said all this in case someone else or Father Commissary may think otherwise. But I don't believe this will happen, for in his order the nuns in many places have confessors who are not their vicars. Our entire existence depends on our keeping out these wicked devotees, destroyers of the brides of Christ. It is

necessary always to think of the worst that can happen in order to remove this occasion of sin, for the devil enters here without our realizing it. This is what can do us harm and that I always fear—as well as our taking in too large a number of nuns. So I beg you to insist that these two things remain firmly fixed in our constitutions.[2] Do me this favor.

4. I don't know why you say we should be silent in regard to the friars being our confessors, for you see how bound we are by the constitutions of Padre Fray Pedro Fernández,[3] and I confess that it is necessary that we be so. Nor do I understand why you must not speak about matters concerning us. I tell you that I have so stressed in my letter the benefit we derive from your visitations—and this is true—that you can readily discuss anything you like in order to help us. You really owe this to these nuns, for you cost them many tears. I would prefer that no one speak of these matters but you and Padre Nicolao, for it is not necessary that our constitutions or that which you ordain for us be dealt with in the chapter or that the others be informed of them. Only between ourselves did Padre Fernández (may he be in glory) and I discuss these matters. And even though some of the eight things that I set down at the beginning seem unimportant, you should realize that they are very important.[4] So, I would not want you to remove any of them. In what regards nuns I can have a say, for I have seen many things.

5. You should know that I wanted to arrange to ask Father Prior and the commissary to appoint masters and *presentados* from those among you who are qualified. This is necessary for some matters and so as not to need to have recourse to the general.[5] But since you say that the commissary has no further authority than to assist at the chapter and draw up constitutions, I let the matter go.

6. It seems they have not granted all that was asked for. It would have been good if they had and done away for some years with any need for us to have recourse to Rome. It will be necessary that you write at once to the general, giving him an account of what is taking place. The letter should be a humble one, submitting to him as his subjects, which is right. And you should write as well to Fray Angel[6] —for you owe it to him—thanking

him for the good things he has done for you and asking him to always consider you his son; and be sure to do this!

7. Now let us deal with what you say of your wish not to be elected or confirmed; in this regard I am writing to Father Commissary. You should know, *mi padre*, that regarding the desire I have had to see you free, I clearly understand that the love I have for you in the Lord is much more at work than the good of the order. From this proceeds a natural weakness that causes me to suffer greatly in seeing that not all understand how much they owe you and how much you have labored; I cannot bear to hear even a word spoken against you. But in considering what could result from this, I see that the general good carries more weight. If, however, Padre Nicolao were elected and then always accompanied by you, I think both wishes could be satisfied. But I truly believe that for this first time it would be better in all respects for you to hold the office, and so I am telling this to Father Commissary. And if this cannot be, then Padre Nicolao accompanied by you would be best because of your experience and knowledge of your subjects, both the friars and the nuns. I tell you that it is for his lack of experience that we consider Macario unsuited to the task. I am giving you good reasons for it all, and I tell you that Padre Fray Pedro Fernández thought this as well, although he did desire very much Macario's election for reasons valid at that time. But now—the damage he would do!

8. I also included the name of Padre Fray Juan de Jesús so that it wouldn't seem that I am limiting myself to only two; although I told the truth in saying that Padre Juan de Jesús didn't have the gift of governing—since in my opinion he doesn't—but that if he had one of the other two for his companion he could pass, for he listens to reason and would take counsel. And so I believe that if you went around with him, he would in no way distance himself from what you tell him; thus I believe he would do well. But I am sure he would not receive the votes. May God so direct things that whatever is for his greater honor and glory will come about, which is what I hope for, seeing that he has already done the greater part. It is a great pity . . .

To Dionisio Ruiz de la Peña, Toledo
Soria, June 30, 1581

Dionisio Ruiz de la Peña was the personal secretary and confessor of the Archbishop of Toledo, Gaspar de Quiroga. Three business matters brought Teresa into communication with Cardinal Quiroga: the Inquisition's examination of The Book of Her Life, *which passed through his hands; a foundation of discalced Carmelite nuns in Madrid; and the thornier problem of his widowed niece's desire to become a discalced Carmelite nun even though she had children who were still minors.*

To the most illustrious Señor Licentiate Peña, confessor of the most illustrious Cardinal Archbishop of Toledo, my lord.

1. Jesus. The grace of the Holy Spirit be with your honor. The day after I sent a private messenger who had brought a letter for me from Señora Doña Luisa,[1] they brought me your letter. I was very sorry because I would have wanted to answer at once and since there is no ordinary mail delivery[2] in this place, I don't know when this letter will go out. I would have wanted it to go quickly so that you would be aware of how little I am at fault, or rather not at all. This is so true that out of respect for the relationship[3] of that person about whom you wrote to me with his illustrious lordship, I did not tell the latter about the efforts I made in this case to impede her entrance into one of these houses. If Padre Baltasar Alvarez, who was provincial of the Jesuits in this province, were alive, he would be a good witness to how I begged him to prevent such a thing, since this lady had more respect for him than for anyone else, and he promised to do so.

2. For some years now I have been standing in her way, and I don't think this is because his illustrious lordship is opposed to her entering, but out of fear that what happened in the case of another lady who entered one of our monasteries, leaving daughters behind, might happen to us. This was done without my approval, for I was far away from that city when she entered.[4] I tell you that ten years of unrest and great trials have gone by (for she entered that long ago), and she is a good servant of God. But since the order of charity,[5] which is obligatory, is not being observed, I think God allows her and her daughters to pay

for such a failure, and the nuns as well. And I have mentioned it so much in these monasteries that I am certain the prioress in Medina becomes upset every time she thinks of what might happen. Consider how although this is true, the devil has found a way in which they can accuse me of the opposite.

3. Our Lord often finds a way of granting me joy in suffering calumnies, which have not been rare for me in this life, but this one in a way has caused me distress. For if I owed his lordship gratitude for nothing else than his having allowed me to kiss his hands there, that would be enough, but how much more do I owe him for so many favors; and in the case of some he does not know that I am aware of them. And knowing what his will is in this regard, I couldn't give my consent now to such a thing, unless I were out of my mind. It is true that sometimes, since this lady cries so much when I tell her many things so as to dissuade her, I may at times have given her some reasons for hope while trying to cheer her up, and perhaps she thought I was in favor of this, although I don't especially remember such a thing.

4. I certainly love her honor very much, and am indebted to her, and so—leaving aside what concerns us—if for my sins what I am speaking of should happen, I strongly desire that she succeed in everything. Yesterday I was told by the prioress of this house (who is from the monastery in Medina, for she is the one with whom this lady frequently communicated) that she had been told by her that the vow she had made to enter contained the condition that she would do so when she could and that if she were told it would be for the greater service of God that she not enter, she would renounce her desire. It seems to me that since she still has children to care for and her daughter-in-law is so young, she is not yet able to enter. If you think it appropriate, tell his lordship about this so that he will understand how the vow was made. Some learned men with whom she speaks disturb her, and the little they say to someone who is so holy is enough to do that.

5. If your letter had come before the one Señora Doña Luisa wrote me, in which she tells me that his lordship has been freed from any illusion about my being at fault in this matter, it would have pained me very much. Blessed be God who so favors me that, without my understanding how, his lordship has come to

know the truth. Never in all my life would I have dreamed of excusing myself since I didn't think I was at fault. I kiss your honor's hands for having informed me of this. I consider it a special favor and consider myself newly obliged to serve you always more with my poor prayers, although up until now I have not failed to do so.

6. As regards the license for a foundation in Madrid, I have begged this of his most illustrious lordship because I think our Lord would be served thereby and because the discalced friars and nuns have urged me, for they say that it would be very useful for everyone to have a house there. But since his illustrious lordship stands in the place of God, I would feel no disturbance if he doesn't think it would be good to grant the permission. I would believe that accepting his denial would be of greater service to God, for I would not be refusing any trials; and I tell you there are many in every foundation.

7. What would be a great trial for me would be the thought that his illustrious lordship is displeased with me on account of calumnies uttered against me, for I love him tenderly in the Lord. And even if this doesn't matter to him, it is a consolation to me that he know the truth, for being loved doesn't matter to our Lord either, yet he is happy with this love alone. Truly, if love is present, it then shows itself in works and in not departing from his will. Through these works I cannot serve his illustrious lordship in any better way than by refusing to oppose him as much as I can. Be certain of this, and do not forget me in your holy sacrifices, as we have agreed.

8. Since you will learn of my travel plans from the Mother Prioress there, I will not mention them. I have better health here than usual, glory to God. It is a great comfort to me to know that his illustrious lordship is in good health. May God give you health, and the holiness I beg of him for you, amen.

From this monastery of the Holy Trinity in Soria, the end of June.

Your honor's unworthy servant,
Teresa of Jesus

To Padre Jerónimo Gracián, Valladolid
Soria, July 14, 1581

The context of the foundation in Soria was a peaceful one. But there were many projects pending, in Avila, Madrid, Burgos, Toledo, and Alba. A major concern was the Carmelite vocation of the widow Doña Elena and the opposition of her uncle, Cardinal Quiroga of Toledo. Future plans included a foundation in Madrid and one in Burgos. Teresa desired to maintain a good relationship with the Carmelite general and to have the text of the nuns' new constitutions put into print. There were some difficult nuns at St. Joseph's in Avila.

To our Father Provincial of the discalced Carmelites, Valladolid.

1. Jesus. The Holy Spirit be with your reverence, *mi padre*. I received a letter of yours dated the feast of St. John and afterward the one that came with Padre Nicolao's.[1] One very long one that you said you wrote me never arrived here. But even though these were short, the happiness they brought me in informing me of your good health was not small, for I was worried. May he, as he can, give you health.

2. I have written you some letters. I wouldn't want the one to get lost where I begged you not to give permission to Doña Elena[2] to become a nun. Now they tell me this messenger for Valladolid, where according to what you say I think you will be, is a very safe one. Since you will be there so close to San Alejo,[3] I thought of sending you these letters from Toledo so that you may see how upset the archbishop[4] is over it, and I do not want us in any way to have him for an enemy. And apart from this, never is there talk about her entering that I do not feel great resistance. For where mother and daughter[5] and other relatives are present, along with what is known about this woman, I fear there will be much disquiet and that she won't be very happy. And so even before I spoke to the archbishop, I had asked Padre Baltasar Alvarez[6] to prevent it, and he promised to do so, for he agreed with me, and he knew her very well. See how it can seem that I persuaded her. I have written to the cardinal that I will inform you, and not to worry, for she will not be received, and that I would be very distressed if her entrance were not prevented.

3. You realize how secret the contents of this letter must be. In any case, tear it up so that no one thinks that it is because of him that we are not accepting her, but that it is because it would not be opportune either for her or for her children, as is true. We already have a lot of experience with these widows.

4. Before I forget, I am afraid that these constitutions are never going to get printed. For goodness' sake do not neglect to do this; see how important it is. By now we could have had a large volume of history published.

5. Now let's take up Burgos.[7] I am enclosing the response, and I am surprised by those who think I can just get up and go there. In my answer to the bishop,[8] I told him that because of my illnesses you ordered me not to go to Burgos at a time in which I would have to be there in winter—you once wrote this to me. This I did so as not to put in doubt the archbishop's[9] intentions and cause hostilities between him and the Bishop of Palencia, something to be avoided. After writing to the Bishop of Palencia, I wrote to the Archbishop of Burgos that because I thought I would be a bother to him if the city did not grant the license[10]— since I thought they would pay little attention to me—I would let the project go until the city authorized it. The hour for this foundation must not have arrived. I think that Fray Baltasar's[11] hour arrived first; so goes the world.

6. A foundation in Madrid is what would now be fitting, and I believe that when the archbishop sees that what he wants is being done, he will authorize it quickly. The bishop[12] here, who is going there in September, tells me that he will give his support. I will be finished here, with God's help, in the middle of August. After the feast of our Lady, if it appears all right to you, I will be able to go to Avila—for it doesn't seem to me that those sisters spoke clearly with Padre Nicolao—for here I have nothing to do. But if there is no big need, it would give me great consolation not to have to remain as prioress,[13] for I am no longer fit for the task. It requires more energy than I have and makes me feel scrupulous.

7. If Padre Fray Gregorio Nacianceno remains there, as I wrote to you, the prioress will suffice[14] since there is no one else there. And although I say "will suffice," I think I am lying because I

don't think there is anyone who can handle the internal affairs of the house. You will see what is best there. The concern I have for that house enables me to give little importance to whatever labor I would have to undergo so as to overcome its difficulties, and the fact that I will be waiting there for the Lord to open the way to a foundation in Madrid will be of some help. But one's human nature will not fail to feel in that place the absence of my brother and friends,[15] and what is worse the presence of the ones who have remained.

8. As for the trip to Rome, I now see that it is very necessary, although there is nothing to fear in going to give obedience to the general.[16] And because of the risk of the journey and our need, I would like to see friars sent who would not be missed so much if anything were to happen. You would certainly miss Padre Nicolao a great deal, although he would be the one who could best smooth everything over. I think that if from time to time you give to the general signs of our obedience and respect-fulness there will be no problem. This is very necessary so that he understand that you are his subjects and that you all realize that you have a superior. Things must not be as in the past, nor the expenses,[17] for this would be a burden for all the houses.

9. I forgot to mention the joy the agreement about the chapel[18] brought me, for it is very well done. Glory to God, some benefit came from delaying.

With that daughter of the Flemish woman,[19] I fear that you will have work for a whole lifetime, as you do with her mother; and please God she won't be worse. Believe me I fear an unhappy nun more than many devils. God pardon the one who took her back. Do not give permission for her profession until I come there, if God desires. I am writing Padre Nicolao to let me know if they have equipment there for travel, for I don't see much here. May God dispose everything for his greater service.

10. Please God you have been able to do something in that matter concerning Beatriz.[20] For some days I have been afflicted over it. I have written a number of letters to her and her mother telling them terrible things that should have been enough for them to make some amends. For although they were without fault, I set before them the dangers that before God and the world

they could have gotten into. In my opinion, though, they are not exempt, and the parents are more to blame because they allow her to give them orders. It's a lost cause, and I believe that if they do not remove the occasion completely, things will go from bad to worse, if such is possible, for they are bad enough now. As for honor, it is already lost, and I am passing over the matter even though it troubles me to do so. I wouldn't want souls to be lost, but I see them, parents and children, so lacking in good sense that I don't find any remedy. May God provide one and give you the grace to bring things to an appropriate conclusion. I see no other remedy than to put her in a monastery, but I don't know how considering their financial situation. It would be a solution if she could remain as a student.[21]

11. I beg you to write and let me know what you did and what you decide about my going to Avila. Given the scarcity of messengers and the brevity of your letters, you need to write in time.

May God preserve you with the holiness I beg of him, amen, amen.

Today is 14 July.

12. The bishop is leaving here within ten days for the synod. The foundress asks me to give you her best regards; consider them received along with those from all the others, for I am tired—although well.

> Your reverence's unworthy servant and subject—
> how gladly I say this,
> Teresa of Jesus

If Padre Nicolao is not there, read the letter that is enclosed for him.

To Don Jerónimo Reinoso, Palencia
Avila, September 9, 1581

Teresa arrived back in Avila unwell after a long and difficult journey. On the very following day the prioress of St. Joseph's, María de Cristo, renounced her office, and Teresa was elected prioress.

---

1. Jesus. The grace of the Holy Spirit be with your honor. I am now in Avila, *mi padre,* where I would most willingly be your daughter again if you were here, for I feel very much alone in this city where I find no one who can console me in my present situation. May God provide a remedy. The more I go on, the less I find in this life that can provide consolation.

2. I was not well when I arrived here, but had a slight fever caused by a certain circumstance. Now I am well, and it seems the body is relieved for not having to go on another trip so soon. For I tell you, these trips are very tiring, although I can't say that about the one from here to Soria. That trip was recreation for me, it being a smooth journey, often with a view of rivers that provided pleasant company. Our good procurator[1] will have told you about this experience.

3. It's a strange thing that not one of those who desire to do me a favor escapes without a good deal of trouble, but God gives them the charity to enjoy it, as he has done with you. See that you do not fail to write me a letter when you have a messenger, even though you may find it tiring to do so, for I tell you there is very little in which to find rest, and many trials.

4. I am delighted that Dionisia[2] has entered. I beg you to tell the chief mail carrier[3] and give him my regards, and don't forget to pray for me. Since I arrived only a short time ago, there is no lack of visitors and so little opportunity to relax by writing to you.

5. I kiss Don Francisco's[4] hands. May our Lord watch over you with an increase in holiness, as I beg of him, amen.

Today is 9 September.

Your honor's unworthy servant and daughter,
Teresa of Jesus

To Sancho Dávila, Alba
Avila, October 9, 1581

Don Sancho was from Avila, a priest, theologian, and professor at Salamanca. In a letter to Teresa he sought her guidance over some problems with his interior life. He had written a biography of his own mother, who had died two years before in the odor of sanctity. After giving him some guidance, Teresa seeks his help for a problem that was causing her much pain. Some calumnies were being spoken against her niece (Beatriz), and nobody seemed to be doing anything about it. After Teresa's death, Beatriz became a discalced Carmelite nun serving the order well in a number of responsible positions.

To the very illustrious Señor Don Sancho Dávila, in Alba.

1. Jesus. The grace of the Holy Spirit be with your honor always. It was a great favor and gift for me to have a letter from you. Yet, since I had been hoping for a visit from you one of these days and I now see that I won't be able to have that joy, the happiness your letter brought me is somewhat diluted. I have praised our Lord and have considered what you hold to be a loss a great favor from him, for no benefit could come to a soul, or health, from such extreme suffering. So you can thank His Majesty, for in taking it away he did not take from her the possibility of serving our Lord, which is what is most important. You do not feel within you that great determination not to offend him, but when the occasion arises to serve him and to reject what could be for you an occasion to displease him you find you are strong—that is the authentic sign of a true desire, in my opinion. And that you are happy to receive the most Blessed Sacrament each day and feel sorry when you do not is the sign of a close friendship, and not as common as you think. Always consider the favors you receive from his hand as given for the purpose of growing in his love, and stop going about looking for all the little subtleties of your miseries, for these show themselves to everyone *en masse*, very much so, especially with me.

2. In regard to being distracted during the recitation of the Divine Office, although I am perhaps much at fault, I like to think it is due to a weakness of the head. And you should think the same,

for the Lord knows well that when we pray we would like to pray very well. Today I confessed this to Padre Maestro Fray Domingo,[1] and he told me not to pay attention to it, and I beg of you the same, for I consider it an incurable evil.

3. Your trouble with your teeth makes me feel very sorry, for I have had much experience with how painful that can be. If one is infected, it usually seems that they all are—I mean that all hurt. I have not found a better remedy than having it pulled, although that doesn't help if the pain is caused by neuralgia. May God take away the pain as I will beg of him.

4. You did very well to write the life of so holy a person.[2] I would be a good witness to the truth of her holiness. I kiss your hands for what you do for me in allowing me to see it.

5. I am getting along better. Compared to last year, I can say that I am well, although not much time goes by that I am not suffering something; and since I see that as long as one lives, suffering is what is best, I bear it willingly.

6. I would like to know if the marquis[3] is there, and to receive some news about Señora Doña Juana de Toledo, his daughter, and about how the marquess is.[4] I beg you to tell them that even though I have gone far away, I do not forget to remember them to our Lord in my poor prayers. I don't do much for your honor since you are my father and lord.

7. I kiss your hands for assuring me that you will be so for me if I need to ask you for help; and I want to do so. Because I am so confident that you will help me, if you see that it is fitting, I want to tell you alone of a great sorrow that I have been bearing for almost a year. It could be that you might be able to provide some remedy. I truly believe that you will know—for they tell me that, for my sins, it is something public—about the great jealousy of Don Gonzalo's[5] wife. They have told her, and she takes it to be true, that her husband is involved in a wicked friendship with Doña Beatriz, my sister's daughter. And she says and asserts this so publicly that the majority of the people believe her. And so, with respect to the young girl's honor, it must now be so lost that there is no point for me to even consider it, but I am concerned about the many offenses committed against God. I am extremely sorry that a relative of mine should be the occasion for this, and

so I have arranged with her parents to have her move away from there, for some learned men have told me the parents have an obligation to do this. And even if they didn't, it seems to me it would be wise to flee as from a wild animal the tongue of a woman inflamed with jealousy. Others tell the family that doing so would make a lie appear to be true, and that they shouldn't move. They tell me that the husband and wife are separated. I see that there is already talk about it by the wife's sister here in Avila, and many calumnies are being spread by those doing the talking. And the talk has extended even to Salamanca. The evil is spreading and neither from one side nor from the other is any remedy being applied. Her parents pay no attention to the things I tell them—which are not a few—but say I am being deceived.

8. I beg you to write me and let me know what I should do so that these offenses against God may stop, for as I say, it would be hard now to salvage her honor in the people's opinion. I had thought of a means, but I would find it hard to put into effect. If you have any dealings with that Don Gonzalo, perhaps you could convince him to leave that place for maybe a year or a half year until his wife returns to normal, since he has a good residence elsewhere and sees the harm that is being done to this girl because of him. And in the meanwhile perhaps the Lord will so arrange that by the time he returns the girl will no longer be there. For without this, the way things are going—and what there is now is already bad—I fear some great evil will arise.

9. I beg you, if you see any way in which you can help me, to take this trial from me. May our Lord do so as he can, and may he give you the holiness that I beg of him for you, amen.

Today is 9 October.

Your honor's unworthy servant and daughter,
Teresa of Jesus

10. I beg you to give greetings for me to Don Fadrique and to my lady Doña María, for my head is in no condition to write to them, and pardon me out of love for God.

To Don Pedro Castro y Nero, Alba
Avila, November 19, 1581

Doctor Castro y Nero was a friend of Gracián's and had been a class-mate of his at the University of Alcalá. A professor at Salamanca, a canon in Avila, he later became Bishop of Lugo and then of Segovia. Teresa had given him a copy of her Life *to read, and in a note she had just received from him, he reveals the powerful impact the book had on him.*

To my lord, Doctor Castro.

1. Jesus be with your honor. The favor that your honor showed me by your letter so moved me that I first gave thanks to our Lord with a *Te Deum laudamus*, for it seemed I was receiving it from the very hands of the one from whom I have received so many other favors. Now I kiss your hands an infinite number of times, and I would like to do so through deeds rather than with words. How great the mercy of God, that through my wicked-ness you should benefit; and with reason, for I am not in hell, which for a long time I have deserved. So, this book is entitled *On the Mercies of God*.[1]

2. May he be always praised, for I had never hoped for less than what he has now accorded me. Nonetheless, every severe word was disturbing to me. I would rather not say more on paper, and so I beg you to come to see me tomorrow, the eve of the Presen-tation, that I might present to you a soul often undone, so that you might bring about all that you understand as fitting for her in order that she please God. I hope in His Majesty for the grace to obey you all my life, for I don't think your absence will let me feel free, nor do I want to, for I have seen changes come about by reason of this desire. It would be impossible for a great good not to come to me through this obedience—provided you do not abandon me, and I don't think you will. As a pledge of this obedience, I am thinking of keeping this note,[2] although I have another more important one.

3. What I beg of you is that for love of our Lord you always keep what I am in mind so as not to pay attention to the favors

granted me by God unless for the sake of considering me even worse than you thought, since I make such poor use of them; clearly the more I receive from him the more indebted to him I am. Repay this Lord of mine, since His Majesty desires to punish me only with favors—which is no small punishment for anyone with self-knowledge.

4. When you finish these papers, I will give you others.[3] On seeing them it will be impossible for you to keep from abhorring someone who should be other than what I am. I think you will like them. May our Lord give you his joy as I beg of him for you.

5. You have not lost any of my esteem by the style of your letters. I ought to be praising you for its elegance. Everything is useful to God when the desire to serve him is at the root. May he be blessed for everything, amen. Not for a long time have I had as much happiness as I have had this night. I kiss your hands many times for the title you give me, which is a very lofty one for me.

To Don Pedro Castro y Nero, Avila
Avila, November 28, 1581

Teresa is writing at night. She had spent a blessed afternoon with St. John of the Cross, who had traveled from Andalusia hoping he could convince Teresa to travel herself to Granada to found the Carmel there. That morning Pedro Castro had surrendered to the nuns' desires and preached a solemn sermon for the profession of Ana de los Angeles (Wasteels).

1. Jesus be with your honor and may His Majesty repay you for the joy and help you have given me today. I also have a desire and if you do not do what you can to fulfill it, I will think it would have been better for me not to have known you, so much will my suffering be. And my trial is this: it doesn't make me happy for you to go to heaven, for you have much to do in God's church. I begged God urgently today not to allow so good a mind to be occupied in anything else.

2. These sisters kiss your hands. You have brought them much consolation. Let me know if you got tired and how you are; but not by mail, for as happy as I would be to receive a letter from you, I wouldn't want to tire you any more than I think necessary, and that is already a lot. I am very happy this evening because of a visit with a father of our order,[1] even though I neglected to send a message to the marchioness,[2] for he is passing through Escalona.

The letter for Alba is going in a very safe way.[3]

And I am your honor's daughter and servant,
Teresa of Jesus

To Madre María de San José, Seville
Avila, November 28, 1581

One of the nuns at St. Joseph's made her profession on this day, and Teresa is now tired after the celebration. St. John of the Cross is in Avila planning with Teresa for a foundation of nuns in Granada, and Teresa begs María de San José to offer two nuns for the new foundation.

---

1. Jesus watch over your reverence for me. I wrote you a long letter today, and so I will not enlarge on this one because of my many other occupations; we had a profession[1] today and I am really tired.

2. For the foundation in Granada I have given the order that they take two nuns from there, and I am trusting that you won't give the worst.[2] So I ask this of you please, for you well know how important it is that they be very virtuous and competent. In this way you will have more room so that you can accept some new nuns and repay me sooner, for it pains me to have to leave for Burgos without any work having been begun on my brother's chapel.[3] And they tell me I am obliged in conscience to have this built. I tell you this so that you will realize that I cannot wait much longer to get the work started.

3. So, do what you can to send me the money, and pray for me, because after Christmas I am going to make that foundation in Burgos—and that region is very cold at this time. If it were close to where you are and I knew I would get to see you, the trip wouldn't bother me at all. But our Lord will arrange that we meet again some day.

4. My health is reasonably good, thanks be to God, for through your prayers and those of all the nuns, the Lord is helping me bear the trials. Teresa[4] sends regards to you and all the sisters.

May His Majesty keep you for me and make you as holy as he can, amen.

From this house in Avila, November twenty-eighth.

Many regards to all the sisters.

Your reverence's servant,
Teresa of Jesus

To Padre Jerónimo Gracián, Salamanca
Avila, November 29, 1581

Teresa had gone to bed at two a.m. and risen with the community at six. She is tired, and she misses those who went with St. John of the Cross to make a foundation in Granada. She had not approved of one of Gracián's choices for Granada. She is also trying to decide which niece to bring to Burgos with her, Teresa (de Cepeda) or Beatriz (de Ovalle), and who to appoint as vicaress at St. Joseph's in her absence. Antonio Ruiz has given her money to send to Gracián—which she is tempted to keep—but St. John of the Cross was unable to give her anything for him.

1. Jesus be with your reverence. Today the nuns left,[1] which was painful for me and leaves me feeling very lonely. The nuns don't feel this way, especially María de Cristo, who is the one who wanted to go most. The plan had already been made public, but the other nun was not suited for this, as you will agree. Nonetheless, I felt very scrupulous since you were the one who told me to send her. Doctor Castro freed me of my scruples.

2. Fray John of the Cross was longing to send you some money and did a good deal of calculating to see if he could give something from what he brought with him for the journey, but he wasn't able to. I think he will get something to send to you.

3. Antonio Ruiz came here three or four days ago and was determined to go with me. He greatly desired to see you, and he is writing to you. He gave me two coins to send you that should be worth about four *escudos*. Of course, I will not send them to you until I have a safe messenger. I am doing all I can not to keep them for myself. The way things are going, it won't be long before I'm tempted to steal them.

4. Inés de Jesús sent me this enclosed letter with others of hers, but the departure will be too soon if it takes place after Christmas. I have already written her that you have to go down there and that they will have to wait. This blessed prioress has to act in such a way because she sees these ladies so filled with ardor. So don't promise to preach there after Advent, for you will have

many occasions to do so here. Doctor Castro wants you to come and spend Christmas at his house, and I too; but few of my desires are fulfilled.

5. Now I believe we cannot fail to bring Teresica,[2] for it seemed a good thing to the learned man I consulted, and she is taking my departure so hard—especially after that of the other sisters—that I think it will be necessary. She is going about a little sad and if some temptation were to assail her while in this state, I don't know what she would do. So it seemed to me well to give her some hope, even though I feel reluctant to do so. Glory to God who wants everything to rain down on me.

6. I am trying hard to see who to leave here in my place,[3] and how well known the desire of Ana de San Pedro[4] was to go. I cannot bear to think of leaving her in charge. It's a terrible thing, because otherwise I think she would do well. Mariana would do well, for she has many talents for the task, if Julián[5] were not in the middle, although he is remaining quite apart for now and not interfering in anything. May God give you light; and when you are here, we will speak about everything.

7. The veil was given yesterday. Mother and daughter are as though mad with joy.[6] It has all tired me very much and I didn't get to bed until two. Those I have designated were the three from here, three from Beas with Anne of Jesus, who goes as prioress, another two from Seville, and two lay sisters from Villanueva who are very good. But the prioress wrote me that it was fitting to send them because they have five lay sisters and it is right to want to help that house in Granada about which so many good things are said. This will not satisfy Anne of Jesus, who likes to direct everything. If it seems all right to you, hold to your decision, for no other better nuns will be found. If not, do as you think best, and remain with God, for I didn't get to bed until two o'clock and then rose early; my head is in bad shape. The rest is going reasonably well.

8. The drawback that now comes to mind is what to do about Teresa if Beatriz needs to be taken with us, for in no way could the two of them come. That would prove a burden, although Teresa would bring me some relief, for she prays well. So, I won't

say anything. But Beatriz must be careful not to be a burden. And in my opinion, it would not be fitting for you to come with Tomasina.[7]

Your reverence's unworthy servant and subject,
Teresa of Jesus

To Doña Catalina de Tolosa, Burgos
Palencia, January 16, 1582

Teresa, who was sixty-seven years old, was on her way from Avila to Burgos. The winter was severe, the roads muddy, and travel slow. She had spent four days in Valladolid and would spend another five in Palencia regaining her strength. Sick with palsy and a serious cold as she writes this, she has been on her way since January 2.

1. Jesus. The grace of the Holy Spirit be with your honor. On our arrival in Valladolid, I arranged for the Mother Prioress there to inform you. I remained there four days because I was not well, for on top of a bad cold, I had a slight attack of palsy. Nonetheless, after improving a little, I departed because I feared making your honor wait, as well as those lords—whose hands I kiss many times. I beg their honors and you as well not to blame me for the delay. If you all knew what the roads were like, you would blame me more for coming. I am also now in pretty bad condition, but I hope in the Lord that this will not prevent me from setting out again shortly if the weather gets a little better. They say that the trip from here to Burgos is an arduous one, and so I don't know if Father Provincial[1] will want to depart until he sees that I am better, even though he is eager to continue the journey. He kisses your hands and has a great desire to meet you. He is very much obliged to pray for you because of all that you do for the order.

2. If it is necessary for you to send us a message, make use of a special messenger, and we will pay the cost here. In matters like this, the cost should not matter much. It could be that if the weather gets better, as it is today, we will leave Friday morning and that a letter sent by ordinary mail will not arrive on time. In case you haven't sent anything or we have already departed, here is how we plan to go.

3. Father Provincial does not want us to fail to see the crucifix[2] in that city, and so they say that before we enter, it is necessary to go there and that from there, or a little before, notify you and go to your house in as hidden a way as possible, and if necessary to wait until nightfall. Then Father Provincial will go to receive the

bishop's blessing so that on the next day the first Mass may be said. You should know that until this is done, it is better that no one knows. This is what I have been almost always doing. Every time I think of how God has done everything, I am amazed and see that it is all the fruit of prayer. May he be ever praised and pleased to watch over you, for he has surely reserved a great reward for you because of your work.

4. I don't think I accomplished a small feat by bringing Asunción[3] with me, considering the resistance to this. She is happy to come, in my opinion. Her sister is well. I have already told you that we will bring her back soon. The prioress here kisses your hands and so too do the nuns accompanying me. We include the five who will remain there and myself and two companions. In sum, there are eight of us traveling. Don't bother about beds, for we can adapt in any arrangement until we get settled. I find that these angels are pleasant and joyful.

5. May God watch over them and give you many years; don't be distressed over my sickness, for I am often like this, and it usually goes away quickly.

Today is the vigil of St. Anthony.

Your honor's unworthy servant,
Teresa of Jesus

To Don Jerónimo Reinoso, Palencia
Burgos, May 20, 1582

The foundation in Burgos had been in existence now a fortnight, but the Jesuits in the city were continuing to oppose it. While Teresa was staying with her nuns in the house of Catalina de Tolosa, they wouldn't come near. Their "despicable interests" were pecuniary, since Catalina de Tolosa, who had previously been a benefactor of the Jesuits, was now a benefactor of Teresa's nuns.

To the illustrious Canon Reinoso, Palencia.

1. Jesus. The grace of the Holy Spirit be with your honor. Whenever I see a letter from you, I feel consoled. And it pains me that I cannot give myself frequently the comfort that comes from writing to you. I know that you realize this, and nonetheless it bothers me not to be able to do more.

2. Through my letter to Father Rector Juan del Aguila,[1] which is enclosed and which Mother Prioress[2] will show you, you will learn something of what is going on with the Society, for it truly seems that a manifest enmity is beginning to take shape. And the devil bases it on accusations of things for which they ought to thank me. Truly serious calumnies are being spread, some of which they themselves are responsible for. It all ends up with these despicable interests that they say I wanted and strove after, and it's a relief that they didn't add "thought about." And since I believe that they wouldn't tell a lie, I see clearly that the devil must have a hand in this muddle.

3. Now they told Catalina de Tolosa[3] that they didn't want her to have anything to do with the discalced nuns lest she be contaminated by our manner of prayer. To the devil it must be very important to promote quarrels between us since he has become so active. They also told her that their general[4] was coming here, that he had already disembarked. I recall that he is a friend of Señor Don Francisco.[5] If he could undo these machinations and establish silence by learning the truth, it would be a great service to God. That people so serious should be engaged in such

childishness is a pity. Would you look into this and in conformity with what you think apply a remedy.

4. Those papers[6] must be really tiring you. I beg you to send them to me, as soon as you find a very safe means, and pray for me to our Lord. May His Majesty watch over you, as I beg of him, amen.

Today is 20 May. I kiss the hands of both Señor Don Francisco and those ladies,[7] your aunts.

Your honor's unworthy servant,
Teresa of Jesus

To Madre Ana de Jesús, Granada
Burgos, May 30, 1582

This has been called "the terrible letter." At the end of November, 1581, St. John of the Cross had gone to Avila to ask Teresa to return to Andalusia and make a foundation in Granada. Although unsuccessful in his attempt to get Teresa to come and make the foundation in Granada, he did return to Andalusia with two nuns from Avila and also one from either Toledo or Malagón. Teresa in the meanwhile had obtained two nuns from Seville and had convinced Anne of Jesus to be the foundress in Granada in her place. Finally, two lay sisters were brought from Villanueva de la Jara. But then Anne of Jesus brought three more nuns from Beas, who had not been a part of Teresa's plan. To make room for these three, the two lay sisters were sent back by Anne to Villanueva. Neither Gracián nor Teresa was being informed of all that was taking place.

---

1. Jesus. May the Holy Spirit be with your reverence. I was amused by the loud complaining of all of you about our Father Provincial[1] and your neglect to keep him informed after the first letter in which you told him that you had made the foundation. And you all acted in the same way with me.

2. Father Provincial was here on the day of the Cross,[2] and he didn't know anything more than what I told him, which came through a letter that the prioress in Seville sent me, in which she said that you bought a house for 12,000 ducats. Where there was so much prosperity, it is not surprising that the patent letters were strictly worded. But down there you're so crafty at not obeying that this latest fact pained me in no small way because of the bad impression it will make in the whole order and also because of the custom that may result by which prioresses will feel independent and will also think up excuses. And since you esteem your hosts[3] so highly, it has been a great indiscretion to stay there with so many nuns. You sent back those poor nuns as soon as they arrived, making them retrace so many leagues—I don't know how you had the heart to do this. Those who came from Beas could have returned there and others with them. It was terribly impolite to stay in that house with so many—especially

knowing that you were a bother; and inconsiderate to bring so many from Beas knowing that you did not have your own house. Certainly I am amazed at the patience of your hosts. Mistakes were made from the beginning, and since you have no other solution than the one you mention, it will be good for you to try it before you end up with greater scandal, seeing that you hold that it would be scandalous to allow one more sister to enter the community. For so large a city this seems a trifle to me.

3. I laughed to myself over the fear you wished to create in us that the archbishop[4] will suppress the monastery. He no longer has anything to do with it; I don't know why you give him such a large role to play. He would die before succeeding. And if the monastery should continue, as is now the case, by introducing into the order principles that show little obedience, it would be much better if it didn't last. Our worth will not come from having many monasteries but in having nuns in them who are saints.

4. I don't know when these letters that have now come for our *padre* can be given to him. I fear that he won't be here for another month and a half, and then I don't know where I can be certain in sending them. He went to Soria from here and from there to many places on visitations. Nothing is known for certain where he will be or when we will have news of him. As I figure it, he will be in Villanueva when the poor nuns arrive. It's very painful for me to think of what he will have to go through when they arrive, and the gossip. The place is so small that nothing is secret, and much harm will be done at the sight of such foolishness. They could have been sent to Beas until informing him. They didn't even have a license to return there for he had already officially made them conventuals in Granada, and they were returning right under his eyes. There must have been some way in which the matter could have been remedied, so the fault is all yours for not having mentioned the number of nuns you were bringing from Beas and whether you included any lay sister. You paid no more heed to our *padre* than you would have if he hadn't received the office of superior.

5. From what he has told me and considering what he has to do, it will be impossible for him to go there before winter. Please God, Father Vicar Provincial will be able to do it, for they just gave me some letters from Seville, and the prioress writes me

that he is struck down by the plague that's afflicting them there—although it's being kept secret—and Fray Bartolomé de Jesús[5] also, which saddened me very much. If you haven't learned of this, pray for them; losing them would mean a great loss for the order. On the envelope of the letter someone wrote that Father Vicar is better, although not out of danger. The nuns are very tired and understandably, since they are martyrs in that house and undergo many more trials than you—although they don't complain as much. Where the nuns are healthy and there is food to eat, being a little crowded won't kill them, especially where they have the support of many sermons. I don't know what the complaining is about, for everything doesn't have to be in perfect shape.

6. Madre Beatriz de Jesús[6] tells Father Provincial that they are waiting for Father Vicar to send the nuns from Beas and Seville back to their houses. The nuns in Seville do not agree with this idea. Besides, Seville is very far and in no way would this be proper. If the need is so great, our *padre* will see to the matter. Regarding those from Beas, it would be indeed the right thing to do. If it were not for my fear of contributing to an offense against God through disobedience, I would send you an explicit order, for in all that regards the discalced nuns I stand in the place of our Father Provincial.

7. In virtue of this authority I tell you and order you that as soon as it can be arranged you send back the nuns that came there from Beas with the exception of Mother Prioress, Anne of Jesus. And this should be done even if you have moved into your own house; at least if you have not a good income that will free you from the straits you're now in. For no reason is it good to have so many nuns living together at the beginning of a foundation, whereas this may be appropriate in other situations.

8. I have prayed to our Lord over this matter during these days—for I didn't want to answer the letters at once—and I find that by your doing things this way, His Majesty will be served, and the more you suffer from this the more you will serve him. For any kind of attachment, even to the superior, is very foreign to the spirit of discalced nuns, nor would they ever grow spiritually in this way. God wants his brides to be free, attached only to him; and I don't want them to begin acting in this house as they did

in Beas. I never forget the letter they wrote me from there when you left office, for a calced nun would not even have written it. This is how cliques begin and many other unfortunate things, although they may not be recognized at the beginning. And for this time, don't follow any opinion but mine, for heaven's sake. For once things are settled and the sisters more detached, they can return if it is fitting.

9. I truly don't know who they are who went, for you kept it really secret from me and from our *padre*, nor did I think you would take so many nuns from there, but I imagine they are very attached to you. Oh, true spirit of obedience, how when seeing someone in the place of God no repugnance is felt toward loving her! For the sake of God I beg you to take care to inspire souls to be brides of the Crucified, that they crucify themselves by renouncing their own will and the pursuit of childish trifles. Look, this is the beginning in a new kingdom, and you and the other nuns are more obliged to behave as valiant men and not as worthless little women.

10. What is this, *madre mía*, that you are paying attention to whether Father Provincial calls you presider, or prioress, or Anne of Jesus?[7] It is clear that if you were not in charge, he wouldn't have reason to give you a title above the others, for they have also been prioresses. You have given him so little news of what is taking place that he doesn't know whether elections have been held or not. Certainly, I am ashamed that in so short a time the discalced nuns are paying attention to these trivialities, and after paying attention to them, making them the topic of their conversations, and that Madre María de Cristo makes such an issue out of it. Either through trials you have all become silly or the devil has introduced hellish notions into this order. And after this she praises you as being very courageous as though acting differently would mean you were not. God desires my discalced nuns to be very humble, obedient, and submissive, for all these other kinds of courage mark the beginning of many imperfections without these virtues.

11. Now I recall that in one of your previous letters you wrote that one of the nuns had relatives there who would be helpful if brought with you from Beas. If this is so, I leave it to the prioress to make the decision, but not the others.

12. I truly believe that you will have many sufferings in the beginning. Do not be surprised, for a work as great as this cannot be done without them since, as they say, the recompense will be great. Please God that the imperfections with which I am doing this do not deserve more punishment than reward, for I always have this fear. I am writing to the prioress of Beas to help with the expenses of the journey. You are so short of means there! I assure you that if Avila were closer, I would be very happy to take back my sisters. That could happen with the passing of time and the help of the Lord. So you can say that once the foundation is made and there is no longer a need there, because nuns will be entering from that area, they may return to the houses from which they came.

13. A little while ago I wrote at length to you and to those *madres*, and to Padre Fray John,[8] and gave you an account of what has been taking place here, and so it seems that I need to write nothing further than what is in that letter, which was meant for everyone. Please God, things being as they are, you will not be offended as when our *padre* called you "presider." Until we had an election here, when our *padre* came, this is the term we used, and not "prioress," and it's all the same.

14. Each time I forget to mention this. They told me that in Beas even after the chapter, the nuns were leaving the enclosure to clean the church. I don't know how they can do that since not even the provincial can give permission for this. The prohibition comes from the pope's *motu proprio*,[9] with severe threats of excommunication, not to speak of the strict prescription of our constitutions. At the beginning this was difficult for us; now we are delighted with it. The sisters in Avila know well that they cannot even go out to lock the door that opens onto the street. I don't know why you were not informed of this. You should take care of this matter, for goodness' sake. God will provide someone to clean the church and there is a solution to everything . . .

15. Every time I think of the crowded conditions in which you have placed your noble hosts, I cannot help but feel bad. I already wrote the other day that you should get a house even if it is not very good or suitable, for you will not be as crowded as you are now, and even if you are it is better that you suffer than to make those who have been so good to you suffer. I am now writing

to Señora Doña Ana,[10] and I would like to have words to thank her for the good she has done us. She will not lose anything with our Lord, which is what matters.

16. If you want something from our *padre*, remember that you have not written to him. For, as I say, it will be late before I can send him letters. I will try. From Villanueva he will be going to Daimiel to receive that monastery, and to Malagón and Toledo; then to Salamanca and Alba, for the elections of I don't know how many prioresses. He told me that he didn't plan to be in Toledo until August. It distresses me to see him have to do so much traveling in places where the weather is so hot. All of you pray for him and try as much as you can to get your own house . . .

17. The sisters could stay there until you have notified the provincial and he decides what the best thing to do might be, for you haven't kept him abreast of anything or written him to tell him the reason you are not taking those nuns.

May God give us light—for without that, there is little one can be sure of—and watch over your reverence, amen.

Today is the thirtieth of May.

Your reverence's servant,
Teresa of Jesus

18. I am writing to Mother Prioress in Beas about the departure of those nuns and that this should be done with as much secrecy as possible. When it comes to be known, it won't matter. Let Mother Subprioress,[11] her two companions, and Padre Fray John of the Cross read this letter addressed to you, for I don't have the head to be writing more.

To Doña Catalina de Tolosa, Burgos
Palencia, August 3, 1582

Although there is mention of the difficulties that Doña Catalina and the Carmelites were having with the Jesuits, the impairment done to the text makes it difficult to read the details of what is being said. Understandably, Teresa shows special interest in Catalina's children.

1. Jesus. May the Holy Spirit be with your honor. I looked at the address and I am grateful that in responding you removed the title "illustrious." I tell you that the nuns and I were very pleased with *mi Lesmes*.[1] May God watch over him and make him a saint. Those two little angels[2] bring me joy. I have asked Maruca to help me pray. She is the portress and does everything well. They both want to see you, just as I do too.

2. May the Lord hear our prayer and repay you for the favor you showed me with your letter, for I was afraid about the condition of your health. I am already desiring to see another letter with news that Beatriz[3] is improving. May God bring this about. The letters I brought still haven't been delivered because I am waiting . . .

What they did wasn't a sufficient reason for giving up all communication with them, even if during a novena that you had in the house, you didn't see any of them present. I mentioned what a bad impression that made in the city. I am taking great care to deliver the letters as soon as possible.[4] Please God no one will send them elsewhere. Tell this to Isabel de Trazanos[5] and give her my regards.

3. You should know that the abbess of Santa Dorotea[6] gave me two ducats without knowing . . .

Remain with God, for I have much to do. . . . My throat is better. I don't know how long this will last.

Today is Friday.

Your honor's servant,
Teresa of Jesus

To Madre Catalina de Cristo, Soria
Valladolid-Medina, September 15–17, 1582

Here Teresa answers various letters from the prioress in Soria, who had presented her with a number of questions concerning the location of the kitchen and refectory; the good conduct of the novices; dealings with the Jesuits; the transfer of a nun to the Carmel in Palencia; and a doubt over possibly delaying profession for the novices. Teresa was about to continue her travels and was very busy. She began the letter in Valladolid and finished it in Medina.

---

1. Jesus be with your reverence, my daughter, and watch over you for me. I received your letters and much happiness along with them. In what regards the kitchen and refectory,[1] I would be delighted if you did so, but you who are there can make the best decision as to the arrangement. Work things out as you wish.

2. I am glad that Roque de Huerta's daughter[2] is pleasant. As regards the profession of the sister[3] you mentioned, I think it is good that it be delayed until when you say, for she's young and it doesn't matter. Don't be surprised if she experiences some setbacks, for at her age these don't amount to much. They happen, but afterward these persons are usually more mortified than others.

3. Tell Sister Leonor de la Misericordia that I would like to do for her what she asks and even more. Would that I could attend her profession. I would do so gladly and it would please me much more than a lot of other things I have to do here . . . may God bring this about, if it be for his service.

4. Regarding the foundation, I will not decide to make it unless there is some income, for I see already so little devotion there that we need to proceed in such a way. And the place is so far from all our other houses that a foundation ought not be made if the community is not provided for. Here one community helps another when it sees there is need. It is good to begin in this way and that you come to know and find devoted people. If the work is desired by God, he will move these persons to do more than is being done at present.

5. I will be only a short time in Avila because I cannot neglect going to Salamanca,[4] and you can write to me there. But if the foundation is made in Madrid[5]—and I am hoping for this—I would prefer to go there since it is closer to us here. Pray for this intention.

6. Regarding that nun about whom you write, if she should want to go to Palencia, I would be delighted, for they need someone in that house. I am writing to Madre Inés de Jesús so that you and she can come to an agreement about it. As for the Theatines,[6] I am happy you are doing what you can with them, for this is necessary, and the good or the bad, and the graciousness we show them . . .

7. Tell Señora Doña Beatriz[7] for me all the things you think would be suitable. I would so like to write to her, but we are about to leave, and I have so many matters to attend to that I don't know where I'm at. May God be served by it all, amen.

8. Do not think that when I mentioned delaying the profession I was giving preference to one novice over the other, for these are worldly considerations that offend me very much, and I wouldn't want you to be looking at things like that. But it is because she is young that I am glad for a delay and so that she may practice more mortification. And if some other interpretation for this delay were made, I would give orders to have the profession at once. For it is good for the humility we profess to be evident in our deeds. I had given precedence to the other knowing that in her humility Sister Leonor de la Misericordia doesn't pay any attention to these worldly points of honor. And this being so, I am truly happy that this child is waiting a little longer before her profession.

9. I cannot enlarge any more, for we are about to leave for Medina. I'm feeling as usual. My companions send you their regards. It wasn't long ago that Anne wrote you the news from here. My best regards to all the sisters. May God make them saints, and you along with them.

Valladolid, the fifteenth of September.

Your reverence's servant,
Teresa of Jesus

10. We are now in Medina and so busy that I cannot say more than that the trip went well. The deferring of Isabel's profession must be done with discretion so that it is not thought that anyone is of higher status, for that is not the main purpose of the delay.

Short Biographies

Ahumada, Juana de (b. 1528). Younger than Teresa by thirteen years, Teresa's sister Juana was also the youngest in the family. When their father died, Teresa took her to live with her at the Incarnation, since there was ample room in her cell, which was really a suite of rooms. For about nine years she was provided for by her sister with much love. Juana married Juan de Ovalle in 1553. She and her husband helped Teresa with the first foundation in Avila as is explained in *The Book of Her Life* (33.11). Her marriage to Juan de Ovalle, nonetheless, resulted in much suffering for her because of his childish and jealous disposition. Three of their five children died in infancy.

Alvarez, Baltasar (1533–1580). Born in Cervera del Rio (Logroño), he entered the Jesuits in 1555 after graduating from Alcalá. He was twenty-six and only one year ordained when he became Teresa's confessor in Avila. He carried out this ministry between 1559 and 1565, a crucial stage in Teresa's spiritual journey. During this time, Teresa began to experience her visions, revelations, and woundings of love. Timid in temperament and easily influenced by those around him, he suffered hesitations and doubts, which were a long time in dissipating entirely. Although he tried to assure Teresa, she could clearly see that he was nervous and apprehensive about her. Neither was he much help to her in the midst of all the troubles she had from her superiors and the townspeople at the time of her first foundation. But during the years he was directing Teresa, he was undergoing problems of his own, scruples, doubts, and fears about his spiritual life, prayer, and ability to direct others. Despite his wavering, Teresa thought of him as a saint and one of her best friends.

In 1565, he was transferred to Medina del Campo as novice master. In 1573, the provincial of Castile, together with Martin Gutiérrez and Juan Suárez, was captured by the Huguenots in the south of France and tortured. Martin Gutiérrez died as a result. Baltasar Alvarez had been left as vice-provincial in Castile, and was forced into frantic efforts to collect 18,000 ducats as ransom money. He was weighed down with worries over the debts incurred. The new general in Rome appointed Juan Suárez as provincial for Castile, and Baltasar Alvarez as rector in Salamanca. Alvarez's arrival in Salamanca filled the Carmelite nuns with hope because they admired his spiritual discernment. But to the great disappointment of Teresa, the provincial Juan Suárez, whom Alvarez had succeeded in ransoming from the Huguenots, paid heed to the accusation that Alvarez was devoting too much care to the nuns in hearing their confessions and began to take action against him. He objected that Alvarez's form of prayer ("learned through his dealings with Madre Teresa and her nuns, in which space is given for the action of God") was suspect. Because of the *alumbrados,* the times were precarious for anyone speaking of quiet in prayer. Later, in his visitation in 1577, Diego de Avellaneda would give the coup de grace, when he ordained that "they [the Jesuits] should not waste time on women, especially Carmelite nuns, either in visits or letters," but "gently and efficaciously" get away from them. The decision was a great sorrow for Teresa.

But Baltasar Alvarez remained her friend until he died. After many other administrative posts, he became provincial of Toledo. He continued throughout his life to support Teresa in her founding new monasteries. While he was in Medina, he began himself to experience infused prayer. But his new mode of prayer gave rise to worries on the part of his superiors. They considered it to be dangerous and foreign to the Spiritual Exercises of St. Ignatius of Loyola. They forbade him to continue with this kind of prayer, and he submitted. Although eighteen years younger than Teresa, he died before her at the age of forty-seven. When word reached her of his death, she wept for over an hour and no one could console her. When asked why she was weeping that much since she was so detached from the things of the world, she replied: "I am weeping because I know what a great loss this is to the Church of God;" and she then went into a rapture for two hours.

Ambrosio Mariano de San Benito (Azzaro) (1510–1594). Born in Bitonto, Italy, he was descended from a noble Neapolitan family and gifted with a high intelligence. In his youth he dedicated himself to intense study, receiving a doctorate in both theology and canon law. Backed by these degrees and his recent studies, he took part in the Council of Trent, where he received important commissions to carry out in certain countries in northern Europe. He met with success in these endeavors and won for himself an element of renown. Invited by Queen Catherine of Austria, the wife of Sigismund II of Poland, to serve as major domo in her palace, Ambrosio felt actually as though in a prison, and he resigned and joined the military. He was later falsely accused of homicide but refused to defend himself, spending two years in prison until ultimately his innocence was acknowledged. Being informed about his extraordinary knowledge in geometry and hydraulics, Philip II employed him in an engineering project. While in Seville, Ambrosio felt touched by a special grace and decided to renounce the world and withdraw into solitude in Tardó, an isolated spot in the Sierra Morena, where a group of hermits were living a life of extraordinary austerity and penance under the direction of Mateo de la Fuente. He lived there for eight years. In 1568, he was called by Philip II to Aranjuez to direct the construction of a large irrigation canal. After finishing this project, he went to Madrid and received hospitality there in the palace of Doña Leonor Mascareñas. At this time, in June 1569, he met Teresa.

It was a providential and decisive meeting for the hermit. Teresa invited him to join her, showing him the constitutions that she had written for her nuns. In the morning of the following day, he informed Teresa that he had decided to embrace her reform. What is more, because of the decree of Pius V, which obliged solitaries to enter orders already established, he had been planning to go to Rome with his companion, Juan Narduch, to obtain from the Holy Father the authorization to live an eremitical life in a solitary place. Coincidentally, Teresa was on her way there to make a foundation of her nuns. One month later, Mariano received the habit of the discalced Carmelite friars and inaugurated the life of the reform there along with Juan de la Miseria and Baltasar de Jesús Nieto. He made his profession the following year, and in 1574, at the urging of Gracián, he was ordained a priest. But he could never detach himself from engineering. As one chronicler put it, he preferred construction to hearing confessions. An admirer of the extraordinary woman penitent, Catalina de Cardona, about whom Teresa wrote a detailed account, he assisted her in her desire to have a monastery of discalced Carmelite friars near her cave in La Roda. Following his inclination to mine under mountains and live underground, he made a passageway so that Catalina could walk in her cave untroubled by cold or heat, with openings for light at intervals. This undertaking depleted funds that had been raised to build a monastery for the friars, and in the end the extensive underground digging weakened the foundations of the friars' monastery, and it collapsed.

He did render important services to both Teresa and Gracián, but because of his impulsiveness and rough manner he caused them suffering as well. Teresa pleaded with him to use discretion and moderation and to be more submissive and respectful toward the general's wishes. In his fascination with the penitential life of Catalina de Cardona, he pushed for austerity within the order. At the chapter of Alcalá, in which the discalced Carmelites became a separate province and were able to elect their own provincial, Ambrosio Mariano supported Antonio de Jesús (Heredia) for provincial, as did some other admirers of Catalina de Cardona. Teresa, of course, strongly favored Gracián, whose ideals for the friars were more like her own, and she grew impatient with Mariano. Fortunately for both friars and nuns, Gracián was elected, but by a margin of only one vote. Mariano next founded a monastery for the friars in Lisbon in 1581, but a year later, a little before Teresa's death, he was called by Philip II to Seville for another construction project. In 1588 and 1590 he was elected to be second councillor to the vicar general, Nicolás Doria. He died in Madrid while serving as prior of the monastery there.

Ana de la Encarnación (Tapia) (d. 1601). A cousin of Teresa's, she was a nun at the Incarnation and went with Teresa on the foundation in Medina del Campo (1567). There her sister, Inés de Jesús, became prioress and she subprioress. In 1570 she went with Teresa on the foundation in Salamanca and became prioress there. In the beginning she had to bear with the constant displeasure of Pedro de la Banda, the owner of the house in which the foundation was made. She remained in Salamanca and was prioress there for many years.

Anne of Jesus (Ana de Jesús Lobera) (1545–1621). Born in Medina del Campo, she entered St. Joseph's in Avila, but made her profession in Salamanca on October 22, 1571. Teresa brought Anne with her to be prioress for the new foundation in Beas in 1575. In 1582, Anne traveled to Granada, accompanied by St. John of the Cross, to make a foundation for nuns there. It was to her that John dedicated his commentary on *The Spiritual Canticle*. In 1586, after Teresa's death, again accompanied by John of the Cross, she made a foundation in Madrid. While prioress there, she enlisted the help of Luis de León to serve as editor for the publication of the works of St. Teresa, which appeared in 1588. Falling into disfavor with Nicolás Doria, the vicar general of the discalced friars and nuns, for having obtained a brief from Sixtus V stating that no one has authority to change or modify the nuns' constitutions (given in Alcalá a year before Teresa's death), Anne was deposed as prioress in Madrid. After Doria died, she was elected prioress in Salamanca in 1596. At the head of five Carmelite nuns from Spain, and in response to the urgent appeals of Pierre de Bérulle, she made a foundation in Paris in 1604. Accompanying Blessed Anne of St. Bartholomew on the foundation in Pontoise in 1605, she some months later made a foundation in Dijon. But noting that Bérulle held firmly to his jurisdiction over the discalced Carmelite nuns in France and was determined to direct them in accord with his own plans, she went to the Spanish Netherlands at the beginning of 1607. Under the jurisdiction of the discalced Carmelite friars, she made foundations in Brussels, Louvain, and Mons. In 1614, she was struck down by illness and for eight years underwent painful bodily sufferings: sore throats, pleurisy, sciatica, paralyses, dropsy, tumors, and burning throughout her entire body. She died in Brussels. The cause for her beatification was introduced shortly after her death, but did not advance.

Banda, Pedro de la. The house in Salamanca where the nuns first established themselves was near both a river and the city reservoir. Because of this and the poor condition of the house itself, the health of the community eventually suffered. The nuns found another house owned by Pedro de la Banda, who was described by the chronicler as ill mannered. The house was from an entailed estate and could not be sold without a royal license. However, the vendor gave his word that the nuns could have it even if the license was not given and that they could do their renovations. Pressured to leave the unhealthy house in which they were living, Teresa moved quickly. The little community spent all they had (over 1,000 ducats) turning this new house into a monastery, complete with cloister, cells, refectory, and chapel. She paid for all of this from the dowries of the nuns who had already entered. But after they had moved in, Don Pedro, who had been away, returned and was furious for what they had done to the house. Teresa decided to let go of the house, but he didn't want that either. What he, or rather his wife, Aldonza Ruiz Maldonado, wanted was money to provide for two daughters. The contract had not required payment of this money until the king's license arrived and was warranted. Don Pedro resorted to a lawsuit, claiming that the contract was null and void for lack of the royal license. Writing about this three years after the event, Teresa remarked that the purchase had not yet been finalized. In fact it took forty-four years, during which the nuns were twice evicted, before the matter was settled.

Báñez, Domingo (1528–1604). Born in Valladolid, he began his studies in Salamanca in 1543 and entered the Dominicans there (San Esteban) in 1546, making his religious profession a year later. He remained in Salamanca, studying philosophy and theology and then teaching these subjects for ten years. In 1561 he was transferred to Santo Tomás in Avila as professor until 1567. During a part of this time in Avila, he was confessor to Teresa and the nuns at St. Joseph's. He fearlessly defended Teresa and her work before the irate city council of Avila. He took his doctor's degree in the University of Siguenza and became professor of theology at Alcalá. In 1573–1577 he was rector at St. Gregory's in Valladolid, then returned to Salamanca as professor. In 1577 he won the chair of Prime at Salamanca University, which he held until 1604. He was a preacher and theologian with great prestige, becoming famous for his debates with the Jesuits over the complex question of predestination and free will. According to witnesses, he always had great admiration and respect for Teresa. As official censor for the Inquisition, he was given the task of examining Teresa's *Book of Her Life*, which had been denounced to that body by the Princess of Eboli. He gave the work his approval and defended Teresa's spirit, also pointing out, however, that the work should be kept secret. After Teresa's death, he published in 1584 his magisterial work of theology, a commentary on the *Summa* of St. Thomas Aquinas. In 1590, he wrote to Nicolás Doria about a controversy that was taking place concerning St. Teresa's constitutions. Since the problem had originated with Anne of Jesus and the nuns at Santa Ana in Madrid, he wrote to Doria, urging him to refrain from any kind of ruthless punishment of the discalced nuns, especially the community at Santa Ana. Báñez died in Medina del Campo.

Braganza, Teutonio de (1530–1602). Son of the Duke of Braganza, Don Teutonio did his studies in Coimbra and Paris. He entered the Society of Jesus in 1549 but later left after a disagreement with St. Ignatius over the removal of Simón Rodríguez, provincial of Portugal. Teresa met him in Salamanca in 1574, and they remained friends for the rest of her life. But he was not as skilled as necessary in carrying out some of the favors Teresa wanted of him. Such was the case with the college for her discalced friars that Teresa wanted in Salamanca. In 1578 he was appointed Archbishop of Evora. In his zeal he committed large sums of money to foundations for works of charity and religion. An author of many works, he also helped in the publication of others including St. Teresa's *Way of Perfection*, printed at his expense in 1583.

Castro y Nero, Pedro. Born in Ampudia (Palencia) in 1541, he was a companion in studies with Jerónimo Gracián in Alcalá and taught philosophy at the University of Salamanca. He later became a canon of the cathedral in Avila, where he first came to know Teresa. Teresa had given him a copy of her *Life* to read, and in a note she had received from him, he revealed the powerful impact the book had on him. She responds with much feeling and begs him to come to see her the following day: "How great the mercy of God, that through my wickedness you should benefit. . . . I would rather not say more on paper, and so I beg you to come to see me tomorrow, the eve of the Presentation, that I might present to you a soul often undone, so that you might bring about all that you understand as fitting for her in order that she please God" (see November 19, 1581). He was later made Bishop of Lugo and then of Segovia, where he died in 1611.

Cepeda, Lorenzo de (1519–1580). Lorenzo, especially after his return from America, was the brother who helped Teresa most and remained closest to her. In fact, she became his spiritual director. Only nineteen when he left for America, he took part with his brothers Hernando, Jerónimo, Antonio, and perhaps Rodrigo in the battle of Añaquito in 1546, fighting on the side of Charles V. In that encounter Antonio died and Lorenzo was seriously wounded. In 1556 he married a wealthy young girl from the nobility, Juana de Fuentes y Espinosa. Holding important offices in Quito, even that of mayor, he turned out to be financially successful. When his wife died in 1567, she left Lorenzo with four living children out of the seven that were born. Later, with the education of his children in mind, Lorenzo decided to return to Spain. He had spent thirty-four years in the work of conquest and pacification of the Indies. He had engaged in the struggle in company with the viceroy, Blasco Nuñez Vela, against Gonzalo Pizarro. Later, after Vela had been killed, he accompanied the priest Pedro de la Gasca from his entry into Peru until he waged battle against Pizarro. When he was chief magistrate in the cities of Loxa and Zamora, Lorenzo had come to the aid of the cities of Loyola and Vallid under siege by the Indians. Having left Panama in May, the Cepedas arrived in Spain in August 1575. Great was his surprise when Lorenzo learned that his sister Teresa was in Seville. He then traveled from Seville to Madrid to make a claim that his remuneration had been insufficient and begged that "he might receive more, according to his many and good services, and his quality; and as he had three small children to be brought up in virtue and good customs, he asked to be excused from returning to that land, while still enjoying the income from his holdings there." But his efforts failed and he returned to Seville sick and discouraged. In March 1576, Pedro left with Lorenzo's two nephews and Teresa's brother-in-law, Juan de Ovalle, for Avila. In June, Teresa, together with Lorenzo and his daughter Teresita, Gregorio Nacianceno, and Antonio Ruiz, left for Malagón on the way to Toledo. Since Teresa had to remain in Toledo for a longer time, Lorenzo departed with Teresita for Avila. Shortly afterward, he enrolled his two sons in the College of San Gil, operated by the Jesuits. In October he bought a piece of farmland and woods six kilometers southeast of Avila in a place called La Serna. Retiring there with his brother Pedro to devote his final years to the care of the land and a life of prayer, Lorenzo tried to follow a daily schedule similar to that of the Carmelites. He sought spiritual direction from Teresa for his life of prayer and also from St. John of the Cross. Becoming one of the victims of the devastating influenza that ravaged Spain in 1580, he died at La Serna in June. After Lorenzo had returned from America, Teresa kept up a correspondence with him in which he sought her counsel and she sought his. He was a generous benefactor of Teresa's, helping her with her foundation in Avila and later with the foundation in Seville and with other projects.

Cerda, Luisa de la (d. 1596). Daughter of the second Duke of Medinaceli, Luisa de la Cerda in 1537 married Antonio Arias Pardo de Saavedra, nephew of Cardinal Pardo de Tavera and one of the wealthiest and most titled men in Castile. His death left his wife so afflicted that the family began to fear for her. Finally, after many other failed attempts to comfort her, the family asked the provincial of the Carmelites to allow Teresa to stay with her in her palace in Toledo. Teresa remained with her for about six months and was able to help free her from the bonds of her affliction, frequent the sacraments, and practice good works. While living in the palace, Teresa was able to observe that nobility and wealth did not free one from the slavery of many human passions. In 1567 Luisa offered to fund a foundation in Malagón if the nuns would pray for her deceased husband. The house that the nuns rented there was poor and inadequate for their needs. Finally, on her return from Seville, Teresa insisted that Luisa build them a new monastery, which she had promised to do. The new monastery, the only one of Teresa's houses that was not an adaptation of some already existing house, was built according to Teresa's own specifications and still exists as a Carmel today, as do all of Teresa's foundations. When the foundation of nuns in Toledo was made, Luisa gave them hospitality in her home while they tried to find a house for themselves. They were very poor and met with serious difficulties, but it doesn't seem that Luisa did anything to help them. Teresa wrote in her *Foundations*, "It will seem impossible that though we had stayed in the house of that lady who loved me so much, we had to enter the new foundation in so much poverty" (15.13). Nonetheless, Teresa continued on good terms with Doña Luisa, sending her little gifts, but also feeling free to ask her for favors when she needed help for herself or someone else. Among these favors was the task Doña Luisa undertook to deliver the precious secret manuscript of Teresa's *Life* to St. John of Avila.

Dávila y Toledo, Sancho. A priest and theologian friend of Teresa's. He studied in Salamanca, taught there, and was at various times rector there. In a letter to Teresa he sought her guidance over some problems with his interior life. After giving him guidance, Teresa sought his help for a problem that caused her much pain. Some calumnies were being spoken against her niece Beatriz; and greatly distressed about it, she sought his assistance. He had written a biography of his own mother, who had died two years before in the odor of sanctity, and which Teresa had expressed a desire to read. He died in 1625.

Daza, Gaspar (d. 1592). This devout and learned priest was one of the first to receive from Teresa an account of her spiritual experiences and remained her friend throughout her life. However, despite his good intentions, his attempts at directing Teresa, as she explains in her *Life*, only caused her greater fears, especially of the devil. At this time in her life, Daza was not the spiritual director she needed. He thought she could change herself according to his directives. Blessed Anne of St. Bartholomew later reported also that he was incredulous when it came to revelations. Daza was the one commissioned by the bishop to give the habit to the first four discalced Carmelite nuns, establish the enclosure, and reserve the Blessed Sacrament in their little chapel in St. Joseph's on August 24, 1562. He was Julián of Avila's confessor and spiritual director. In the absence of Teresa, who in the beginning was not allowed to live in the new community, he took charge of directing the first novices and giving them the veil. At the time that the Bishop of Avila was appointed to Palencia, Teresa wrote and asked the bishop with wonderful courtesy and tact that he give Gaspar Daza a canonry or some other benefice. Daza, at his own expense, had a side chapel constructed in the chapel of St. Joseph's in Avila that was built after Teresa's death. He died in 1592 and is buried in the floor of this chapel close to the tomb of Julián de Avila.

Enríquez, Ana. A friend of Teresa's and collaborator with her on several foundations. She knew many of Teresa's friends: María de Mendoza and the bishop, Don Alvaro; Dona Guiomar, Baltasar Alvarez, and Domingo Báñez. Together with Doña Guiomar they had planned a foundation in Zamora. She sent a statue for the foundation in Palencia for which Teresa thanks her: "You have honored us greatly with the statue you donated, which stands alone on the main altar, and it is so well done and large that there is no need for others."

Gaytán, Antonio. When Teresa began to have dealings with him in Alba de Tormes in 1573, he was already a widower and enjoyed a life free from financial worry. Teresa thought highly of him, as is clear from what she reports in her *Foundations* (21.6). Through his friendship with Teresa, he became a fervent Christian. In 1574, he accompanied her on the foundation in Segovia. She also entrusted to him the secret and demanding mission of leading fourteen nuns in their escape from Pastrana and the Princess of Eboli to Segovia. In 1575, he accompanied Teresa on her journey to Beas. While she was there, she sent him and Julián de Avila to Caravaca to negotiate for a foundation there. It proved a long, tedious journey for the two in bad weather and on miserable roads. As is evident from Teresa's letters, he approached her as a spiritual director and sought her advice. In the summer of 1577, he asked her if the nuns in Alba de Tormes would receive his daughter, who was still a child only seven years old, as she had done in the case of her niece Teresita and Gracián's little sister, Isabelita. He promised to pay for her sustenance and also a special dowry. Recommending the idea to Gracián, Teresa asked for his permission. She wrote: "I tell you these little angels edify us and are refreshing. With no more than one in each house, I don't see any obstacle but a benefit." At the beginning of 1581, Antonio Gaytán married again. Under the influence of his new wife, it seems, he became remiss in sending what he had promised for the sustenance of his daughter, and the nuns began to fear they would not receive the dowry he had promised to give when the time for her profession came. In 1581 Teresa had to write and urge him to keep his commitments to the nuns. It seems that in the end he took care of the matter. His daughter, taking the name Mariana de Jesús, made her profession in 1585, and later in Tarazona became novice mistress, subprioress, and prioress. After the death of Teresa, no more mention is made in the chronicles of Antonio Gaytán.

Huerta, Roque de. Teresa's friend and collaborator from Madrid, starting in 1577, Huerta was the chief forest guard in the nation, but he fulfilled other charges as well in the court in Madrid. It was through Jerónimo Gracián that Teresa came to know him and become his friend. In the beginning he was the means by which Teresa was able to send letters to Gracián. But he went on to serve Gracián, the discalced Carmelites, and Teresa, not only in delivering mail, but in many other confidential or delicate matters. He kept Teresa informed of decisions made by the nuncio Filippo Sega and, for example, sent her a copy of the royal ordinance favoring Gracián and his visitations. Teresa in her turn kept him informed, positively and negatively, of how matters were proceeding with the discalced Carmelites. She sent him a long letter about the unfortunate second chapter at Almodóvar (see October 24, 1578). This letter shows how much Roque had won Teresa's total confidence. In 1581, his daughter María, a young girl of only fifteen, entered the Carmel of Soria and took the name María de la Purificación. Teresa gave her the habit on the eve of her departure for Soria. Teresa alludes to both father and daughter in her last letter, a few days before her death: "I am glad that Roque de Huerta's daughter is pleasant." Roque de Huerta has left us sixteen letters from Teresa, more than we have from any other of her secular friends.

Inés de Jesús (Tapia) (d. 1601). She and her sister, Ana de la Encarnación, were Teresa's cousins and belonged to the community of the Incarnation in Avila. She helped Teresa in the foundation of St. Joseph's in Avila and was present when the first four discalced nuns received the habit. Accompanying Teresa on the foundation in Medina del Campo, she was named prioress of that new community, but remained a calced nun. At one point she was removed from her office of prioress and sent to the new foundation in Alba de Tormes, but subsequently she returned to her post in Medina. Not until 1581 did she renounce the mitigated rule and become a discalced Carmelite. In that same year, she joined Teresa for the foundation in Palencia, where she was elected prioress. In 1588, she went on the foundation in Zaragosa, later returning again to Medina. She died on the same day as her sister Ana, April 22, 1601. Teresa was particularly attached to her and placed great confidence in her. Her remains are buried next to those of St. John of the Cross's mother (Catalina Alvarez) in Medina del Campo.

Jerónimo de la Madre de Dios (Gracián) (1545–1614). Although Gracián was not the first discalced Carmelite friar, Teresa saw him as ideal, one sent by God just at the right moment for the renewal of the observance of the primitive rule. He represented for her both its salvation and the future of the discalced friars. Born in Valladolid, he was one of the twenty offspring of Diego Gracián Alderete and Juana Dantisco. His father was secretary for both the emperor Charles V and the king Philip II. His grandfather on his mother's side, Juan Dantisco, was ambassador to the Spanish court for Sigismund I of Poland. Jerónimo Gracián began his studies at age six with private tutors. When he was fourteen, the family had to move to Toledo. His father wanted him to prepare for a career as secretary to the court and carry on in the family tradition. But Gracián desired to go on for university studies. The family had to raise the money from benefactors for this venture, among whom was Philip II himself. Beginning his studies at the University of Alcalá in 1560 at age fifteen, Gracián received his bachelor of arts degree in 1563, and a year later his master's. After finishing his studies in the arts, he registered in the school of theology, finishing in 1568. He then went on for a four-year doctorate course in theology. In 1572, with only one remaining test to undergo for the doctorate, when at the very point of receiving what many ambitioned but only a few achieved, he oddly abandoned everything. During his studies for the doctorate, he was ordained to the priesthood.

At this time he became friendly with the Jesuits and was thinking seriously of joining them. One day, on the feast of St. Francis in 1571, he went to celebrate Mass for the Franciscan nuns, but by mistake went to the discalced Carmelite nuns in

Alcalá, a community founded not by Teresa but by María de Jesús. Presuming they were Franciscans, he preached on St. Francis. After Mass the foundress spoke to him, explained the difference, and gave him a copy of Teresa's constitutions. He grew enthused about them and actually wrote to Teresa without ever having met her. These incidents led to his study of the Carmelite order. Subsequently, at the age of twenty-seven, he entered the novitiate of the discalced Carmelites in Pastrana. It was a bad year to enter the novitiate in Pastrana. It was precisely the time when the novice master was introducing a number of absurd ascetical practices. Teresa once remarked that Gracián had learned how to govern by way of contrast, treating others just the opposite of the way he was treated in Pastrana. Despite his being only a novice, at Teresa's request, he preached and gave spiritual direction to her nuns in Pastrana.

A few months after his profession on April 25, 1573, he was named by Francisco Vargas as visitator of the Carmelites of the observance in Andalusia. Vargas delegated his own powers to Gracián. Before a year was up, Vargas named him vicar provincial of all the Carmelites in Andalusia. In view of the difficulties that arose regarding the legality of this appointment, the pope's nuncio to Spain, Nicolás Ormaneto, named Vargas and Gracián visitators in solidum, thus responding to the revocation obtained by the general of the order on August 13, 1574. But the chapter of Piacenza in May–June of 1575 was to cause further difficulties for the discalced friars and nuns. At this same time, Gracián, in Beas, finally met Teresa. From a theological and spiritual point of view, this was the most decisive meeting in the history of the Teresian Carmel after her meeting with St. John of the Cross in Medina del Campo. Something that happened to Fray John of the Cross now happened to Gracián: a direct communication of the Teresian charism. Gracián from then on found a spiritual support in Teresa for all the burdens that had been laid on him. Impressed by his learning and his access to the king, Teresa was, above all, highly impressed by his spirituality and his gentle mode of governing. At this first meeting the affinity between them became clear almost instantaneously. They concurred in all their points of view. The two were adaptable, had a gift for getting on well with people, and were open to broad horizons. Shortly after meeting him, wanting to do something more in the service of the Lord, Teresa made a vow of obedience to Gracián in honor of the Holy Spirit for a wonderful favor received on the vigil of the feast of Pentecost. After this, Gracián, in turn, made a decision to consult Teresa in all matters. This wise practice resulted in his being criticized and even calumniated for taking up business matters with a woman and letting himself be ruled by one.

Countering the chapter of Piacenza, Ormaneto enlarged the faculties of Gracián on August 3, 1575, naming him commissary and reformer of the Andalusian Carmel and of the discalced friars and nuns of Castile. Gracián's work turned out to be decisive for the advance of the Teresian Carmel. Nonetheless, the persecutions, calumnies, and Carmelite family struggles ended in his being deposed by the new nuncio, Felipe Sega, and his being confined in a monastery in Alcalá. In October 1578, the discalced friars and nuns were put under the jurisdiction of the provincials of the Carmelites of the observance. Since this move created further conflicts and even public scandals, the king intervened and appointed a commission to deal with the whole matter. This commission placed Angel de Salazar, a former provincial of the observant Carmelites in Castile, in charge of the discalced friars and nuns. He was, in Gracián's view, a gentle and discreet man whose main concern was to console the afflicted and promote peace. Salazar then named Gracián commissary and visitator of the discalced friars and nuns in Andalusia. Finally, through the intervention of Philip II, Gregory XIII, in the brief *Pia consideratione* (June 22, 1580), allowed the discalced Carmelites to form a separate province, which, in Teresa's words, "was all that we were desiring for the sake of our peace and tranquility."

On March 4, 1581, in the chapter of Alcalá, Gracián was elected the first provincial of the Teresian Carmel. But not all were in favor of Gracián, and the vote was anything but unanimous. At the end of her life Teresa herself warned Gracián against being arbitrary and authoritarian. He governed until 1585, attending to the organizational and juridical needs of the new province, extending the discalced friars' presence outside of Spain and opening the first mission in Africa. He was forty years old at the time, and had been superior for as many years as he was a professed religious. Not all the friars shared Teresa's judgment of Gracián as "the one who was best able to bring about a union between religious perfection and gentleness." On finishing his provincialate, Gracián presented to the chapter of Lisbon (May 1585) a detailed defense of his government. According to the opposition, he had been too soft, should have given fewer dispensations, and done more to correct abuses in the strict observance. It seems there were always those who wanted him to do more punishing and threatening. Gracián proposed Nicolás Doria as his successor. He was accepted and Gracián was elected as his first councillor. When the chapter continued in Pastrana, Gracián was elected vicar provincial of Portugal.

At the end of 1586, Gracián published a work zealously promoting the missions, which marked the beginning of trouble with the new provincial. He was ordered to withdraw the book from publication. Furthermore, Gracián had begun to oppose the new form of government devised by Doria at the end of 1585, called the consulta. This was to be a government consisting of a body of five members who would decide matters by vote. He also supported those nuns who opposed changes in Teresa's constitutions. The result was a plan to send Gracián to Mexico to serve there as vicar. While Gracián was in Seville preparing to go to Mexico, orders came from the religious authorities in Portugal, commissioning him to make some visitations in Portugal. There was fear that the English would invade, and it was rumored among Castilians that the Carmelite prior in Lisbon, Padre Antonio Calderón, was an Antonista hiding arquebuses and making plans for betrayal. Gracián's task was to find the friars favoring the revolution, calm them down, and urge them to stay out of politics. This new commission, of course, prevented his going to Mexico.

When the nuns obtained a brief from Sixtus V confirming their desire that the constitutions of St. Teresa not be changed, it was seen as opposition to Doria's government. Gracián was reputed to have given his strong support to the nuns. After he finished his two-year visitation in Portugal, the time seemed ripe for Gracián's brethren to begin a process against him.

He was imprisoned in the monastery of San Hermengildo in Madrid and forbidden to write any letters without permission from Doria. The investigations and interrogations went on for six months. On February 17, 1592, the sentence was pronounced against Gracián. He was declared incorrigible, ordered to remove the habit of the discalced Carmelite friars, and expelled for sowing discord and opposition to the superiors. After much reflection and counsel from others, Gracián decided to defend himself and take his case to the supreme authorities in Rome. Traveling in the habit of a hermit and as a pilgrim, he did so with the determination to defend the good name of the nuns as well. He was forty-seven at the time. By June 1592, he was in Rome only to find that the ambassador of the king had taken Doria's side, favoring the more austere elements of religious life. Gracián could do no more than give Pope Clement VIII his side of the story and leave the matter in the hands of God. After doing so, he went on to Naples, but the viceroy there rejected him, so he was forced to go to Sicily, where the Countess of Olivares received him warmly. Gracián carried on an intense apostolic activity throughout Sicily, even giving courses in scripture in Palermo. While he was immersed in these activities, the decision of Rome reached him. He was forbidden to enter any monastery of the order again and advised to take the habit of the discalced Augustinians. Hoping to get a reversal of the decision, he took a boat for Rome. But it was captured by Turks. Gracián was stripped and chained and his feet branded. He had to work at the oars in the galleys. The ship went about its pillaging throughout the month of October and then landed in Tunis in November. Gracián was held captive for two interminable years in the midst of indescribable suffering and hardship. While held bound by four twenty-five-pound iron weights in a dark and fetid dungeon, he began a correspondence with his friends trying to raise money for his ransom. After a first amount of money arrived, he was allowed more freedom of movement so that he could preach and hear confessions among the hundreds of Christian prisoners. In 1594–1595, he worked intensely in this ministry, also saying Mass daily. By the beginning of August 1595, he was able to leave Africa and captivity behind.

From Genoa he wrote to the general in Spain, Elías de San Martín, asking once more to be readmitted into the order, but he received no answer. While waiting for a response, he spent his time working for captives in Africa, trying to raise money for them and to interest the authorities in helping them. In mid-October, he went to Rome to plead his case. While in Rome he also devoted his time to preaching, spiritual direction, working on behalf of the poor captives in Africa, and, what comes as no surprise, promoting the cause for beatification of Teresa. In this latter regard, he found more enthusiasm for Teresa's cause in Italy than he did in Spain. On March 16, 1596, he received a pontifical brief absolving him from any penalties and censures he may have incurred and authorizing him to return to the discalced Carmelites. Because of the hard opposition to him in Spain, it was recommended that he remain in Italy. There he was warmly received by the vicar general of the Carmelites of the observance, who granted him permission to live among them and wear the discalced habit. Not long after this, he was named by Cardinal Daza an official theologian of the Holy Office.

In 1614, Gracián's health began to weaken. Five months before his death, on April 24, 1614, he was able to share in the joy of Teresa's beatification. In September, he was struck down by a strange illness outside the city of Brussels, while on a journey of priestly ministry, and had to be lodged in a nearby house. He died the next day on September 21 at the age of sixty-nine.

Gracián always bore more of the dove in him than the serpent, but he was tenacious in his ideals. With an enormous capacity for work and an extraordinary physical resistance, he would give all his powers to a task if he judged it was good and noble. A few hours of sleep were enough and he was ready to go again. Everywhere, he made friends, but his friendship with Teresa is what history remembers him most for. His esteem for her is clear through his many letters from her that we now possess. For himself and for posterity, he took the pains to save them. Not for a moment did he ever doubt that she was worthy of being canonized or that she was the foundress from whom the discalced Carmelites, both friars and nuns, received their spirit.

On December 15, 1999, the Discalced Carmelite order, after thorough study, officially revoked the sentence of expulsion from the order issued against Padre Jerónimo Gracián. It did this as an authoritative gesture to restore his good name and set right the injustice of which he was victim. The following year the order took the first steps to introduce his cause for canonization.

John of the Cross, St. (1542–1591). The first of the discalced Carmelite friars, John was born in Fontiveros (Avila), the third son of Gonzalo de Yepes and Catalina Alvarez. John was little more than two years old when his father died. In need of a better means of livelihood for her sons, John's mother moved to Arévalo and then Medina del Campo. In 1551 good fortune came John's way when he was enrolled in a catechism school in Medina for poor boys. This led to his employment as both an orderly and beggar for a hospital in the city. The new responsibility enabled him to enter a school operated by the Jesuits and study the humanities under their guidance. But unexpectedly he entered the Carmelites at the age of twenty-one, taking the name Juan de Santo Matías. After his novitiate he was sent for studies to Salamanca. Ordained a priest in 1567, he returned to Medina to sing his first Mass. There he met Teresa, who recruited him for a contemplative way of life for Carmelite friars similar to that of her nuns, with the exception of preaching and other priestly ministry. She brought him with her on their new foundation in Valladolid and there taught him and allowed him to see and experience the new style of Carmelite life established by her. At this time she made him a new habit, which she especially designed for the discalced Carmelite friars. The first house for friars was opened in Duruelo on November 28, 1568. John served as master of novices for the discalced friars in Duruelo, Mancera de Abajo, and Pastrana. In 1571 he was appointed rector of the new college in Alcalá for the discalced friars who would be pursuing studies. But soon after, he was named by the nuncio Ormaneto confessor at the Incarnation in Avila to help Teresa in her work of reform there. He remained in this office until 1577 when, in early December, as a result of the chapter of Piacenza, he was unjustly seized as a renegade and imprisoned in the Carmelite monastery of the observance in Toledo. There he suffered until he managed a dramatic escape at night on August 15, 1578. While in prison he composed most of the majestic stanzas of his poem *The Spiritual Canticle*. After his escape he was sent to Andalusia as vicar of El Calvario. There he began his work of spiritual direction of the discalced Carmelites, both friars and nuns, which led to his classic commentaries: *The Ascent of Mount Carmel*, *The Dark Night*, and *The Spiritual Canticle*.

In 1579 he was named rector of a new house of studies in Baeza for discalced Carmelites, living in the south of Spain. In 1582, he was elected prior of the house in Granada. He had previously gone to Avila, in 1581, to urge Teresa to come down to Granada to make a foundation for her nuns there, but since she had other commitments at the time, she directed him to assist Anne of Jesus in making this new foundation, which the two of them did in January 1582. It was later in that same year that Teresa died. While in Granada (1582–1588), John did most of his writing. In 1585 he was elected vicar provincial of Andalusia, but continued to live in Granada. This office kept him busy with much travel and a number of new foundations. During those years, crowded with many responsibilities demanding his attention, in the space of two weeks he composed his loftiest work, *The Living Flame of Love*. In 1588 he was called back to Castile to serve as prior of the house in Segovia and serve on the council of the vicar general for the discalced friars and nuns, Nicolás Doria. Because of disagreements among Doria, Gracián, and some of the discalced Carmelite nuns, he was considered a dissenter, set aside from the central government, and destined for the missions in Mexico. While plans were being made for this mission to Mexico, he withdrew to a solitary house in La Peñuela in Andalusia in June of 1591. At this time, Diego Evangelista began gathering any information he could that might be useful in calumniating him and having him expelled from the order. On September 12, John grew seriously ill with fever and an infection in his leg. Transferred to Ubeda where he could receive medical attention, he grew progressively worse until after much suffering he died on December 14, 1591. In 1593 his body was transferred to Segovia. He was beatified on October 6, 1674, and canonized on December 27, 1726. He was declared a Doctor of the Church in 1926.

Since none of Teresa's letters to John of the Cross have reached us, we are missing an important source of knowledge. But generally we can say that, for Teresa, John of the Cross was an expert exponent of spirituality, a spiritual, learned, and experienced man. She asserted that she had gone about here and there looking for light and then found it all in "little Seneca." In her letter to Anne of Jesus, she calls him a "divine and heavenly man" and affirms that in all Castile she had not found another spiritual director like him. For her, "he was a candid and pure soul, a man without malice or cunning," and "one of the purest souls in the Church." However, although she conceded absolute primacy to John in the area of spiritual direction, her preferred three in the area of government seem to have been Gracián, Doria, and Juan de Jesús Roca. It is hard to give any clear reason for this. In their spiritual teaching, John and Teresa were mutually influential. After her death, insofar as we know, John was the first promoter of the publication of her writings. In his *Spiritual Canticle* he praised her writings, and in his *Living Flame of Love* he praised her mystical graces and charism.

María Bautista (Ocampo) (1543–1603). The celebrated prioress of Valladolid and great friend of Teresa's was born in Torrijos (Toledo) to Teresa's cousin Diego de Cepeda. Her mother, Beatriz de la Cruz y Ocampo, died when she was five years old. She was then taken into the care of her aunt and uncle in La Puebla Montalbán (Toledo). Teresa met her there in 1549 when she made her pilgrimage to the Shrine of Guadalupe. Later she brought María to the Incarnation, where her sister Leonor was already being educated. When in 1560 Teresa began to plan her reform project, María offered a thousand ducats from her inheritance. She entered St. Joseph's in 1563 and made her profession in 1564. Teresa took her with her for the foundation in Medina del Campo in 1567, and two years later, at the request of María de Mendoza, María transferred to Valladolid. She became prioress of Valladolid in 1571, at the time Teresa was made prioress of the Incarnation. Gifted with an uncommon combination of qualities, she was virtuous, intelligent, cautious, discreet, well organized, and a good administrator. She enjoyed a close friendship with Teresa, sharing with her as well a friendship with the renowned theologian Domingo Báñez. She felt perfectly at ease in giving her cousin advice, which sometimes Teresa found to be amusing. But Teresa sometimes had to reprove her lest she misuse her talents, turning them into a means of satisfying her own interests. What turned out to be unfortunate was the way Teresa was treated by her on her return in ill health from Burgos at the end of her life. María disdainfully sided with Beatriz de Castilla, who was determined to break Lorenzo's will and gain the inheritance destined for St. Joseph's in Avila. Teresa, of course, firmly resisted both María and Beatriz. Anne of St. Bartholomew, who was Teresa's nurse and companion in those last days, reported that María, who was prioress at Valladolid when Teresa and her nurse passed through, was loved very much by Teresa, but, on this occasion, reciprocated with no respect and ordered Teresa out of the house.

In the last years of her life, María was afflicted with a paralysis and rheumatism and much suffering. It is said that Teresa appeared to her, comforted her, and told her that this was fitting because, since she loved her so much, she wanted her to be close to her in heaven.

María de Cristo. A nun at St. Joseph's in Avila, professed there in 1568, she was the first prioress to be elected after the transfer of the Carmel to the jurisdiction of the order in 1577. She renounced her office in 1581 and in her place Teresa was elected. Before that, Teresa had written to Gracián: "the prioress will suffice since there is no one else there. And although I say 'will suffice,' I think I am lying because I don't think there is anyone who can handle the internal affairs of the house" (see July 14, 1581). She was sent on the foundation for Granada in 1581, traveling to it with St. John of the Cross. She was subprioress in Granada, and in 1585 was made prioress in Málaga, where she died in 1590. Only one letter to María de Cristo from Teresa has come down to us (see April 16, 1580), but she is mentioned negatively in the "terrible" letter to Anne of Jesus (see May 30, 1582).

María de San José (Salazar) (1548–1603). She was undoubtedly one of Teresa's most intimate friends. Gracián said of her that she was one of the holiest, purest, and most prudent women he had known in the order, and the one who suffered the most opposition in standing firm against a change in the laws left by Teresa.

Born in Molina de Aragón (Guadalajara) or, according to others, in Toledo, she received an education characteristic of those who lived in the households of the Castilian nobility. When a little girl, she entered into the service of Doña Luisa de la Cerda and lived in her palace. There she met Teresa, who in 1562 was sent by her superiors as a companion to Doña Luisa to comfort her after her husband's death. Fourteen years old at the time, María developed a great admiration for Teresa and sometimes was a witness of her ecstasies. Six years later when Teresa returned to Toledo to arrange for a foundation in Malagón with Doña Luisa, María decided to join Teresa and her companions. It was not until two years later, however, that she received the habit. The investiture took place in Malagón in 1570 when she was twenty-two. In 1575, Teresa took her on the foundation in Beas with the intention of making her prioress of a further foundation that was planned for Caravaca. When Gracián intervened to order a foundation in Seville, Teresa chose instead to make her prioress there. Because of her intelligence, education, and other talents, she was referred to by Teresa as the "provincialess." And when nearing the time of her death, Teresa thought that María would be perfectly capable of taking her place. María saved a great number of Teresa's letters. In them she is forever being urged to take care of her health and try the various remedies prescribed by Teresa for her different illnesses. In some of her letters, Teresa joked with her over one display or another of her erudition. She also would accuse her of being crafty and lacking in openness. Teresa became most upset with her when she complained to the nuns in Seville that the house bought for them there and considered ideal by Teresa was unhealthy. Strange to say, in this matter, María de San José was probably more right than wrong. Teresa acknowledged that María de San José was cut out for dealing with Andalusians.

Despite any limitations she may have had, the prioress of Seville was a great figure among the nuns of the Teresian Reform. To none of the other nuns did Teresa express so much praise and cordial and intimate friendship. In 1578, Diego de Cárdenas, the provincial of the Carmelites of the observance in Andalusia, deposed her from the office of prioress because of false accusations that were made against her by Beatriz de la Madre de Dios. In the following year, Angel de Salazar was named vicar for the discalced friars and nuns. In reviewing the process against María, he concluded that removal from office was without foundation and restored her rights. On June 9, 1580, she was reelected prioress.

Her fidelity to Padre Gracián after Teresa's death brought her many troubles. They both felt the lack of Teresa's endorsement when they were in need of it. In December 1584, Gracián sent María as prioress on a new foundation in Lisbon. Later, the chapter, which elected Nicolás Doria in the place of Gracián, was held in Lisbon. The dissension between Gracián and Doria that was to follow had its repercussions on María de San José. Though she tried to be a peacemaker, she was ordered by Doria in 1588 to have no more communication with Gracián, whom she had come to know well in Seville. She played a role with Anne of Jesus in obtaining the brief from Sixtus V entitled *Salvatoris* (1591). The brief stated that no one has the authority to change or modify the constitutions received from Teresa. It riled Doria that there were efforts to preserve Teresa's constitutions from any changes that might be made by him, but not until 1593 were measures taken against her. She was confined to the monastery prison and deprived of Communion for nine months, but then Doria died unexpectedly. The new general, Elías de San Martín, put an end to María's trials. She was elected prioress again in 1597. She was among those nuns desired by Jean de Brétigny for a foundation of Teresa's nuns in France, but the next general, Francisco de la Madre de Dios, opposed their going to France. Since authorization was then obtained by the French to take nuns from Portugal for a foundation in France, María de San José was transferred by the general out of Portugal to Talavera and then on to Cuerva, where she was received coldly by the prioress. María died shortly afterward. She left a number of writings that are highly regarded for their thought and charming style.

Mendoza, Alvaro de (d. 1586). The bishop who was closest to Teresa and from whom she received the most favors, he came from a highly influential family in Spain. He was appointed Bishop of Avila in 1560. A robust man, he nonetheless, at the same time, manifested much piety and charity, sponsoring many humanitarian and social works. In 1562, influenced by

Peter of Alcántara and won over by Teresa herself, he gave her decisive support in her endeavors. Accepting her new foundation in Avila under his authority when the provincial refused to grant it, he even provided the bread for the community. Yet at first he did oppose the foundation, fearing that Avila was too poor to support another community of nuns. He protected and defended Teresa against detractors and helped her with unbounded generosity. In 1577, he was appointed Bishop of Palencia and, at his urgings, Teresa founded a monastery in Palencia in 1580, and then through his mediation, she founded one in Burgos in 1582. When the persecution of Teresa was at its peak, he had the delicacy to write to King Philip II, defending Teresa and her work. So great was his love and esteem for her that he arranged to be buried on the epistle side in the sanctuary of the new chapel in St. Joseph's in Avila to which he had contributed.

Nieto, Inés. A good friend of Teresa's, she was the wife of Juan de Albornoz, secretary to the Duke of Alba, living at times in Madrid and at other times in Alba. An exchange of correspondence and favors took place between Teresa and Doña Inés. Doña Inés had recommended to Teresa a friend of hers, Isabel de Córdoba, for the Carmel in Valladolid. Teresa also wrote to console Inés at the imprisonment of her husband and at the death of her friend the Marchioness of Velada. In her turn, Teresa asks Inés to intercede to have her nephew Gonzalo de Ovalle removed from the list of pages in the service of the Duchess of Alba, and also thanks her for a statue of our Lady: "The more I look at the statue, the more beautiful it seems."

Ortiz, Diego (d. 1611). An inhabitant of Toledo and one of the founders of the Carmel there, very demanding and punctilious. Teresa records: "I immediately began to take up the business matters with Alonso Alvarez and a son-in-law of his, named Diego Ortiz. The latter, although very good, and a theologian, was more unyielding in his opinion than Alonso Alvarez. He did not readily soften his demands. They began to ask for many conditions that I didn't think I could easily agree to" (*Foundations* 15.4). Ortiz continued to make all kinds of demands for the foundation. In 1571 he wrote Teresa a letter whose difficult tone we can guess from Teresa's response: "You show me so much kindness and charity through your letters that even were your last letter more severe, I would have felt well repaid and obliged once more to serve you" (see May 27, 1571). A few years later he wrote through Gracián to ask Teresa for help with a business matter he had in Madrid. He also sent her images of our Lady and St. Joseph for the foundation in Andalusia. In a postscript to the manuscript of Madrid of *The Way of Perfection* Teresa writes: "This was approved and seen by Padre Fray García de Toledo and by Doctor Ortiz, an inhabitant of Toledo." At the time of his death in 1611, he had read Teresa's writings and her biography by Ribera.

Osorio, Inés and Isabel. These two sisters from Madrid were begging Teresa for permission to enter Carmel, but Teresa wanted them to wait because of the troubles in the order at the time (1578) and because of her hopes for the foundation of a Carmel in Madrid. Inés (de la Encarnación) chose not to wait and entered the Carmel in Toledo. There she lived at times with Teresa, who once wrote to her sister: "Certainly she is an angel. She rejoiced to be with me." Inés died in Toledo in 1635. Isabel, on the other hand, Teresa kept urging to wait for the foundation in Madrid. But then Isabel became sick herself, although she persisted in her desire to be a Carmelite. Teresa died before a Carmel in Madrid was ever founded. Of the letters that have come down to us, one is addressed to the two sisters together, and three to Isabel.

Ovalle, Juan de (d. 1595). Teresa's brother-in-law was born in Alba de Tormes and served under Charles V in Germany before marrying Juana. Though he had a difficult temperament, unstable, suspicious, and jealous, he and his wife made an effort to live a pious Christian life, and were generous in giving alms and caring for poor orphans. But in their efforts to sustain a status equal to that of the *hijosdalgo*, they never fared well and were often in financial difficulty. Teresa gives the impression that he was touchy and self-important but well-meaning.

Philip II (1527–1598). King of Spain, son of the emperor Charles V and Isabel of Portugal, he ascended the throne of his father in 1556. He never felt any contradiction between his profound Catholic belief and his high-handed actions with respect to the

Church. His continuous hostility to aspects of papal policy was inherited from his father. "Secular princes," he emphasized to his ambassador in Rome, "are not bound to carry out the mandates of the pope in temporal matters." An unswerving supporter of the spiritual authority of the papacy, he could not brook its refusal to support him blindly. Within Spain, Philip felt himself completely free to act as he liked in church matters. When he gave support to reforms within the Church in Spain, he did not hesitate to sanction the use of troops against monasteries and convents. Possessing total control over appointment of bishops, he nonetheless always consulted carefully before naming to sees. He also came to accept the inevitability of toleration in specific circumstances. If England were invaded, he decided in 1576, there must be no religious persecution. He was also able to move towards accepting a form of toleration in the Netherlands. Likewise he accepted—albeit reluctantly—the need to coexist with Muslims (in Spain) and Jews (in Italy and North Africa) as subjects. His confessors, like those of other Catholic rulers, occupied a special place in government. They were always allotted a place on committees where moral questions were on the agenda. Philip was by temperament tranquil, subdued, and ever in control of himself. He spoke little, and when he did he always expressed himself carefully and courteously. It was precisely his silence that unnerved others. They were given the right to speak first, which made them feel immediately under scrutiny. A story goes around that even Teresa was unnerved in his presence: "I began to speak to him when his penetrating gaze, of those that penetrate to the soul, settled on me, so I lowered my eyes and rapidly stated what I wanted." But the story is unauthentic. The king's reserve, however, was natural, not affected. Teresa had to turn to him on various occasions for help with the trust of someone seeking help from a father. At times seeking protection for her reform, at other times for individuals, such as John of the Cross or Gracián, who were being either persecuted or calumniated, she happily found that Philip II did not disappoint her hopes. He even went so far as to pay all the expenses of the chapter of separation. Teresa asserted that had it not been for the king, all of her work would have collapsed. After her death, he seemed to favor Doria in the latter's conflict with Gracián. On the whole, Philip II refused to engage in any propaganda battle to enhance his reputation, and thus he left the field wide open to the English and the Dutch. Their journalism produced an image of him and Spain that has since been characterized as "the Black Legend."

Reinoso, Jerónimo. A canon of the cathedral in Palencia and friend and servant of Teresa's. "He is very discreet, holy, and shows good judgment in everything, even though he is young" Teresa wrote of him, in her *Foundations*. He had done his studies at Salamanca. Besides being a canon in Palencia, he was also the provider for the hospital of San Antolín. Serving as one of Teresa's confessors, six letters of hers to him have come down to us. Of special interest is the last one dealing with some of the problems with the foundation of the Carmel in Burgos (see May 20, 1582). Reinoso died in Palencia in 1600.

Rubeo, Juan Bautista (Giovanni Battista Rossi) (1507–1578). An untiring apostle, he was born in Ravenna and entered the Carmelites at the age of ten. He received his doctorate in Padua. In 1546 he was named procurator general of the order and began lecturing at the Sapienza in Rome. The Carmelite general chapter in 1564, under the presidency of St. Charles Borromeo, unanimously elected him general. He lost no time in obtaining faculties from the Holy See to visit, reform, and correct the houses of the order. His cherished desires were to bring the order back to its origins, and to stress solitude, affective prayer, devotion to Mary, and the apostolate. This appealed to him much more than merely promoting fulfillment of the laws newly set forth by the Council of Trent. In 1564 he began his visit to Spain, and on June 10, 1566, he had an audience with Philip II. Proceeding to Andalusia, where the Carmelites were torn by rival factions and resistance to reform, he convoked a provincial chapter for September 22 at which over two hundred Carmelites took part. His efforts to correct abuses angered the guilty parties and caused them to make appeals to the king, complaining of Rossi and calling on the king himself to set up a visitation. As a result, Philip II lost confidence in Rossi and initiated his own plans for the reform of religious orders in Spain. Unaware of the king's attitude, Rossi began his visitation of Castile and on April 27, 1567, authorized Teresa to found other houses for her nuns, provided they be under the jurisdiction of the order, and the number in each community be restricted to no more than twenty-five nuns. A month later he limited the region where the new houses could be founded to Castile, but later he extended this to all parts. Because of the troubles among the friars in Andalusia, he did not want to grant permission for new foundations of discalced friars. But at Teresa's request on August 10, 1567, he wrote from Barcelona giving her permission to found two houses of "contemplative Carmelite friars" in Castile. In 1569 in a letter to the prioress of Medina, Rossi wrote: "She [Teresa of Jesus] does more good for the order than all the Carmelite friars in Spain together." Teresa esteemed him just as highly. But later, because of the many jurisdictional complexities that arose from the king's desire to reform the Carmelites in Spain, passions were aroused and Rossi was so misinformed that he approved measures harmful to what Teresa was trying to bring about. She never lost her high esteem for Rossi and explained and appealed to him through her letters.

Rossi died unexpectedly on September 4, 1578, as a consequence of an accident in which he fell from his mule and broke his leg. Teresa was deeply saddened when she received the news and always lamented the pain she thought she had caused the general because of the misunderstandings that had arisen and her inability to explain things to him personally or get her letters through to him.

Ruiz de la Peña, Dionisio. A priest, confessor, and personal secretary to the Archbishop of Toledo. Teresa turned to him to mediate with the archbishop in certain matters. Two in particular were of concern to her: the foundation in Madrid and the vocation of Elena, the archbishop's niece. Concerning the latter she writes: "I don't know when this letter will go out. I would have wanted it to go quickly so that you would be aware of how little I am at fault, or rather not at all. This is so true that out of respect for the relationship of that person about whom you wrote to me with his illustrious lordship, I did not tell the latter about the efforts I made in this case to impede her entrance into one of these houses. If Padre Baltasar Alvarez, who was provincial of the Jesuits in this province, were alive, he would be a good witness to how I begged him to prevent such a thing, since this lady had more respect for him than for anyone else, and he promised to do so" (see June 30, 1581).

Salcedo, Francisco de (d. 1580). Born in Avila, he married a cousin of Teresa's aunt. He studied theology for twenty years at the Dominican school in Avila. The first one in whom Teresa confided when her mystical life began in full, he was the one who was also most skeptical about her experiences and caused her the greatest suffering. He was convinced of the devil's involvement. Peter of Alcántara had to go to great lengths to assure him that Teresa's experiences were indeed from God. In the end, since he was always well intentioned, he did change his opinion and was ever faithful in trying to help Teresa with her undertakings. She wrote of him in *The Book of Her Life*: "This gentleman is so prayerful and charitable that his goodness and perfection shine throughout the whole town" (23.6). When he started referring to himself as being old and infirm, Teresa in one reply joked with him: "Don't keep telling me that you are old, which leaves me in total dismay. As though there were some security in being young!" In 1570, after his wife died, he was ordained a priest. In 1576 he got tangled up in a troublesome lawsuit in which he lost a great part of his possessions. Teresa wrote to her brother in Avila urging him to show much kindness to Don Francisco, and regretted that he didn't bear the trial with greater courage. She believed it was sent to him by the Lord. When he died, the rumor went around that he had left the nuns a fortune and so their benefactors stopped trying to help them. The poor community ended up in dire straits, for the legacy they received was much too small to meet their needs.

Toledo, García de. A typical aristocrat in soul and blood, García de Toledo was a nephew of the Count of Oropesa. He went to America with the viceroy of Mexico and made his profession as a Dominican there in 1535. Returning to Spain, he became subprior in 1555 at Santo Tomás, the Dominican house in Avila, and served as one of Teresa's trusted confessors. Suddenly and unexpectedly, he entered the pages of Teresa's *Book of Her Life* when she met him in a church in Toledo in 1562. To him we owe the expanded version of her *Life*, with its extra little treatise on prayer (chs. 11–22) and its final chapters on the foundation of St. Joseph's (chs. 32–40). Once, Teresa received a message from

God for him. The message was brief but all from God. And the witness said, "he began to weep, for it penetrated to the depths of his being. And he is a tough man who could rule the world." In 1569 he accompanied his cousin Francisco to Peru, where the cousin had been appointed viceroy. He became provincial there besides having held other offices. He returned to Spain in 1581 and retired to the Dominican house at Talavera de la Reina, where he died.

Tolosa, Catalina de. Teresa introduces Catalina in this way: "There lived in this city of Burgos a holy widow named Catalina de Tolosa . . . I could go on at length telling about her virtues, her penance as well as her prayer, her generous almsgiving and charity, her good intelligence and courage" (*Foundations* 31.8). Born in 1538, she had nine children, one of whom had died before Teresa first met the family. When the small caravan of Carmelites arrived in Burgos to make the foundation there, they first got installed in the home of Catalina de Tolosa, who had been desiring the foundation of a Carmel in Burgos. Teresa ended up attracting to Carmel Catalina's daughters and two sons. Eventually the mother herself entered the Carmel of Palencia at age forty-nine. In the Carmel she became a subject of her own daughter, Isabel of the Trinity, who was prioress of the community, and of her son, Sebastián, who was provincial of Castile at the time. She herself also became prioress of the community. She died in 1608. Again, Teresa wrote of her: "But Catalina de Tolosa did everything so well, because she was so generous and showed so much good will, that she provided us all in a room where we were secluded with food for a month, as though she were mother of each one" (*Foundations* 31.24). Of the many letters between Teresa and Catalina, only two have come down to us (see January 16, 1582, and August 3, 1582).

Notes

To Don Lorenzo de Cepeda, Quito (Ecuador)
Avila, December 23, 1561

1. Teresa's younger brother Lorenzo de Cepeda departed for America in 1540 and took up residence in Quito, where he became a wealthy man.

2. Guiomar de Ulloa was the widow of Francisco Dávila, a large property owner, who left her a small fortune, which she used mostly for charitable works.

3. Teresa placed her first foundation under obedience to the Bishop of Avila on account of the difficulties the Carmelite provincial had about accepting it.

4. The project suffered a delay so that the foundation did not take place until August 24, 1562.

5. Teresa's older sister María, the widow of Martín de Guzmán y Barrientos, had shown Teresa hospitality on their farm in Castellanos de la Cañada when Teresa had become sick as a young nun.

6. Juan de Ovalle, Teresa's brother-in-law, was the husband of Juana de Ahumada.

7. All this litigation in the family stemmed from the fact that Alonso de Cepeda had not divided his goods equally between the children of his first and second marriages.

8. Teresa's sister and brother-in-law had come from Alba de Tormes to Avila to help Teresa with her new foundation.

9. Toribia worked for Don Alonso as a housemaid.

10. Teresa became acquainted with Guiomar de Ulloa through her daughter, Antonia de Guzmán, who was a nun with Teresa at the monastery of the Incarnation in Avila. Antonia, sometimes accompanied by Teresa, used to leave the monastery for long visits with her mother. A close friendship then began between Teresa and Doña Guiomar.

11. Juana de Fuentes y Espinosa was Lorenzo's wife. Born in Peru (1539), she married Lorenzo in 1556. She died in childbirth in 1567, leaving seven children behind.

12. The little boy, probably Lorenzo's oldest son, died in 1563.

13. In Spain, the Jesuits were at first called Theatines.

14. These patent letters were given by the chancery of Valladolid in favor of Teresa's father and uncles after suit was brought against them for not paying taxes. They claimed exemption because of their noble status (1519–1522).

15. It was December 24. In Avila the new year began on Christmas Day, until 1564 when the date for beginning the new year was changed to January 1.

16. Teresa's younger brother (1522–1575), who was returning from Spain to America.

17. Hernando (1510) and Pedro (1521) are Teresa's brothers. Both went to America; only Pedro returned, in 1575.

To Juan de San Cristóbal, Avila
Avila, April 9, 1564

1. The Octave Sunday of Easter.

To Padre García de Toledo, Avila(?)
Avila, 1565

1. The service was either her having written for him or having sent him *The Book of Her Life*.

2. Padre García encouraged Teresa to give free rein to her pen.

3. Teresa is referring to St. John of Avila. In the end, with the help of Doña Luisa de la Cerda, she sent him the autograph itself rather than a copy.

4. This date, according to Domingo Báñez, refers to the completion of the first redaction. The second redaction was finished toward the end of 1565.

To Don Gaspar Daza, Avila
Toledo, March 24, 1568

1. She is alluding to the solemn transfer of the relics of Justus and Pastor from Huesca to Alcalá, March 7.

2. The nuns at St. Joseph's in Avila.

3. She was probably the *demandadera* (one who serves an enclosed monastery of nuns by answering the door and running errands).

4. The abbess of the Cistercian nuns in Avila.

5. The foundation in Malagón.

To Doña Luisa de la Cerda, Antequera
Toledo, May 27, 1568

1. It seems Velasco resigned from the service of Doña Luisa.

2. Juan Pardo de Tavera, Doña Luisa's son, and the others in their circle.

3. Alonso de Cabria Pecellín, a priest in the service of Doña Luisa, who enjoyed a benefice in Paracuellos.

4. She arrived from Malagón on the 19th and will leave for Escalona on the 28th.

5. Gabriel de Reolí, a Toledan and friend of Teresa's. (The form of the name used in text is the affectionate diminutive.)

6. The licentiate Juan Bautista.

7. Doña Luisa's administrator, Juan de Huidobro de Miranda.

8. Doña Luisa's brother, Hernando de la Cerda.

9. Doctor Bernardino Carleval, a disciple of St. John of Avila's and professor at the university of Baeza. The manuscript is illegible here for about three lines.

10. The Carmelite Tomás de Carleval.

11. The Jesuit Pablo Hernández.

12. An expression referring to a woman given to acts of piety and under the guidance of Jesuits, who at first were called Theatines.

13. Probably Tomás Carleval, confessor at the Carmel in Malagón.

14. Teresa now wanted the Mass to be said each day by the Carmelite, Padre Carleval. She was trying to find another, better benefice for the former chaplain.

15. Teresa had consigned *The Book of Her Life* to Doña Luisa, who was to care for its safe delivery to St. John of Avila.

16. Fray Domingo Báñez, who had already rendered his official judgment of the book and didn't see any need to submit it for an opinion to St. John of Avila.

17. The group of theologians and directors in Avila who had already approved the book.

18. Doña Juana Lucas de Toledo, the Marchioness of Villena and the Duchess of Escalona, a near relative of Padre García de Toledo's.

19. Padre García de Toledo, one of the Avila group who approved the *Life*.

20. Ana de Thienlloye, wife of Doña Luisa's brother, Hernando de la Cerda.

21. Pedro Niño de Conchillos y Rivera, an in-law of Doña Luisa's.

22. Margarita de Centellas y Borja, St. Francis Borgia's sister.

23. Ana de Silva, directress of a school for young ladies from the nobility.

24. The prioress of the Jeronimites of San Pablo.

25. Juana Manuela de Portugal, who died May 1, 1568.

26. Antonia del Espíritu Santo, one of the original nuns from San José in Avila, who accompanied Teresa on her journeys.

27. A humorous yet respectful name for the Jesuit Pablo Hernández.

28. Probably the daughter of the founder of Teresa's monastery in Toledo, Alonso Ramírez.

Doña Luisa de la Cerda, Antequera
Avila, June 9, 1568

1. In the previous letter.

2. The priest from Malagón, the licentiate Juan Bautista.

3. Fuentepiedra, a spring near Antequera from which Doña Luisa's son, Don Juan Pardo de Tavera, was seeking a cure from kidney stones.

4. Doña Teresa de Toledo, the daughter of the Marchioness of Velada, Doña Lucas de Toledo, joined the Cistercian nuns of Santa Ana in Avila.

5. *The Book of Her Life*, which she wanted delivered to St. John of Avila.

To Doña Luisa de la Cerda, Antequera
Avila, June 23, 1568

1. *The Book of Her Life*, which she wanted St. John of Avila to read.

2. St. John of Avila.

3. The Dominican theologian Domingo Báñez.

4. She is being facetious here. Thinking his approval was sufficient, Báñez did not want her *Life* to be read by others.

5. The Jesuit Gaspar de Salazar, former rector in Avila.

6. Teresa's Carmelite foundation in Malagón, which Doña Luisa had endowed.

7. Tomás de Carleval.

8. The Carmelites of the observance in Toledo.

9. Juan Pardo, Doña Luisa's son.

10. Doña Luisa, by reason of the endowment, is considered the foundress and patroness of the Carmel in Malagón and Don Juan, its patron.

To Don Francisco de Salcedo, Avila
Valladolid, September 1568

1. Fray John of the Cross, who is preparing for the discalced life in Duruelo.
2. *Aloja* was a popular drink made from water, honey, and spices.
3. Antonia del Espíritu Santo (Henao), one of the first four nuns at St. Joseph's in Avila.
4. Mencía del Aguila, Francisco de Salcedo's wife and a relative of Teresa's.
5. One of Salcedo's maids, the oldest. She was much respected and given the title "Lady."
6. Maridíaz was Teresa's friend and known in Avila for her penance and recollected life. The Flemish woman was Ana Wasteels, who became a Carmelite at St. Joseph's (Ana de San Pedro). María Dávila, the latter's daughter, also became a Carmelite at St. Joseph's (Ana de los Angeles).
7. Ana de Mendoza (the Princess of Eboli) was in a hurry for Teresa to make a foundation in Pastrana. Teresa did not pass through Avila until February or the beginning of March.

To Doña Juana de Ahumada, Alba
Avila, Middle of December 1569

1. Juana's husband, Juan de Ovalle, who was returning from Seville to Alba.
2. Juan de Ovalle.
3. The money sent by Lorenzo.
4. Gonzalo de Ovalle.
5. She is alluding to the money brought for her by her brother-in-law from her brother Lorenzo in Seville.
6. The monastery of the Incarnation in Avila.
7. Juan de Ovalle had some investment plans in mind.
8. Juana's daughter.
9. Gonzalo Godínez, Juan de Ovalle's brother.

To Diego Ortiz, Toledo
Toledo, Middle of August 1570

1. Teresa wanted the sung Masses, stipulated in a contract made with Diego Ortiz, to be the responsibility of the chaplains; that is, the priest celebrating Mass would sing the usual parts without any sung response from the nuns. According to her own constitutions (no. 2), but not the rule, the nuns were to sing at Mass on Sundays and feast days.
2. A secretary was writing this letter for Teresa.
3. He was the son of Diego Ortiz and Francisca Ramírez. Teresa told the nuns that whenever "Martinico" came to the monastery they should call her. She enjoyed speaking with him because he was a very virtuous young man.
4. Diego Ortiz did not yield to Teresa's wishes, as might have been expected. He was a difficult man to deal with.

To Doña Catalina Hurtado, Toledo
Avila, October 31, 1570

1. Juana del Espíritu Santo, one of Doña Catalina's two daughters, who was a discalced Carmelite nun in Toledo.

2. María de San Jerónimo, subprioress of St. Joseph's in Avila.

To Doña Isabel de Jimena, Segovia
Salamanca, End of 1570

1. A Jesuit residing at the time in Segovia where Isabel lived who had highly recommended her to Teresa.

2. For a dowry she brought 3,000 ducats as well as other things for the church. This was the Isabel (de Jesús) who, as a novice in Salamanca, sent Teresa into ecstasy with her singing so beautifully a song about how hard life is without God.

3. Cf. Mt 19:21.

To Diego Ortiz, Toledo
Avila, May 27, 1571

1. The discalced Carmelite Ambrosio Mariano de San Benito.

2. The prioress of the Carmel in Toledo, Ana de los Angeles.

3. Alonso Alvarez Rodríguez, another one of the founders in Toledo.

4. Diego Ortiz's children.

5. Giovanni Battista Rossi, who had already approved the contract for the foundation.

6. The Dominican Pedro Fernández.

7. Diego Ortiz's wife.

To Doña Luisa de la Cerda, Paracuellos
Avila, November 7, 1571

1. Teresa had taken over her office of prioress at the Incarnation in Avila on October 6. Insisting on their right to vote for a prioress, the nuns in Medina, despite the provincial, received permission from the visitator Fernández, a higher authority, to vote for Teresa. After Teresa was elected prioress of Medina, the provincial, in apparent retaliation, managed to convince the visitator to appoint Teresa as prioress of the Incarnation in Avila. The nuns at the Incarnation vehemently resisted having Teresa imposed on them as prioress, without an election. They tried to bar the provincial from entering their monastery. Not until they were asked by the provincial did they agree to accept Teresa.

2. The place was Paracuellos del Jarama, between Madrid and Alcalá.

3. She had been appointed prioress by the apostolic visitator, Pedro Fernández.

4. Juana de Toledo Pacheco was the daughter of the second Count of Oropesa.

5. Padre Duarte, from Alcalá de Henares, was a Jesuit confessor to Doña Luisa.

To Doña Juana de Ahumada, Galinduste
Avila, February 4, 1572

1. The monastery of the Incarnation in Avila.

2. A probable reference to Lorenzo de Cepeda, who could have had some official business at the court.

3. Apparently the Ovalle brothers were in opposition to the nuns' receiving from the municipality a narrow passageway on the border between the monastery and the Ovalle houses. The passageway served for drainage, and they feared that if given to the monastery it would be enclosed, which would put their houses in danger of flooding.

4. The Incarnation was suffering from such lack of material resources that there was not enough food to provide all the nuns with their daily ration. At the Incarnation a good percentage of the nuns came from families of a high social class, and the nuns were not obliged to give up certain possessions. There was a distinction between goods held in common and individual goods. In speaking of the poverty of the monastery, one is referring to what was held in common.

To Doña Juana de Ahumada, Alba de Tormes
Avila, September 27, 1572

1. The monastery of the Incarnation in Avila. Teresa has been prioress there for a year.

2. It seems she is alluding to the house in Alba that was the cause of a litigation between the Ovalles and the Carmelite nuns in that city.

3. The brother referred to is Lorenzo de Cepeda, who in fact did not return from the Americas with this fleet. The Perálvarez house belonged to Pedro Alvarez Cimbrón, who was soon to become a good friend of Lorenzo's.

4. The prioress was Juana del Espíritu Santo, superior of the Carmel in Alba de Tormes. She had transferred to the discalced Carmelites from the Incarnation and accompanied Teresa on the foundation in Toledo. She was prioress in Alba when Teresa died there.

5. Cristóbal Chacón was an old friend of Teresa's father. His three daughters were Ana, Sancha, and Inés. The latter two were nuns at the Incarnation.

6. The portress had a room, or sometimes a chair, next to the turn where she communicated unseen with people who came to the monastery.

7. Although there were rich monasteries, the Incarnation was a poor one. The daily ration of food for each nun in 1565 was 5 1/4 ounces of bread and about 4 ounces of meat. This does not mean that all the nuns lived on this ration alone.

8. She is alluding to the severe orders given her by the visitator Pedro Fernández regarding the reform of the Incarnation.

9. Teresa had arranged for St. John of the Cross to come to the Incarnation as confessor to the large community.

To Madre Inés de Jesús, Medina del Campo
Avila, Beginning of May 1573

1. Sister Isabel de San Jerónimo (Alvarez) died November 23, 1582, of a brain illness from which she suffered for a number of years. According to Alonso de la Madre de Dios, John's early biographer (1600), St. John of the Cross, "on seeing her, concluded that her affliction was not a work of the devil but the beginning of an illness that would cause insanity. Afterward, when it grew worse they understood its nature." The last two sentences are missing from some copies of this letter.

To King Don Philip II, Madrid
Avila, June 11, 1573

1. She alludes to the Carmels she has been founding and also to the Incarnation, from where she writes this letter.

2. The queen is Anne of Austria; the prince, Don Fernando, born December 5, 1571, and pronounced heir in May of 1573. He died at the age of seven, October 18, 1578.

3. Juan Calvo de Padilla, a zealous reformer.

To Pedro de la Banda, Tozos (Salamanca)
Salamanca, August 2, 1573

1. Pedro de la Banda was not very cooperative; he didn't return until a month later. When he did come and saw what the nuns had done, Teresa writes, he "was so furious that I didn't know what to do with him."

To Pedro de la Banda, Salamanca
Salamanca, October 8, 1573

1. This prayerful wish may have been prompted by Pedro de la Banda's angry reaction on his return to Salamanca at finding the nuns in his house.

To Padre Domingo Báñez, Valladolid
Salamanca, Beginning of January 1574

1. In the quartan fevers, the fever returned every fourth day.

2. The letters referred to were those in which the visitator, Pedro Fernández, deferred the matter of the school for young women in Medina to the decision of Báñez and Teresa. Fernández and Báñez had been companions together in the novitiate.

3. In her *Foundations* (ch. 11), Teresa tells the story of Casilda de Padilla, how she escaped from her family and entered the Carmelite cloister in Valladolid before she had reached the age of twelve. The family in their great opposition finally got a court order to take her out of the monastery. They had recourse to Báñez and tried to get him to overcome Teresa's resistance. Eventually, Casilda escaped again and entered the monastery. She was professed a week after her fifteenth birthday, January 13, 1577.

4. When the Prince of Eboli died, the princess announced that she was going to become a nun and entered the monastery of the discalced Carmelites in Pastrana, bringing her maids with her and totally disrupting the

contemplative life of the nuns. Growing to dislike the prioress and the rest of the nuns, she eventually left, but continued to cause them trouble.

5. Casilda de Padilla.

6. This refers to the actual situation in which the family, wanting to keep her outside of the monastery for thirty days, sought the help of Báñez.

7. The business refers to the purchase from Pedro de la Banda of a house for the nuns in Salamanca.

8. The house actually belonged to Pedro de la Banda's wife. She wanted it sold so she could use the money to help her two daughters.

9. The Dominican prior of Atocha in Madrid, Hernando del Castillo, a friend of the deceased prince, went to Pastrana to try to appease the princess, but in vain.

10. The discalced Carmelite friars in Pastrana, a foundation that had also been patronized by the prince and princess.

11. Bartolomé de Medina, a Dominican professor at Salamanca, had strongly opposed Teresa, but as he got to know her he softened his attitude.

12. One of Báñez's directees and admirers.

13. Beatriz Sarmiento de Mendoza, the sister of Don Alvaro de Mendoza, Bishop of Avila.

To Madre Ana de la Encarnación, Salamanca
Alba de Tormes, Middle of January 1574

1. In the Carmels founded by Teresa there were little chapels or cells in the garden or on the top floor of the house; there the nuns could enjoy a more intense solitude. From this hermitage Teresa had a view of the river Tormes.

2. Quiteria Dávila (1526–1607) was a nun from the Incarnation whom Teresa brought with her to Salamanca.

3. The Dominican professor of theology at the University of Salamanca who had at first opposed Teresa.

4. Juana de Jesús (Guerra) received the habit in Avila in 1570 and then was transferred to Salamanca, where she made her profession.

5. One of Teresa's messengers.

To Don Alvaro de Mendoza, Valladolid
Alba de Tormes, January–February 1574

1. The prioress in Valladolid.

2. Teresa adds this sentence in the margin of the letter.

3. The matter in question was the planned marriage of the duke's heir, Don Fadrique, with Doña Magdalena de Guzmán, a lady from the royal court. The marriage never took place, and the attempt to proceed without the royal permission brought about the imprisonment of Don Fadrique and Don Fernando, the duke.

4. María de Mendoza, Don Alvaro's sister. Despite her friendship and close contact as benefactress with the nuns in Valladolid, she avoided any confrontation with the wealthy members of Doña Casilda's family.

5. Casilda de Padilla.

6. The sinner is Teresa.

7. Doña Beatriz is Don Alvaro's sister. The duchess is Leonor Ana de Guzmán of Osorno.

8. Teresa will be passing through Avila on her way to the foundation in Segovia. She needs permission from Pedro Fernández, the visitator, to stay with the nuns of her first foundation in Avila. She is still officially prioress of the Incarnation. María Bautista is the prioress in Valladolid.

To Some Aspirants, Avila
Segovia, Middle of March 1574

1. Mariana Juárez de Lara did finally enter St. Joseph's in Avila in 1574.

2. San Gil was the Jesuit school in Avila.

To Antonio Gaytán, Alba de Tormes
Segovia, May 30(?), 1574

1. The owner of the houses rented by Antonio Gaytán and Julián de Avila for the foundation in Segovia. The houses did not meet with Teresa's approval.

2. The chaplain at St. Joseph's in Avila, who frequently accompanied Teresa on her foundations.

3. The negotiations were successful, and the nuns moved to the new house, where they are still located.

To Madre María Bautista, Valladolid
Segovia, End of June 1574

1. Inés de Jesús.

2. Isabel de los Angeles, whom Teresa admired, was the niece of Simón Ruiz, a well-known banker in Medina del Campo.

3. Domingo Báñez.

4. María de León, prioress of the Dominican convent in Valladolid.

5. A medicinal herb.

6. Isabel Bautista Ortigosa, a lay sister in Valladolid.

7. Doña Guiomar de Ulloa was a collaborator with Teresa in the foundation of St. Joseph's in Avila.

8. Probably Isabel de San Pablo, who at this time was helping Teresa with her correspondence.

9. The rest of the text is missing.

To Don Teutonio de Braganza, Salamanca
Segovia, July 3, 1574

1. Although Teresa was careful to use the pompous titles of the times in addressing others, she did not want anybody using them with her.

2. Baltasar Alvarez, then rector of the Jesuits in Salamanca.

3. Luis de Santander, rector of the Jesuits in Segovia.

4. The house for the foundation in Segovia, accepted by Padre Santander in the name of the Carmelite nuns.

5. Baltasar Alvarez.

6. Diego de Acosta, who was a Jesuit professor of theology in Salamanca and later provincial.

7. Baltasar Alvarez.

8. Pedro Fernández. The matter concerning a foundation for discalced Carmelite friars in Salamanca had to be discussed with him.

9. By his interest in helping toward the foundation in Salamanca.

To Madre María Bautista, Valladolid
Segovia, July 16, 1574

1. Domingo Báñez,whom she calls *mi padre* throughout the rest of the letter.

2. In the constitutions for the discalced Carmelite nuns of 1581, the number of lay sisters was not to exceed three. The Dominican Pedro Fernández was the visitator.

3. The saintly María de Velasco y Aragón, with whom Teresa had a close friendship.

To Madre María Bautista, Valladolid
Segovia, September 11, 1574

1. The cathedral chapter of canons.

2. Probably Lorenzo de Cepeda, who had sent Teresa money from America.

3. The monastery of the Incarnation in Avila was in dire need of funds. Teresa's term as prioress at the Incarnation was to expire on October 6.

4. A Dominican professor at Salamanca, Bartolomé de Medina.

5. Pedro Fernández was a Dominican provincial as well as the apostolic visitator of the Carmelites in Castile.

6. She in fact did get to see María Bautista before the trip to Beas. At the end of December, the matter concerning Casilda de Padilla required Teresa's presence in Valladolid.

To Padre Domingo Báñez, Valladolid
Avila, December 3, 1574

1. María Bautista, the prioress in Valladolid, was this nun who called herself *poca cosa* (of little worth). Báñez also began referring to her in this way. She was afraid the nuns would reelect her as prioress. As things turned out, she was reelected.

To Doña Ana Enríquez, Toro
Valladolid, December 23, 1574

1. The prioress of Valladolid, María Bautista.

2. A Jesuit and former confessor to Teresa.

3. Estefanía de los Apóstoles, a lay sister.

4. Casilda de la Concepción.

5. As an example, one day the king, Philip II, visited the monastery and entered the cloister and asked Sister Estefanía what she would like. She answered that she would like a little hermitage next to the kitchen where she could go and be recollected in prayer when free in the kitchen. When they agreed, she suggested: "Your reverence has so many business matters to attend to that I'm afraid you'll forget; let me tie a knot in your scarf so that you will remember." The hermitage still exists and is dedicated to Our Lady of Mount Carmel.

6. Pedro Fernández, the Dominican provincial and visitator of the Carmelites.

7. María Bautista.

8. She had been planning to make a foundation in Beas. She journeyed to that foundation by way of Medina, Avila, and Toledo the first part of January.

9. She is referring to the Dominican, Domingo Báñez; actually his election was not confirmed and he remained in Valladolid.

To Doña Inés Nieto, Madrid
Valladolid, December 28, 1574

1. A widow for twenty years, she was being recommended to the Carmel by Juan Albornoz. In the end, she entered the Carmel of Santa Ana in Madrid.

2. María Bautista (Ocampo), a relative of Teresa's, was prioress.

3. Juan de Albornoz, the husband of Doña Inés.

4. The Bishop of Avila's sister, who helped Teresa with the foundation in Valladolid.

To Don Teutonio de Braganza, Salamanca
Valladolid, January 2, 1575

1. A house founded in poverty did not have a benefice attached to it. The patron or "founder" of a house established with a benefice would agree to endow the monastery with assets that would provide a fixed income. Teresa found that the patron would often be reluctant to endow the monastery with sufficient income.

2. The Jesuit Francisco de Olea was opposed to Teresa in certain matters, but the passage is puzzling to historians. Also puzzling are the previous words about the marquis.

3. Don Teutonio had recommended a reliable messenger to Teresa. He had also spoken in her favor in Madrid to those who were criticizing her for her travels outside the cloister.

4. In a patent letter of April 6, 1571, Father Giovanni Rossi, the general of the Carmelite order, commissioned Teresa to found as many monasteries as she could. She took this commission seriously and mentions it a number of times in her *Foundations*.

5. In Valladolid.

6. Fray Junípero was that companion of St. Francis of Assisi known for his simplicity.

7. The new foundation she was planning to make in Beas. She traveled there as planned, but instead of returning to Salamanca, she went on to Seville, under obedience, and made a foundation there.

8. Don Teutonio was helping Teresa's nuns in Salamanca in their difficulties over the lawsuit with Pedro de la Banda.

9. Don Teutonio turned to Teresa for spiritual direction.

To Padre Luis de Granada, Lisbon
Beas, May 1575(?)

1. It is not known which of the books written by Fray Luis de Granada that Teresa read. In her *Constitutions*, she recommends them in general.

2. Deceived because of his high esteem for her.

To Padre Juan Bautista Rubeo, Piacenza
Seville, June 18, 1575

1. Giovanni Battista Rossi, the prior general of the Carmelite order, wrote his name in Latin as Johannes Baptista Rubeus. Thus Teresa used a Latinized form for his last name: Rubeo.

2. Beas lay within the civil jurisdiction of Castile, but at the same time it belonged under the ecclesiastical jurisdiction of Andalusia.

3. Ambrosio Mariano de San Benito was a discalced Carmelite who came down to Andalusia from Pastrana.

4. Baltasar Nieto de Jesús was a troublesome Andalusian Carmelite who after being punished by the general managed to join the discalced friars and become prior of the discalced monastery in Pastrana.

5. The Carmelite chapter of Piacenza, May 1575, gave orders that the monasteries founded without permission in Andalusia were to be abandoned and that those friars made superiors be removed from office.

6. Teresa refers to the Carmelites of the observance as "calced" friars to distinguish them from the "contemplative" friars who came to be known popularly as discalced friars because they did not wear shoes but went about barefoot or in sandals as a sign of reform and return to the primitive rule. "Calced Carmelites" has never been the official title of the Carmelites of the Ancient Observance, but "Discalced Carmelites," after Teresa's death, became an official title for the discalced friars of the Teresian Carmel. In her letters Teresa often uses the popular terms "calced" and "discalced" to distinguish the Carmelite friars of her time.

7. Rubeo in his patent letter wanted them to be called the "contemplative" rather than "discalced" friars.

8. Cristóbal de Rojas y Sandoval. At this time he was still opposed to Teresa's foundation in Seville.

9. In this letter (April 6, 1571) he gives her faculties to make as many foundations in all regions as she could and orders her under holy obedience to devote herself to the work. The visitators (Pedro Fernández and Francisco de Vargas) were appointed August 20, 1569.

10. Fray Gabriel de la Peñuela had been punished by Rubeo in 1566.

11. Padre Antonio de Jesús had sought permission from the general for the foundation in Almodóvar del Campo and received a positive reply June 21, 1574.

12. Fray Gaspar Nieto (brother of Fray Baltasar Nieto), former provincial of the Carmelites in Andalusia, who was also troublesome and punished by Rubeo.

13. Teresa is alluding to the monastery San Juan del Puerto (Huelva) of the Carmelites of Andalusia that was given over to the charge of the discalced

friars by Vargas in October 1572. But the project failed and Gracián returned the monastery to the Andalusian Carmelites, October 18, 1573.

14. The rest of the text is missing.

To King Don Philip II, Madrid
Seville, July 19, 1575

1. The edifice is her reform.

2. On November 2, 1535, Teresa entered the Incarnation, a Carmelite monastery of nuns in Avila.

3. Teresa simply thought the king had all the powers necessary to issue such orders. King Philip II and Rossi had divergent views about matters of reform.

4. Jerónimo Gracián de la Madre de Dios was thirty years old at the time and had been a priest for five years, but he had been a professed Carmelite for only two years.

5. In her *Foundations*, Teresa tells of her writing to the king asking that a license be given so that the foundation would be subject to the Carmelite order rather than the council of the Order of Knights, as the first license prescribed. This letter has been lost.

To Padre Baltasar Alvarez, Salamanca
Seville, October 9, 1575

1. Julián de Avila was the chaplain at St. Joseph's in Avila; the Maestro was Maestro Gaspar Daza, a priest in Avila and friend of Teresa's. Juan de Avila de la Vega was a gentleman from Salamanca.

2. Lorenzo de Cepeda, recently back from America, went to Madrid on business in October and then returned to Seville, staying there until June 1576.

To Padre Jerónimo Gracián, Toledo
Seville, October 1575(?)

1. She is speaking about the transfer of a nun to another monastery, perhaps from Toledo to Malagón. That nun could travel with those who were on their way from Segovia to make a new foundation in Caravaca. They would be passing through Toledo and Malagón.

2. The prioress was Ana de la Encarnación. She had previously been a member of the community at the Incarnation in Avila and was one of the original nuns of the first foundation, St. Joseph's in Avila.

3. "The cats" was a code name, probably for the Carmelites of the observance.

4. Giovanni Battista Rossi (Rubeo).

5. The prioress in Malagón, Brianda de San José, had received these permissions because Teresa had taken a number of nuns from Malagón for the foundations in Beas, Seville, and Caravaca.

6. Seneca is Teresa's code name for St. John of the Cross. Seneca, Lucius Annaeus (4 B.C.– A.D. 65), born in Córdoba, was a Roman Stoic philosopher whose writings both in verse and prose reached a high ethical and religious standard. In the sixteenth century, countless editions, translations, and commentaries sprung up. Luis de Granada, O.P., used him in his sermons and

spiritual writings. Stoic teaching seems to lie in the background of some of John's observations (cf. *Ascent of Mount Carmel*, Bk. 3, ch. 6). Teresa often used the diminutive "mi Senequita."

7. Gracián was not good at riding animals; on the other hand, he admired the way Teresa rode.

8. Elías is Padre Juan Evangelista, prior of the Carmelites of the observance in Seville.

To Madre María Bautista, Valladolid
Seville, December 30, 1575

1. Domingo Báñez.

2. Jerónimo Gracián had returned to Seville and resumed, with much opposition, the visitation of the Carmelites of the observance.

3. The general of the order, Giovanni Battista Rossi (Rubeo). She is alluding to the decision of the recent general chapter in Piacenza (May 1575) to suppress the foundations made by the discalced Carmelites in Andalusia without permission from the general and the orders she received in Seville toward the end of 1575 to retire to one of her monasteries in Castile.

4. The Council of Trent established rules for the enclosure of nuns as a tool of reform.

5. The Carmelites of the observance.

6. Domingo Báñez.

7. Jerónimo Gracián.

8. Lorenzo de Cepeda, who had gone to Madrid on business.

9. The Jesuit school of San Gil in Avila.

10. Domingo Báñez.

11. María Bautista was a great friend of Padre Báñez's.

12. The founding nuns of Caravaca arrived there December 18, 1575.

13. One of the first four nuns at Teresa's first foundation in Avila.

14. Antonia del Espíritu Santo was also one of the first four nuns in Avila. Teresa had desired that María Bautista obey the subprioress in matters that pertained to her health.

15. From the Incarnation in Avila, she had been the first prioress of Valladolid. But when Teresa was appointed prioress at the Incarnation (1571), she called her back to be subprioress there.

16. St. Pius V, Philip II, Nicolás Ormaneto, and Jerónimo Gracián.

17. The Archbishop of Seville, Don Cristóbal de Rojas y Sandoval.

18. Don Lorenzo had been thinking of joining the discalced Carmelite friars.

To Padre Juan Bautista Rubeo, Cremona
Seville, January–February(?) 1576

1. Only one of these letters has been preserved, that of June 18, 1575.

2. The Mantuan Congregation was a Carmelite reform that at the time had forty-two houses scattered through northern and central Italy.

3. The houses founded in poverty had no established income but depended on alms and what could be earned through spinning and other handiwork. This, though not always possible, was Teresa's ideal.

4. Antonio Gracián, one of the king's secretaries.

5. She is alluding to the opposition of the Carmelites in Seville to Gracián as visitator.

6. It seems that despite Teresa's insistence neither Gracián wrote to the general nor the general to Gracián. But Ambrosio Mariano de San Benito, the one least apt to write a tactful letter, did write and succeeded in offending him.

7. Padre Antonio de Jesús (Heredia) had been sent from Almodóvar del Campo to be prior of the discalced Carmelite friars at Los Remedios in Seville.

8. Angel de Salazar was the provincial of Castile, and Miguel de Ulloa was the prior of the Carmelites of the observance in Seville.

9. Neither the decrees of the Council of Trent nor those of the pope.

10. The nuncio, Nicolás Ormaneto, had given these faculties to Gracián September 22, 1574. Fray Angel de Salazar, the provincial.

11. Fray Alonso de Valdemoro was prior of the Carmelites of the observance in Avila. The discalced friars at the Incarnation were St. John of the Cross and Francisco de los Apóstoles (or Germán de San Matías). They had been seized by Valdemoro and held captive in Medina del Campo until the nuncio intervened and ordered that they be released and return as confessors to the Incarnation.

To María de San José, Seville
Malagón, June 15, 1576

1. Gregorio Nacianceno, who accompanied her to Seville and on the return trip to Malagón.

2. Doña Luisa de la Cerda, the founding patron of Malagón, who on this day informed Teresa that she was sending a good workman.

3. The subprioress in Seville was María del Espíritu Santo.

4. Leonor de San Gabriel had been Teresa's nurse in Seville.

5. Garciálvarez was a secular priest who helped with the Seville foundation, but he later caused many difficulties for that Carmel.

6. The lawsuit was occasioned by the demand that the nuns pay the excise on purchasing the house in Seville.

7. Jerónimo Gracián was returning from Castile to resume his visitation of the Andalusian Carmelites of the observance.

8. Isabel de San Francisco was chronicler for the community.

9. The Carmelites of the observance in Seville.

10. Teresa de Ahumada, daughter of Lorenzo de Cepeda.

11. She had lived with the sisters in Seville for several months.

To María de San José, Seville
Malagón, June 18, 1576

1. Gregorio Nacianceno.

2. An obligation arising from the purchase of the house.

3. Elvira de San Angelo, who made her profession in Malagón. Her sister, whose name is unknown, lost interest, it seems, in the thought of becoming a Carmelite.

4. Jerónimo Gracián.

5. Beatriz de la Madre de Dios (Chaves), who made her profession September 29, 1576.

6. The mother, Juana de la Cruz, entered the Carmel of Seville also, making profession October 10, 1577.

7. Lorenzo de Cepeda.

8. Lorenzo's daughter.

9. The aspirant who was fourteen years old.

To Don Lorenzo de Cepeda, Avila
Toledo, July 24, 1576

1. Lorenzo had left for Avila fifteen days ago.

2. She is probably referring to Lorenzo's housekeeper, Jerónima de Aranda.

3. She was hoping to go there without delay, for she was the prioress of that monastery. In fact, she was not able to return until July of the following year.

4. Juan de Ovalle was Teresa's brother-in-law from Alba de Tormes. Cimbrón was Pedro Alvarez Cimbrón, a cousin of Teresa's and now Lorenzo's confidant. Teresa's sister Juana was kept in Alba by her husband when perhaps her brother Lorenzo was expecting to see her in Avila. Guiomar de Ulloa was Teresa's friend who collaborated with her and Juan de Ovalle in the foundation of St. Joseph's in Avila.

5. Another name for Cimbrón.

6. An *agnusdei* is a disk made from the wax of Easter candles stamped with the figure of a lamb. *Agnusdeis* are blessed by the pope in the first year of his pontificate and every seven years after. The rings were emerald brought by Teresita from the Americas. The items were lost but later found. Thinking that she would soon be returning to Avila, Teresa had sent ahead with a muleteer her mantle, the first chapters of her *Foundations*, and other private papers.

7. The visitator was Padre Gracián, who ordered her to continue writing her *Foundations,* which she had interrupted after chapter 19.

8. The prioress of Valladolid was María Bautista. María de Mendoza was the bishop's sister. The book formerly in the bishop's possession was Teresa's autograph of the *Life*, which had been confiscated by the Inquisition the previous year. A copy was made surreptitiously at Doña María's request.

9. She is referring to the special faculties she had been given in matters pertaining to her vow of poverty.

To Padre Jerónimo Gracián, Almodóvar
Toledo, September 5, 1576

1. Angela is a code name for Teresa herself. The prior of La Sisla was Diego de Yepes, a Jeronimite and future biographer of Teresa's.

2. Joseph is a code name for Jesus Christ.

3. The Jesuit Gaspar de Salazar.

4. Ana de los Angeles.

5. Alonso Velázquez.

6. A friar of the observance who had transferred to the discalced friars and was acting as Gracián's secretary.

7. The note has not been preserved.

8. A code name for Gracián.

9. Alonso Velázquez.

10. Diego de Yepes.

To Padre Jerónimo Gracián, Almodóvar
Toledo, September 5, 1576

1. Antonio Figueredo was the chief courier of Toledo, not a brother but a cousin of a Carmelite nun in Segovia.

2. Jerónimo Tostado was appointed visitator for the Spanish Carmelites.

3. Padre Juan de las Infantas was named prior of San Juan del Puerto by Gracián.

4. Pedro González de Mendoza was a canon and treasurer of the cathedral. After his escape from prison, St. John of the Cross was cared for by him.

5. The discalced friars would be returning from the chapter in Almodóvar. It had been convoked by Gracián on August 26. The Duke of Alba was Fernando de Toledo.

6. Antonio de Jesús (Heredia), who received a license to found a monastery in Almodóvar. It was given by the general on June 21, 1574.

7. The friars at the chapter followed Teresa's wish and sent Juan de Jesús and Pedro de los Angeles to Rome.

8. Antonio Ruiz from Malagón.

To Madre María de San José, Seville
Toledo, September 20, 1576

1. Jerónimo Gracián, whom she presumes is in Seville.

2. Brianda de San José, who had been hemorrhaging from the lungs a few days before.

3. Lorenzo de Cepeda, a great benefactor of the Carmel in Seville.

4. Ana de los Angeles, prioress of Toledo.

5. Hernando de Pantoja, the prior of the Carthusians of Las Cuevas who was then old and ailing.

6. The nuns of Seville had requested the Franciscan friars allow them to tap water from their property.

7. The Carmel of Seville owed the Carmel of St. Joseph's in Avila forty ducats.

To Padre Jerónimo Gracián, Seville
Toledo, October 5, 1576

1. Antonio de Jesús (Heredia), prior of the discalced Carmelite monastery in Seville, who attended the chapter in Almodóvar.

2. Code name for Gracián.

3. Gracián's official visitation of the Carmelites in Andalusia.

4. Another code name for Gracián.

5. Code name for Jesus.

6. She resumes the written account of her foundations at Gracián's request. She had gotten as far as chapter 19. She wrote chapters 20–27 within the next month, finishing on November 14, 1576.

7. Gracián had given a report of all he had done as apostolic visitator to the conventual chapter of the Carmelite friars of the observance in Seville.

8. She is referring to those friars of the observance who left the order before being expelled.

9. The discalced friars had their own monastery (Los Remedios) in Seville.

10. The identities of David and Esperanza are unknown.

11. Diego de Buenaventura, visitator of the Franciscans.

To Madre María de San José, Seville
Toledo, October 5, 1576

1. Jerónimo Gracián.

2. Through the chief courier of Toledo, Antonio Figueredo.

3. Ambrosio Mariano de San Benito, who arrived in Toledo on September 25.

4. Antonio de Jesús (Heredia), the prior in Seville who had attended the chapter in Almodóvar.

5. The litigation over the excise had been going on since the purchase of the house.

6. Lorenzo de Cepeda.

7. Leonor de San Gabriel, who was Teresa's nurse in Seville.

8. A well-to-do aspirant was discouraged by the Jesuits from entering the Carmelites because she did not have a strong constitution.

9. A priest friend of both the Carmelites and the Jesuits in Seville.

10. The Carthusian prior, Hernando de Pantoja.

11. Diego de Acosta, a Jesuit in Seville.

To Padre Ambrosio Mariano, Madrid
Toledo, October 21, 1576

1. The Jesuit Francisco de Olea is recommending an unsuitable aspirant. He will end up becoming angry with Teresa over this question.

2. Padre Olea had harsh words for the prioress in Valladolid for not having procured a favorable vote for the novice.

3. Jerónimo Gracián.

4. Nicolás Ormaneto.

5. Jerónimo Manrique, a canon in Toledo, who was highly regarded by Philip II.

6. Alonso Valdemoro, prior of the Carmelites of the observance in Avila.

7. Diego Mejía de Ovando, Count of Uceda, a relative of Don Alvaro de Mendoza's.

8. The Archdeacon of Toledo, Francisco de Avila.

9. The dean of the cathedral in Toledo, Diego de Castilla.

10. Doña Luisa de la Cerda, Teresa's friend in Toledo.

11. Jerónimo Tostado.

12. Juan de Jesús María Roca, prior of Mancera. The Salamancan project consisted of a house for discalced Carmelite friars in front of a women's refuge. Teresa preferred that they have a house of studies in Salamanca.

13. The Bishop of Salamanca, Francisco Soto y Salazar.

14. Repentent women living in the house of refuge and rehabilitation.

15. Juan Calvo de Padilla.

16. Don Teutonio de Braganza, who was also interested in the foundation in Salamanca.

17. Another foundation project of the discalced friars not yet realized.

18. She is referring either to the prior of the Carmelites of the observance in Madrid, Francisco Ximénez, or to Baltasar de Jesús Nieto, prior of the discalced friars in Pastrana.

19. Teresa's mail carrier.

20. Ana de Jesús (Lobera).

21. The discalced Carmelite friars of La Peñuela transferred to El Calvario, not far from Beas, in November of 1576.

22. Don Iñigo López de Mendoza.

23. The nuns in Beas opened a window in the wall connecting their house to the parish church so they could listen to the sermons preached there and attend other church functions. But the priest was contesting their right to do such a thing.

To Padre Jerónimo Gracián, Seville
Toledo, November 1576(?)

1. Teresa's new Carmels.

2. Gracián.

To Padre Jerónimo Gracián, Seville
Toledo, November 1576

1. An allusion to the legend of Santa Marina, who lived a solitary life disguised as a monk. When accused of being the father of a child, she bore the calumny in silence. Only after her death was the truth discovered.

To Madre María de San José, Seville
Toledo, November 19, 1576

1. María de San José knew how to write Arabic numerals but is not doing so, perhaps out of false humility.

2. María de San José sent her letter to Ambrosio Mariano de San Benito without sealing it so that Teresa could read it.

3. Teresa continues to speak in jest. When she was in Seville, Gracián ordered her to make a general confession, which proved to be a burdensome mortification for her. On the other hand, María de San José had done the same without any difficulty.

4. The prioress of Caravaca, Ana de San Alberto, who had previously gone with Teresa for the foundation in Beas and Seville. As with María de San José, she began to appreciate Teresa's affection only after their separation.

5. Monasteries that were endowed and thus had to live on a fixed income.

6. Beatriz de Jesús (Cepeda y Ocampo) was appointed vicaress of Malagón by Madre Brianda.

7. The Spanish proverb is, "For want of good men, my husband is mayor."

8. El Carmen was the monastery for the Carmelite friars of the observance in Seville, and Los Remedios for the discalced Carmelite friars in Seville.

9. Evidently a letter from Gracián to Teresita, Teresa's niece postulant in Avila, was unsealed and read by both María de San José and Teresa.

10. Julián de Avila, the chaplain of the discalced nuns in Avila.

11. Little Isabel Dantisco, eight years old, was residing in the Carmel of Toledo at Teresa's side. She wrote the letter mentioned.

To Padre Jerónimo Gracián, Seville
Toledo, Around December 1576

1. Antonio de Jesús (Heredia).

To Lorenzo de Cepeda, Avila
Toledo, Christmas Season 1576–77

1. The persons alluded to are St. John of the Cross and Lorenzo's son Francisco. The Incarnation is the name of the Carmelite monastery of nuns in Avila.

To Don Lorenzo de Cepeda, Avila
Toledo, January 2, 1577

1. This paper written by Gracián was meant for Garciálvarez, the chaplain for the Carmel in Seville, limiting his powers as confessor. María de San José sent it to Teresa from Seville. It is of interest to Lorenzo because of his close ties with the nuns in Seville.

2. According to legend, the letters IHS were found impressed in gold on St. Ignatius of Antioch's heart after his martyrdom.

3. The nuncio was thinking of forming a province of the houses founded by Teresa.

4. The key to the small chest.

5. *The Way of Perfection* is the book in which she reflects on the Our Father and in chaps. 30–31 deals with the prayer of quiet. The other book is *The Book of Her Life*, where she treats of the prayer of quiet in chaps. 14–15.

6. Lorenzo had taken Teresa as his spiritual director and promised obedience to her. Now, without consulting her, he has made a vow of doing always the more perfect thing.

7. Teresa had made a "vow of perfection," but with certain conditions that her brother hadn't taken into consideration. Her confessor was Alonso Velázquez.

8. The privileges of the Holy Year of 1570–71 were extended to the entire Catholic world by Gregory XIII for the year 1576.

9. La Serna, about three miles from Avila, was a property purchased by Lorenzo. Now he was thinking of selling it to be free of administrative responsibilities and have more time for prayer.

10. Francisco de Salcedo was a friend of Teresa's of whom she speaks in her *Life*, and who had since become a priest after his wife's death.

11. Lorenzo's oldest son, Francisco de Cepeda, who was then seventeen.

12. She is referring to the answers given to the words "Seek yourself in Me," of which she wrote a satirical critique according to the custom of the time (see *A Satirical Critique* in vol. 3 of her *Collected Works*, pp. 357–362).

13. He questioned the humorous way in which the critique of the answers was to be made.

14. To keep the fish fresh in those days it was wrapped in slices of bread.

15. She kept the Advent fast and abstinence.

16. Guiomar de Ulloa. They were together a good deal during the years 1558–62.

To Padre Ambrosio Mariano de San Benito, Madrid
Toledo, February 28, 1577

1. Teutonio de Braganza, the future Archbishop of Ebora.

2. Nicolás Ormaneto. It had been rumored that he was going to be relieved of his office.

3. Mariano was living outside the monastery because he wanted to have more freedom to deal with the business of the discalced friars. The nuncio had disapproved of this.

4. The Carmelites of the observance.

5. The answer to a petition probably made by the discalced friars that the directive issued against them be withdrawn.

6. Jerónimo Gracián, who is carrying out his commission as visitator of the Carmelites in Andalusia.

7. She is referring to calumnies uttered against the discalced Carmelites in Andalusia.

8. Only now does she inform Mariano of the illness she has suffered from overwork and that she must not be writing letters.

To María de San José, Seville
Toledo, March 1–2, 1577

1. She had been suffering for about a month from an illness that was brought on through overwork.

2. Luisa de la Cerda's administrator, Juan Huidobro de Miranda.

3. María de San José had made her profession in Malagón.

4. The Portuguese nun was Blanca de Jesús María; her mother was Leonor de Valera.

5. Beatriz de la Madre de Dios, a nun in the Seville Carmel.

6. Isabel de San Jerónimo, one of the three who went to help reform the community in Paterna. She and Beatriz showed a certain lack of balance in their prayer experiences.

7. One of the prioresses in Castile before Isabel de San Jerónimo went south to Andalusia.

8. One of her confessors told Isabel to write down her experiences in prayer. One of her pages was mislaid and fortunately landed in the hands of the prioress in Paterna, Isabel de San Francisco.

9. Jerónimo Gracián.

10. Ana de Jesús (Anne of Jesus); it was she for whom St. John of the Cross wrote his commentary on *The Spiritual Canticle.*

11. Isabel de San Francisco.

12. The Jesuit Diego de Acosta.

13. It seems those discalced nuns who went to reform the community in Paterna started out by demanding more than what the nuns were obliged to by their constitutions.

14. Luisa de la Cerda.

15. Isabelita Dantisco, Gracián's young sister living in the Carmel in Toledo.

16. She wrote *catamaca* instead of *tacamaca*. It was a resin that was used as a sedative.

17. These were the answers to the question about the meaning of the words "Seek Yourself in Me."

18. The prior of the discalced friars in Seville, Antonio de Jesús, and Nicolás Doria.

19. Lorenzo de Cepeda.

20. What follows was written on the outside next to the address.

To Lorenzo de Cepeda, Avila
Toledo, January 17, 1577

1. She is referring to Peralta's house, near the discalced Carmelite nuns in Avila, which Lorenzo had bought.

2. A reference to the contents of her *Life* and other private writings about her spiritual life.

3. The two are St. John of the Cross and Francisco de Salcedo.

4. Lorenzo did not understand the first stanza of the poem Teresa had sent him, "Oh Exceeding Beauty": Oh Beauty exceeding / All other beauties! / Paining, but You wound not / Free of pain You destroy / The love of creatures.

5. Without wounding you cause pain, and without pain you wear away the love of creatures.

6. María de Cepeda, Teresa's cousin, was a nun and ill at the Incarnation in Avila.

7. She is alluding to Lorenzo's generosity in financing the foundation in Seville.

8. The bishop was Don Alvaro de Mendoza, and the book was a copy of her *Life*.

9. The prioress of Valladolid was her cousin María Bautista. The merchant was Agustín de Vitoria, who will later help Teresa with the foundation in Palencia.

To Don Lorenzo de Cepeda, Avila
Toledo, February 27–28, 1577

1. Francisco de Cepeda, Lorenzo's son.

2. She is referring to the ecstasies she was beginning to experience in public again some days previous to this.

3. Lorenzo's daughter, living in the monastery of St. Joseph's in Avila.

4. The chaplain for the discalced nuns in Avila.

5. She is alluding to 1 Sm 15:22: "Obedience is better than sacrifice and submission than the fat of rams."

6. The "papers" were the autograph of her *Life*. The manuscript had been in the possession of the Inquisition since 1575. The Grand Inquisitor was Gaspar de Quiroga. Doña Luisa de la Cerda was Teresa's friend and benefactor from Toledo.

7. Actually, the Inquisition did not return Teresa's manuscript to her.

8. The bishop is Don Alvaro de Mendoza. It was he who had to send the autograph of Teresa's *Life* to the Inquisition.

9. The prioress was María de San José of Seville. Teresa was interested in paying off the debt on the monastery in Seville without touching the dowries of Beatriz de la Madre de Dios and her mother, Juana de la Cruz.

10. Agustín de Ahumada, Teresa's brother, lived in America. The Marchioness of Villena, Juana Lucas de Toledo, was a niece of the Viceroy of Peru, Francisco de Toledo, under whose rule Agustín was subject.

11. Agustín de Ahumada, with his fiery and warlike temperament, was a cause of anxiety for Teresa; she feared for his eternal salvation.

12. Some of the discalced Carmelite nuns from Seville, through Gracián's initiative, were engaged in reforming a monastery of nuns at Paterna.

13. It seems Francisco de Salcedo had compared Teresa to his housekeeper, Señora Ospedal, and Lorenzo mentioned this to his sister.

To Madre María de San José, Seville
Toledo, July 11, 1577

1. María del Espíritu Santo, the subprioress in Seville.

2. Like going off to the land of the Moors (cf. *The Book of Her Life* 1.4).

3. Brianda de San José, residing in Toledo because of illness.

4. Jerónimo Gracián.

5. Doubts had arisen whether or not Gracián's faculties continued in force after the death of the nuncio.

6. Don Cristóbal de Rojas, the Archbishop of Seville and friend of Teresa's.

7. Nicolás Doria, a novice with the discalced Carmelite friars at Los Remedios.

8. Gregorio Nacianceno at Los Remedios, who was considering along with Madre María the possibility of moving to a new house.

9. Beatriz de la Madre de Dios (Chaves) and her mother, Juana de la Cruz.

10. Padre Gracián, who had been a support to the community.

11. Many nuns from the monastery of the Incarnation in Avila joined Teresa's first communities.

12. Antonio de Jesús (Heredia), prior at Los Remedios in Seville.

To King Don Philip II, Madrid
Avila, September 18, 1577

1. She is referring to his canonical visitations.

2. The two discalced Carmelite friars were the lay brother Miguel de la Columna and Padre Baltasar de Nieto.

3. She is referring to the Carmelites of the observance.

4. Gracián was the son of Diego de Alderete, the king's secretary.

5. Jerónimo Tostado, appointed visitator for the Carmelites in Spain at the general chapter.

6. Baltasar de Jesús (Nieto).

7. These chapters were meetings of the entire community called by Gracián during his canonical visitations for the correction of faults. It was customary for visitators to enter the enclosure on occasions like this.

To Madre María de San José, Seville
Avila, October 22, 1577

1. Jerónimo Gracián was commissioned as visitator and apostolic commissary.
2. The calced Carmelite friars in Andalusia.
3. Fray Miguel de la Columna, a lay brother; Baltasar de Jesús (Nieto).
4. Philip II.
5. Teresa's former monastery of the Incarnation in Avila.
6. Jerónimo Tostado, visitator of the Carmelites in Spain.
7. The provincial of the Carmelites in Castile was Juan Gutiérrez de la Magdalena.
8. Doña Ana de Toledo, who obtained 34 votes.
9. The Council of Trent. The nuns remained excommunicated for about two months.
10. This reflects the orders she received from the general chapter of Piacenza to retire to a monastery in Castile and not leave it.
11. The monastery of the Incarnation.
12. Teresita de Ahumada (Cepeda), her niece.
13. Doña Ana de Vaena.
14. Doña Luisa de la Cerda, Gaspar de Quiroga, and Philip II.

To Padre Jerónimo Gracián
Avila, November 1577

1. Gracián.
2. That is, Gracián should tell himself (Paul).
3. Jesus Christ.
4. Teresa.

To Padre Jerónimo Gracián
Avila, December 1577(?)

1. Gracián.

To King Don Philip II
Avila, December 4, 1577

1. Teresa had been prioress at the Incarnation 1571–1574. The nuns attempted to elect her again on October 7.
2. Pedro Fernández, who had appointed her prioress at the Incarnation.
3. St. John of the Cross.
4. Germán de San Matías.
5. Hernando Maldonado, prior of the monastery in Toledo. He went there for the purpose of absolving those who voted for Teresa from the excommunication imposed on them.
6. The confessors were John of the Cross and Germán de San Matías.
7. Jerónimo Gracián.
8. John of the Cross.
9. Hernando Maldonado was the superior. Antonio de Jesús (Heredia), one of the first two friars to become discalced (the other being John of the Cross),

had accompanied Teresa and Gracián on their recent trip from Toledo to Avila. On his return, Antonio was ordered by Maldonado to remain sequestered in Toledo.

10. Jerónimo Tostado.

To Don Juan de Ovalle and Doña Juana de Ahumada, Alba
Avila, December 10, 1577

1. Juan de Ovalle was seeking help from intermediaries to obtain a position.

2. Luisa de la Cerda's brother was Fernando de la Cerda.

3. She wonders why they don't spend the winter in Galinduste as in previous years. It would be cheaper for them. Beatriz was Juana's daughter.

4. The nuns, though absolved from the excommunication, were still insisting on their rights to have Teresa for their prioress. The Carmelites of the observance in Castile had taken away as prisoners the confessors John of the Cross and Germán de San Matías, which explains Teresa's strong language.

5. The two brothers are Lorenzo and Pedro. Teresa is her niece who was residing at St. Joseph's in Avila.

To Madre María de San José, Seville
Avila, December 10, 1577

1. An aromatic resin from the Indies having medicinal properties.

2. St. John of the Cross and Germán de San Matías.

3. The prior of the Carmelites in Avila, Alonso Valdemoro.

4. A small town between Avila and Medina del Campo where the Carmelite friars had another monastery.

5. Gregorio Nacianceno, a discalced friar at Los Remedios in Seville.

6. Her brother Lorenzo had advanced a large sum of money for the foundation.

7. Juan Evangelista had been appointed prior of the Carmelites of the observance in Seville by Gracián in his apostolic visitation. In the uprising he was deposed and a vicar was appointed.

8. An ironic statement about the first house, highly praised by Padre Ambrosio Mariano. The first house would have proved a disaster, and fortunately the purchase fell through.

To Padre Jerónimo Gracián, Pastrana
Avila, February 16, 1578

1. Teresa fell down the stairs on Christmas Eve in 1577 and broke her left arm. It wasn't reset until May.

2. Antonio de Jesús (Heredia) was sick in Seville; Ambrosio Mariano de San Benito was staying in Madrid; and Bartolomé de Jesús was Gracián's secretary.

3. The Jesuit provincial was Juan Suárez. Carillo was a code name for Gaspar de Salazar, a Jesuit residing in Granada.

4. Gaspar de Salazar's proposal was to leave the Jesuits and transfer to the discalced Carmelites.

5. The provincial reproached Teresa for using her supposed revelations to persuade Salazar to transfer.

6. Gonzalo Dávila was the Jesuit rector at San Gil in Avila who brought Suárez's letter to Teresa.

7. Cf. the papal bull *Licet Debitum* of Paul III (1549).

8. Catalina Machuca, a protégée of the Princess of Eboli. The latter wanted to impose her on the Carmel of Pastrana without obtaining Teresa's consent.

9. Catalina de Jesús was one of the sponsors of the foundation in Beas and was also inclined toward the extraordinary. (See *Foundations* 22.4–24.)

10. Code name for Jesus Christ.

11. Juan Calvo de Padilla, a priest who was very much involved in the reform of religious orders.

12. Joanes could be a code name for Gracián. The ravens are the Jesuits.

13. Code name for Gracián.

14. María de San José (Salazar).

15. Blanca de Jesús (Freire). Her sister María de San José made profession in the Carmel of Seville on January 1, 1583.

16. Lorenzo de Cepeda.

17. Guiomar de Ulloa, Teresa's friend and collaborator.

18. Francisco de Jesús.

19. Roque de Huerta, Teresa's connecting link in Madrid for the safe transport of her letters.

20. It seems that Gracián decided to hold on to Teresa's letter to Salazar.

21. Juan Suárez.

To Roque de Huerta, Madrid
Avila, March 8–12, 1578

1. The provincial of the Carmelites in Castile, Juan Gutiérrez de la Magdalena. These were the days in which he was pressuring the nuns with threats to withdraw the accusations made against him to the Royal Council.

2. On March 1 the royal secretary Juan Chacón notified the provincial of the royal provision that he must absolve the nuns at the Incarnation from the censures and excommunications imposed on them by himself. Teresa was enclosing copies of the documents.

3. The provincial had feigned absence from Avila. Alonso Valdemoro was the former prior of the monastery of friars in Avila.

4. Juan Calvo de Padilla, who will be taken under arrest on June 27.

5. Jerónimo Tostado, the Carmelite visitator.

6. John of the Cross had been seized during the first days of December 1577 and was at the time held in the monastery prison of the Carmelites of the observance in Toledo.

To Padre Jerónimo Gracián, Alcalá
Avila, March 10–11, 1578

1. The Carmelites of the observance.

2. The Carmelite nuns at the Incarnation who were being threatened by Gutiérrez and Valdemoro.

3. The two confessors, Fray John of the Cross and Fray Germán de San Matías.

4. Roque de Huerta and Juan Calvo de Padilla.

5. Germán de San Matías.

6. She was probably Isabel de la Cruz from Ciudad Rodrigo. She made her profession in Alba de Tormes August 22, 1579.

To Madre María de San José, Seville
Avila, March 28, 1578

1. She makes this remark in a humorous vein.

2. Isabel de San Francisco had been prioress in Paterna for some months.

3. Isabel de San Jerónimo, a member of the community in Seville, though good intentioned was somewhat unbalanced.

4. Teresa (Teresita) de Jesús, Lorenzo's daughter and Teresa's niece.

5. Good Friday.

6. Julián de Avila, the chaplain at St. Joseph's in Avila.

To Padre Jerónimo Gracián, Alcalá
Avila, May 7, 1578

1. The woman was a bonesetter from Medina sent by Inés de Jesús, the prioress there.

To Padre Jerónimo Gracián, Alcalá
Avila, May 8, 1578

1. The previous letter, above.

2. It seems she is referring to Padre Antonio de Jesús, always resentful of her. Now he failed by being too credulous in his visitation of the community in Malagón.

3. The nuns at the Carmel in Malagón.

4. These words supply for what Teresa later crossed out. She is referring to the licentiate Gaspar de Villanueva, confessor and chaplain for the nuns.

5. Gracián had given orders to the nuns' Carmels not to provide meals for the discalced friars.

6. "The one who is there" is Gaspar de Villanueva.

7. She is referring to the charity of Ana de la Madre de Dios.

8. Brianda de San José.

9. Malagón was a small town, but on an important main road leading from Castile into Andalusia.

10. The prioress of Segovia, who was formerly prioress in Pastrana and had to deal with the erratic Princess of Eboli.

11. Gracián had given Padre Antonio, without any forewarning, faculties to make the visitation.

12. The "N" was inserted by the copyist in place of the name written by Teresa. She seems to be alluding to Brianda de San José.

13. Bartolomé de Jesús had been Gracián's secretary. Francisco de la Concepción had transferred to the discalced Carmelites from the Carmelites of the observance. Antonio Ruiz was a merchant friend of Teresa's from Malagón.

14. Antonio de Jesús and Ana de la Madre de Dios.

15. María de San Jerónimo (Dávila) had been vicaress at St. Joseph's in Avila during Teresa's absence there.

To Madre Anne of Jesus, Beas
Avila, August 1578(?)

1. Catalina de Jesús (Sandoval) was one of the founding patrons of the Carmel in Beas and a future directee of St. John of the Cross.

To Padre Jerónimo Gracián, Madrid
Avila, August 21–22, 1578

1. He was taken prisoner during the night of December 3, 1577, and escaped from his prison in the night of August 17, 1578.

2. Fray Germán de San Matías was a confessor for the nuns at the Incarnation along with John of the Cross. He was taken prisoner at the same time as John, but very soon afterward broke free from his captors.

To Roque de Huerta, Madrid
Avila, October 24, 1578

1. Angel de Salazar, the provincial of Castile.
2. Alonso Velázquez.
3. We don't know what she is referring to here.
4. It is not clear what he is bound in conscience to do; it may be to reconvene the chapter.
5. The chapter members.
6. Submission of either Padre Gracián or Antonio de Jesús to the nuncio.
7. This probably refers to Antonio de Jesús.
8. This could be either the nuncio or the provincial.
9. Either the nuncio or the provincial.
10. Jerónimo Gracián.
11. The discalced friars.
12. Jerónimo Gracián.
13. A Dominican friar who was at the time confessor to Philip II.
14. Members of Roque's family household.

To the Discalced Carmelite Nuns, Seville
Avila, January 31, 1579

1. She is alluding probably to news given by a messenger rather than by letter.
2. Her analogy refers to the fact that it was from Seville that boats set sail for the Americas and their treasures.
3. Allusion to 1 Cor 10:13.
4. Allusion to Mt 8:25–26.
5. An allusion to the plays that were a custom in the community in which the nuns would act as Christians in a foreign land longing to suffer martyrdom.
6. Allusion to Ex 14:28.
7. Probably they had written a report documenting the events of the process to which they had been subjected by the provincial.
8. This process was carried out by Diego de Cárdenas in the Carmel of Seville in November–December 1578. An account of it is given in María de San José's *Libro de Recreaciones*.

9. Jerónimo Gracián, the main casualty of the process.

10. Garciálvarez, the community's former confessor who, because he had been dismissed as confessor by María de San José, joined ranks with the provincial.

To Padre Jerónimo Gracián, Alcalá
Avila, Mid-April 1579

1. Teresa was hoping that soon the discalced Carmelites would be allowed to become an autonomous province with a provincial of their own.

2. Gregorio Nacianceno, a discalced Carmelite sent by the nuncio to Andalusia.

3. A nun in the Carmel of Seville who had also been punished by Diego de Cárdenas.

4. Allusion to the nuns who had come from Castile for the foundation in Seville.

5. Diego de Cárdenas.

6. Juan de Jesús Roca was in Avila preparing for his secret trip to Rome to plead the cause of the discalced Carmelites.

7. Diego de Montoya from Avila, the king's canonist in Rome. His mother, residing in Avila, was María de Montoya.

8. Juan de Jesús Roca.

To Don Teutonio de Braganza, Evora
Valladolid, July 22, 1579

1. *The Way of Perfection*, which Don Teutonio will arrange to have printed in Evora. It wasn't actually published until 1583, a number of months after Teresa's death.

2. Diego de Yanguas. The 1583 edition of *The Way of Perfection* has as an appendix the text entitled *Vida y milagros del glorioso padre San Alberto* (The Life and Miracles of our Glorious Father St. Albert). Diego de Yanguas dedicated this life to St. Teresa and at her insistence wrote: "Many unhistorical things are added here for the greater glory of this glorious saint." St. Albert, Patriarch of Jerusalem, gave the hermits on Mount Carmel their rule sometime between 1206 and 1214.

3. She is referring to the establishment of a separate province for the discalced Carmelites. On July 15, 1579, the nuncio Sega with his advisors proposed the erection of a separate province.

4. When the young king of Portugal was killed in battle, the nearest male heir was his great-uncle, Cardinal Enrique. The cardinal was Don Teutonio's uncle and had preceded him as Archbishop of Evora. The principal claimants to the throne were King Philip II and Don Juan, Duke of Braganza, Don Teutonio's nephew. Philip was threatening a possible military and naval intervention.

To Madre María de San José, Seville
Toledo, April 3, 1580

1. From the middle of February she had traveled to Malagón, La Roda, Villanueva de la Jara, and Toledo, where she arrived on March 26.

2. Nicolás Doria, who stopped off in Toledo on his way back from Seville to Pastrana, where he was prior. The grille was a grating in the parlor separating the enclosed nun from her visitor.

3. She is referring to the conflict over the successor to the king's crown.

4. Guiomar Pardo de Tavera, the daughter of Luisa de la Cerda and wife, after her first husband's death, of Juan de Guzmán, son of the Count of Alba de Liste.

5. Jerónimo Gracián, who is on the way to be prior in Seville after having been elected unanimously on February 19, 1580.

6. These probably contained an account of all the troubles that took place in the community the previous year.

7. Beatriz de la Madre de Dios, who played a role in causing the troubles.

8. The dispatches representing the king and the nuncio had arrived in Rome. They were awaiting a favorable response from the Holy See, which would be obtained on June 6, 1580.

9. The monastery of the discalced Carmelite friars in Seville.

10. Roque de Huerta was the king's chief forest guard.

11. The prioress in Toledo, Ana de los Angeles.

12. The prioress of Villanueva de la Jara, María de los Mártires.

13. Brianda de San José, the former prioress of Malagón.

14. Hernando de Pantoja, who in January was hurt in a fall and no longer held the office of prior.

To Doña Isabel Osorio, Madrid
Toledo, April 8, 1580

1. The desire for a foundation in Madrid.

2. Valentín López, a Jesuit from Madrid; probably Isabel's confessor.

3. Baltasar Alvarez, named provincial in Lent of 1580.

4. Isabel's sister.

5. Gabriel de la Asunción, who was prior of La Roda, near Villanueva de la Jara.

To Madre María de Cristo, Avila
Toledo, April 16, 1580

1. The vicar general is Angel de Salazar.

2. Lorenzo de Cepeda, in Avila.

3. Nicolás Doria, prior of Pastrana.

4. The prioress in the Carmel of Toledo, Ana de los Angeles.

5. Teresa's cousin, who was a nun in the Carmel of Avila.

6. The subprioress.

7. Teresa's niece, Lorenzo's daughter.

To Padre Jerónimo Gracián, Madrid
Toledo, May 5, 1580

1. The dispute revolved around the obligation in conscience of someone on his deathbed to become reconciled with an offender. The question was complicated by ideas concerning "points of honor," and a budding moral probabilism.

2. An epidemic of influenza, from which Teresa had been suffering, was passing through Castile in those days.

3. The letter was a notice given by Abbot Bernardinus Briceno to Philip II that Gregory XIII had granted permission for the discalced Carmelites to establish a separate province.

4. Angel de Salazar, the Carmelite vicar general, had given Gracián some official commissions: prior of Los Remedios in Seville and visitator of the discalced Carmelite friars in Almodóvar del Campo.

5. Baeza, where at the time St. John of the Cross was rector.

6. The brief from Rome.

7. The Archbishop of Toledo, Gaspar de Quiroga.

8. The prioress was Isabel de Santo Domingo.

9. Responding to the request of the Bishop of Palencia, Don Alvaro de Mendoza, Angel de Salazar gave Teresa orders to go to Valladolid and Palencia.

10. Juan Vázquez de Velasco, who won favor in Madrid for the discalced Carmelites, and Gracián in particular, was the Carmelite aspirant's brother.

To Padre Jerónimo Gracián, Madrid
Toledo, June 3, 1580

1. The angel was the Grand Inquisitor, Gaspar de Quiroga, the Archbishop of Toledo.

2. Angel de Salazar, their vicar general, whom she wanted to meet in Madrid. He was to travel from Salamanca to Valladolid and then to Madrid. Teresa's plan was to travel through Madrid to Segovia.

3. Hernando del Castillo, a Dominican from Madrid who was a great friend of Teresa's and had intervened in the case against the Princess of Eboli.

4. Ana de Mendoza, the widow of Ruy Gómez de Silva, became suspect of having had a role to play in the murder of Juan Escobedo, secretary to Don Juan of Austria. She had been confined to the castle of Santorcaz by order of the king and then moved to the family palace at Pastrana. More than once Teresa sent Gracián to Santorcaz and Pastrana to try to comfort her.

5. Pedro Juan de Casademonte, a merchant from Medina del Campo.

6. She is referring to the strange delays that kept them from setting out on their journey to Madrid and Segovia.

To Padre Jerónimo Gracián, Seville
Valladolid, November 20, 1580

1. Gracián's mother.

2. Gracián's sister, who was a Carmelite in Valladolid.

3. Her nephew Francisco de Cepeda, who suddenly left the novitiate in Pastrana without having received the habit.

4. The desire to become a discalced Carmelite.

5. Nicolás Doria, prior of Pastrana, was somewhat abrupt in saying goodbye.

6. It was on the feast of the Presentation of Our Lady in the Temple that Gracián presented the papers to the Carmelites in Seville that authorized him to make an official visitation. This created such an uproar that Teresa feared for his life.

7. She had dictated what preceded (nos. 1–4) and now, in nos. 5–6, writes in her own hand, and then again probably in no. 9.

8. Blessed Anne of St. Bartholomew, Teresa's secretary. She will sign her name in no. 8.

To Doña Juana de Ahumada, Alba
Palencia, January 13, 1581

1. She arrived in Palencia on December 28, 1580, with five nuns, among whom was her nurse, Blessed Anne of St. Bartholomew. She was still suffering from the effects of the perilous influenza that spread through Spain the previous year and left her gravely ill in Toledo and then again in Valladolid.

2. Francisco de Cepeda, Teresa's nephew, after a brief attempt at the discalced Carmelite life in Pastrana, got married to Doña Orofrisia de Mendoza y Castilla in Madrid. His mother-in-law, Doña Beatriz de Castilla y Mendoza, was soon to clash with Teresa over money matters. Pedro de Ahumada, Teresa's brother, who until the death of Lorenzo had been dependent on him, was now left to himself.

3. Don Francisco's marriage took place hastily, and Teresa is seeking to prevent her sister from becoming angry at not having been informed properly.

4. Inés de Jesús was Teresa's cousin, who came with her to Palencia and will remain there as prioress.

To Padre Jerónimo Gracián, Alcalá
Palencia, February 1581

1. Vicars were superiors who had authority over a community of nuns, delegated by either the ordinary or the provincial. Teresa did not want vicars for her communities.

2. Gracián complied with this request.

3. She is referring to decisions made by Pedro Fernández at the time when he was the apostolic visitator.

4. Teresa must have written to the chapter or to the commissary stressing the effectiveness of Gracián's official visitations of the discalced Carmels of nuns. It is not certain whether these eight points were in that letter or at the beginning of this letter, which is a fragment.

5. Giovanni Battista Rossi. The brief *Pia consideratione* did not grant the presider at the chapter the powers to confer the degrees of master and *presentado* as Teresa wanted.

6. Angel de Salazar, who had been acting as vicar general of the discalced friars and nuns.

To Dionisio Ruiz de la Peña, Toledo
Soria, June 30, 1581

1. Luisa de la Cerda, a friend of Cardinal Quiroga's.

2. When there was no ordinary (or official) mail delivery, one had to contract a personal messenger.

3. She is alluding to Doña Elena de Quiroga, who was the cardinal's niece and who wanted to enter the Carmel in Medina where her daughter was already a professed nun.

4. She is referring to the Flemish woman Ana Wasteels, who was widowed at age thirty-one, with two daughters, and entered St. Joseph's in Avila, taking the name Ana de San Pedro.

5. She has in mind the theological doctrine that the first ones to whom our love should be directed are children and parents.

To Padre Jerónimo Gracián, Valladolid
Soria, July 14, 1581

1. Nicolás Doria, who accompanied her to Soria and was now on his return, either in Avila or Valladolid.

2. Elena de Quiroga, niece of the Cardinal Archbishop of Toledo, Gaspar de Quiroga, who wants to be a discalced Carmelite nun against the desires of her uncle.

3. A monastery of friars on the outskirts of Valladolid.

4. The Archbishop of Toledo, Gaspar de Quiroga.

5. Doña Elena, a widow, wants to enter the Carmel of Medina where her daughter, Jerónima de la Encarnación, is a nun.

6. Her former Jesuit confessor.

7. She is referring to a plan for a foundation of discalced Carmelite nuns in Burgos.

8. The Bishop of Palencia, Alvaro de Mendoza, who interceded in favor of the foundation.

9. The Archbishop of Burgos, Cristóbal Vela, had promised to give permission for the foundation, but he doesn't seem disposed to carry through on his promise.

10. She had to obtain a license from the city of Burgos first.

11. A troubled Carmelite who had transferred to the discalced friars, and disliked Gracián, was working to make a foundation in Madrid.

12. Alonso Velázquez, Bishop of Osma.

13. Prioress of St. Joseph's in Avila, a monastery that was having serious difficulties. In fact, she had to accept the charge as soon as she arrived back (September 10).

14. The prioress in Avila was María de Cristo. Teresa had proposed Padre Gregorio Nacianceno for confessor to her discalced nuns in Avila.

15. An allusion to the recent deaths of Francisco de Salcedo and Lorenzo de Cepeda.

16. The general of the Carmelite order, Giovanni Battista Caffardo.

17. She is referring to both the conflicts the discalced friars had with the central government of the order and the expense of their trips to Rome to negotiate their becoming a separate province.

18. She is alluding either to the chapel in Alba or the one for St. Joseph's in Avila willed by her brother, Lorenzo de Cepeda.

19. The Flemish woman was Ana Wasteels (Ana de San Pedro), a nun at St. Joseph's in Avila; her daughter, Ana de los Angeles, after spending a year with the Bernardan sisters in Avila, also entered St. Joseph's.

20. Her niece Beatriz de Ovalle had been the victim of a calumny at that time.

21. As one living in a convent school, receiving an education.

To Don Jerónimo Reinoso, Palencia
Avila, September 9, 1581

1. Pedro Ribera, who accompanied Teresa on the long journey from Soria to Avila.
2. Dionisia de la Madre de Dios entered the Carmel of Palencia and made her profession the following year.
3. Diego Reinoso, Jerónimo's brother, was the chief mail carrier.
4. Francisco Reinoso, Jerónimo's brother.

To Sancho Dávila, Alba
Avila, October 9, 1581

1. The Dominican Padre Domingo Báñez.
2. Sancho Dávila had written a biography of his mother, Doña Juana Enríquez de Toledo. She was a highly esteemed friend of Teresa's.
3. The Marquis of Velada, Gómez Dávila, Don Sancho's brother.
4. The Marquess of Velada, Ana de Toledo y Monroy. The daughter was Juana de Toledo.
5. Don Gonzalo is someone who appears often in Teresa's last letters to her sister Juana de Ahumada. His wife became extremely jealous of him and Teresa's niece.

To Don Pedro Castro y Nero, Alba
Avila, November 19, 1581

1. *The Book of Her Life.* After having examined this work by Teresa, the Inquisition decided to keep it out of circulation. Teresa was here using a manuscript copy of it that had been in the possession of the Duke and Duchess of Alba.
2. The note that Dr. Castro had sent her.
3. These papers probably refer to her *Life.* The "others" could refer to *The Interior Castle* or to some of the *Spiritual Testimonies.*

To Don Pedro Castro y Nero, Avila
Avila, November 28, 1581

1. This was St. John of the Cross, who had traveled from Andalusia to arrange with Teresa for a foundation of her nuns in Granada and to bring her with him on the foundation, if possible.
2. The Marchioness of Villena, Doña Juana Lucas de Toledo.
3. The letter will be delivered by Padre Ambrosio de San Pedro, prior of Almodóvar, who will meet Padre Gracián in Salamanca.

To Madre María de San José, Seville
Avila, November 28, 1581

1. The profession was made by Ana de los Angeles (Wasteels).
2. The two nuns given for the foundation in Granada were María de Jesús and María de San Pablo.
3. Her brother left orders in his will that, with money he was owed, a chapel should be built at the Carmel of St. Joseph's in Avila.

4. Teresa's niece, Teresita.

To Padre Jerónimo Gracián, Salamanca
Avila, November 29, 1581

1. Two of the three from Avila who were chosen for the foundation in Granada: María de Cristo and Antonia del Espíritu Santo.

2. *Teresica* was one of the names Teresa used for her niece, Teresa de Jesús (Teresita), who was a novice at St. Joseph's in Avila and who would accompany Teresa and the other nuns for the foundation in Burgos.

3. She is wondering whom to leave in her place as prioress at St. Joseph's in Avila.

4. Ana de San Pedro Wasteels, the Flemish nun.

5. Julián de Avila, the confessor and chaplain of the community.

6. Ana de San Pedro and Ana de los Angeles (both Wasteels). The daughter (Ana de los Angeles) had made profession the previous day.

7. Tomasina Bautista (Perea), from the Carmel in Alba, destined for the foundation in Burgos.

To Doña Catalina de Tolosa, Burgos
Palencia, January 16, 1582

1. Jerónimo Gracián, who had been accompanying Teresa since the departure from Avila.

2. A famous crucifix in Burgos that at the time was venerated in the church of the Augustinians; and now, in the cathedral.

3. Catalina de la Asunción, a daughter of Catalina de Tolosa, who made her profession in Valladolid. The prioress, María Bautista, opposed this plan.

To Don Jerónimo Reinoso, Palencia
Burgos, May 20, 1582

1. The Jesuit rector of the Society's college in Valladolid. He had been Teresa's confessor.

2. The prioress of Palencia, Inés de Jesús.

3. A noblewoman in Burgos who was supporting Teresa's foundation there.

4. The general of the Society of Jesus, Claudio Acquaviva. His arrival in Spain was pure rumor.

5. Don Francisco Reinoso, Don Jerónimo's uncle and future Bishop of Córdoba. He had spent several years in Rome and there came to know Claudio Acquaviva.

6. She may be alluding to her *Spiritual Testimonies*.

7. These are Don Jerónimo's uncle and aunts: Don Francisco Reinoso and Doñas María and Leonor Reinoso, three very good friends of Teresa's.

To Madre Ana de Jesús, Granada
Burgos, May 30, 1582

1. Jerónimo Gracián.

2. May 3.

3. Doña Ana de Peñalosa and Don Luis de Mercado, St. John of the Cross's very good friends, who provided lodging for the nuns while they looked for a place in Granada where they could live.

4. The Archbishop of Granada, Juan Méndez de Salvatierra.

5. A discalced Carmelite friar in Seville who had been a secretary for Gracián at one time.

6. One of the founding nuns in Granada who had come from either Toledo or Malagón.

7. She is referring to the patent letter in which Gracián appointed her to make the foundation in Granada.

8. St. John of the Cross.

9. She is alluding to the pontifical decrees on enclosure issued after the Council of Trent: *Circa pastoralis officii* of Pius V (Jan. 1, 1566); *Decori et honestati* of Pius V (Feb. 2, 1570); and *De sacris virginibus* of Gregory XIII (Dec. 30, 1572).

10. She had turned over a large part of her house to the nuns for their temporary quarters.

11. María de Cristo; her two companions from Castile were Antonia del Espíritu Santo and Beatriz de Jesús.

To Doña Catalina de Tolosa, Burgos
Palencia, August 3, 1582

1. Doña Catalina's son, still a small child, who later became a discalced Carmelite.

2. Doña Catalina's two daughters, nuns in the Carmel of Palencia: María de San José (Maruca) and Isabel de la Trinidad. Or, she could be referring to Catalina's two youngest children: Lesmes and Beatriz.

3. Beatriz de Jesús (Arceo), who was sick in the Carmel in Burgos.

4. She is alluding to letters entrusted to her by Catalina to be delivered in Palencia. A damaged passage follows and several lines are then intentionally effaced in the autograph.

5. The identity of this person is unknown.

6. The canonesses regular of St. Augustine in Burgos.

To Madre Catalina de Cristo, Soria
Valladolid-Medina, September 15–17, 1582

1. Teresa had suggested they move the kitchen and refectory to the ground floor to save the cook extra work.

2. María de la Purificación, sixteen years old, to whom Teresa gave the habit before leaving Soria.

3. Isabel de la Madre de Dios (Medrano), seventeen years old.

4. She changed her itinerary on the following day by order of Padre Antonio de Jesús (Heredia), who was waiting for her in Medina and wanted her to go at once to Alba.

5. She was never able to realize her plan for a foundation in Madrid.

6. The Jesuits.

7. Beatriz de Beamonte, the founding benefactress of the Carmel in Soria.

St. Teresa of Avila (1515–1582) was a Carmelite nun, reformer, theologian, mystic, and author of many essential spiritual classics of the Catholic tradition, including *The Interior Castle* and *The Way of Perfection*. She was canonized in 1622 by Pope Gregory XV and Pope Paul VI named her a Doctor of the Church in 1970.

Sr. Regina Marie Gorman, O.C.D., is vicar general of the Carmelite Sisters of the Most Sacred Heart of Los Angeles.

Rev. Kieran Kavanaugh, O.C.D., is a member of the Institute of Carmelite Studies and the English translator of the writings of St. Teresa of Avila and St. John of the Cross.

AVE

AVE MARIA PRESS

Founded in 1865, Ave Maria Press,
a ministry of the Congregation of
Holy Cross, is a Catholic publishing
company that serves the spiritual and
formative needs of the Church and its
schools, institutions, and ministers;
Christian individuals and families; and
others seeking spiritual nourishment.

For a complete listing of titles from

Ave Maria Press

Sorin Books

Forest of Peace

Christian Classics

visit www.avemariapress.com

AVE MARIA PRESS
Notre Dame, IN
A Ministry of the United States Province of Holy Cross